Self-Study of Teaching and Teacher Education Practices

Volume 25

Series Editor
Julian Kitchen, Brock University, Hamilton, Canada

Advisory Editors
Mary Lynn Hamilton, University of Kansas, Kansas, USA
Ruth Kane, University of Ottawa, Ottawa, Canada
Geert Kelchtermans, Katholieke Universiteit Leuven, Leuven, Belgium
Fred Korthagen, Utrecht University, Utrecht, The Netherlands
Tom Russell, Queen's University, Kingston, Canada

Important insights into varying aspects of teacher education emerge when attention is focused on the work of teacher educators. Teacher educators' observations, explorations and inquiries are important as they offer access to the intricacies of teaching and learning about teaching so important in shaping the nature of teacher education itself. For (at least) this reason, research of the kind found in self-study of teacher education practices (S-STEP) is increasingly pursued and valued by teacher educators. In so doing, self-study also encourages others to look more closely into their own practices.

For many, self-study has become an empowering way of examining and learning about practice while simultaneously developing opportunities for exploring scholarship in, and through, teaching. Self-Study allows educators to maintain a focus on their teaching and on their students' learning; both high priorities that constantly interact with one another. This interplay between practice and scholarship can then be quite appealing to educators as their work becomes more holistic as opposed to being sectioned off into separate and distinct compartments (e.g., teaching, research, program evaluation, development, etc.). However, just because self-study may be appealing, it is not to suggest that the nature of self-study work should simply be accepted without question and critique. There is a constant need to examine what is being done, how and why, in order to further our understanding of the field and to foster development in critical and useful ways so that the learning through self-study might be informative and accessible to others.

This series has been organized in order so that the insights from self-study research and practice might offer a more comprehensive articulation of the distinguishing aspects of such work to the education community at large and builds on the International Handbook of Self Study in Teaching and Teacher Education (Loughran, Hamilton, LaBoskey & Russell, 2004).

Self-study may be viewed as a natural consequence of the re-emergence of reflection and reflective practice that gripped the education community in the last two decades of the 20th century (see for example Calderhead & Gates, 1993; Clift et al., 1990; Grimmett & Erickson, 1988; LaBoskey, 1994; Schön, 1983, 1987). However, self-study aims to, and must, go further than reflection alone. Self-study generates questions about the very nature of teaching about teaching in teacher education (Korthagen & Kessels, 1999) and is important in conceptualizing scholarship in teaching as it generates and makes public the knowledge of teaching and learning about teaching so that it might be informative to the education community in general.

This series offers a range of committed teacher educators who, through their books, offer a diverse range of approaches to, and outcomes from, self-study of teacher teacher education practices. Book proposals for this series may be submitted to the Publishing Editor: Claudia Acuna E-mail: Claudia.Acuna@springer.com

Adrian D. Martin

Editor

Self-Studies in Urban Teacher Education

Preparing U.S. Teachers to Advance
Equity and Social Justice

 Springer

Editor
Adrian D. Martin
New Jersey City University
Jersey City, NJ, USA

ISSN 1875-3620   ISSN 2215-1850   (electronic)
Self-Study of Teaching and Teacher Education Practices
ISBN 978-981-19-5429-0   ISBN 978-981-19-5430-6   (eBook)
https://doi.org/10.1007/978-981-19-5430-6

This Springer imprint is published by the registered company Springer Nature Singapore Pte Ltd.
The registered company address is: 152 Beach Road, #21-01/04 Gateway East, Singapore 189721, Singapore

This volume is dedicated to all educators and teacher educators committed to equity and social justice.

Foreword

Springer's Self-Study of Teaching and Teacher Education Practices series is designed to deepen and extend understanding of self-study and teacher education more generally. Volume 25, *Self-Studies in Urban Teacher Education: Preparing U.S. Teachers to Advance Equity and Social Justice*, edited by Adrian D. Martin, contributes to deepening understanding of social justice in teacher education through self-study while extending the conversation to include more diverse voices.

In "Preparing Preservice Teachers for Social Justice Teaching: Designing and Implementing Effective Interventions in Teacher Education," Kitchen and Taylor (2021) argued "that preparing preservice teachers for social justice teaching is critical to reducing inequity in an increasingly diverse world" (p. 977). This can best be achieved, we continued, through programs explicitly designed around "effective interventions," "deep understanding of social justice," and "sophisticated professional understanding of teacher education and social justice teacher education" (p. 977). We concluded, "While this is challenging work, the possibilities are promising" (p. 977). The chapter "Self-Studies in Urban Teacher Education," individually and collectively, offers promising insights grounded in rich understandings of social justice teacher education and specific possibilities for implementation with teacher candidates. As importantly, the interventions are targeted to the particular needs of urban education and urban teacher education in the United States.

Martin's opening chapter, "Self-Studies in Urban Education: An Introduction," defines key terms and issues, makes a strong case for self-study as an approach to understanding urban education and improving urban teacher education, and introduces the four sections of the book and ten chapters that follow.

"Urban," as Martin notes in the opening chapter, is a proxy for qualities associated with cities, particularly "inner-cities," such as higher rates of racial diversity, immigration, poverty, and crime. While urban education takes place largely in cities, it is more about the differentiated access to social goods and opportunities due to racial /cultural identities and lower socio-economic circumstances than the geographic location. For example, in my home city of Toronto in Canada, the downtown core (where I have lived for 40 years) has become increasingly "gentrified," but "urban" concerns persist with most marginalized people now residing in high-density suburban areas. "Urban education" focused on addressing the specific challenges of urban learners and communities is critical to fostering the equitable outcomes for diverse students and communities. Key to addressing these needs is "urban teacher education" designed specifically to prepare teacher candidates for the needs of students in these communities. Particularly vulnerable in these times of nativism and polarization are people of color living in urban communities drawing on multiple funds of knowledge to overcome many challenges. Yet, as Cochran-Smith and Villegas (2016) observed, while students of color account for around 50% of learners in American schools, the "teaching force continues to be overwhelmingly White, middle class, and monolingual native English speaking (p. 445). Clearly these teachers need to be educated for the diverse urban realities of school and more teachers need to be recruited from urban communities.

As Martin writes, this volume "expands and builds on the knowledge base in the teacher education scholarly literature." In particular, it draws on self-study as an entry point that centers inquiry on teaching practices, identities, and experiences of teachers and teacher educators. Martin suggests that self-study "provides fertile ground" for exploring the "multiple dimensions" of urban education and teacher education adapted to the needs of these communities. The powerful inquiries in the chapters that follow validate Martin's claim that self-study is well suited to inquiry into social justice in teacher education and to addressing urban education in the United States generally.

Self-Studies in Urban Teacher Education: Preparing U.S. Teachers to Advance Equity and Social Justice extends the work of other edited volumes that have employed self-study to examine teaching for social justice, such as the Self-Study and Diversity series of books.

As Tidwell and Fitzgerald (2006) did in *Self-Study and Diversity*, Martin brings together respected self-study practitioner-researchers to frame the challenges that confront established teacher educators. A notable example of this is "Who Gets to Ask 'Does Race Belong in Every Course?': Staying in the Anguish of White Teacher Educators," in which Madigan Peercy and Sharkey make themselves vulnerable as White teacher educators by struggling authentically with their complicity in a system that has not served urban communities well. This dimension is most evident in the final section of three chapters on rethinking boundaries in urban education. Morettini, in "Reimagining My Self-in-Practice: Relational Teacher Education in a Remote Setting," engages in similar self-questioning as she adjusts to her relational approach to teaching about urban education online. This is followed by consideration of the boundary between rural and urban education in Rice and Casteñon's "Not to Simply Intervene, but to Enact the Between: Urban Education as an Intra-Active Process" and Martin and Mills' "Materiality, Affect, and Diverse Educational Settings: A Collaborative Inquiry Between Urban and Rural Teacher Educators."

Martin, like Kitchen, Tidwell, and Fitzgerald (2016) in *Self-Study and Diversity II*, introduces powerful new racialized voices speaking from their places within diverse communities. This is particularly evident in "Teaching Black: Common Eyes All See the Same," in which Hannon and four colleagues critically reflect on their professional experiences as Black urban educators disrupting the traditionally

White space of the classroom (even in urban schools). The two explorations of academic content areas in urban education offer fresh first-hand accounts by new voices. In "A Self-Study in PreK-4 Science Teacher Preparation: Supporting Teacher Candidates' Professional Development," Burrell demonstrates how she considered the collective experiences of local communities in striving to make science learning relevant. Harmful racial and mathematics ideologies are critiqued and disrupted in Odom Pough and Willey's "A Closer Look at Equitable Outcomes: A Self-Study in Urban Mathematics Teacher Education."

This volume is strikingly similar to Kitchen, Fitzgerald, and Tidwell's (2022) *Self-Study and Diversity III* in the authors' sense of urgency writing at a time when inclusion and diversity are being questioned. Monica Taylor and Michael Diamond (2020), in "The Role of Self-Study in Teaching and Teacher Education for Social Justice," wrote:

> We worry about these who are marginalized, invisible, and voiceless: children and young people in our schools, the teachers who work with them, our school families and communities, our preservice teacher, and ourselves as teacher educators in schools, community, colleges and university settings. (p. 510)

In "Collectively Caring: Co-Creating a Critical Community of Justice-Oriented Teacher Educators," Taylor and colleagues convey their worries during a time of social tension and demonstrate how we might attend to self and others while engaged in the critical work of urban teacher education. This chapter is followed by two chapters that use self-study to puzzle over the nature of urban education: "Tourist Teachers and Layers of Colonization: Lessons from New Mexico" by Haniford and Sanchez and "How Do We Do Praxis: Becoming Teachers of Diverse Learners in Urban Environments" by Edge and Vipperman.

It is an honor to include this timely and important book in our Self-Study of Practice series. I also look forward to future volumes that deepen the conversation about urban education and social justice education in the United States and extend those conversations to other countries.

Professor, Faculty of Education   Julian Kitchen
Brock University, Hamilton, ON, Canada

References

Cochran-Smith, M., & Villegas, A. M. (2016). Research on teacher preparation: Charting the landscape of a sprawling field. In D. H. Gitomer, & C. A. Bell (Eds.), *Handbook of research on teaching* (pp. 439–547). American Educational Research Association.

Kitchen, J., & Taylor, L. (2021). Preparing preservice teachers for social justice teaching: Designing and implementing effective interventions in teacher education. In C. Mullen (Ed.),

Handbook of social justice intervention in education (pp. 955–980). Springer. https://doi.
org/10.1007/978-3030-29553-0_70-1

Kitchen, J., Fitzgerald, L., & Tidwell, D. (Eds.) (2022). *Self-study and diversity III: Inclusivity and diversity in teacher education.* Brill Sense.

Kitchen, J., Tidwell, D., & Fitzgerald, L. (Eds.). (2016). *Self-study and diversity II: Inclusive education in a changing world.* Sense.

Taylor, M., & Diamond, M. (2020). The role of self-study in teaching and teacher education for social justice. In J. Kitchen, A. Berry, S. M. Bullock, A. R. Crowe, M. Taylor, H. Gudjonsdottir, & L. Thomas (Eds.), *International handbook of self-study of teaching and teacher education practices* (2nd Ed., pp. 509–543). Springer. https://doi.org/10.1007/978-981-13-1710-1_16-1

Tidwell, D., & Fitzgerald, L. (Eds.). (2006). *Self-study and diversity.* Sense.

Contents

Chapter 1
Self-Studies in Urban Teacher Education: An Introduction

Adrian D. Martin

Abstract This chapter serves as an introduction to this volume. Urban schools in the United States often reflect the confluence of social issues, challenges, and opportunities that confront individuals and communities in the twenty-first century. Given the breadth of cultural, linguistic, and socio-economic diversity characteristic of urban communities, teachers in these settings are challenged to provide meaningful and relevant learning experiences to a diverse body of P-12 students. Thus, teacher education must prepare teachers to engage in pedagogical practices and to possess dispositions that are inclusive, affirmative, and responsive to the learning and socio-emotional needs of urban students. Such work serves to not only support the academic learning of P-12 urban students, but can also facilitate an equitable education. This chapter provides an overview of urban schooling and urban education in the United States. Features of the urban context are discussed in relation to pedagogy and the institutional context of urban schools. The chapter discusses the role of teacher education in relation to preparing educators for urban schools. It establishes the relevance and necessity for teacher education research and, more specifically, for self-study research, in urban teacher education. The chapter provides a synthesis of prior self-study research that has attended to urban education. It concludes with a discussion of the self-studies collected in this volume and highlights the insights put forth by the contributing authors.

Keywords Self-study · Urban education · Literature review · Social justice · Equity · United States

The word "urban" is defined as "of, relating to, characteristic of, or constituting a city" (Merriam-Webster, n.d.), a chief characteristic of which is that it is a highly populated area. Based on this definition, urban education refers to institutional

A. D. Martin (✉)
New Jersey City University, Jersey City, NJ, USA
e-mail: amartin6@njcu.edu

© The Author(s), under exclusive license to Springer Nature Singapore Pte
Ltd. 2022
A. D. Martin (ed.), *Self-Studies in Urban Teacher Education*, Self-Study of
Teaching and Teacher Education Practices 25,
https://doi.org/10.1007/978-981-19-5430-6_1

systems of teaching and learning in densely populated contexts. Yet this term, and the pedagogical practices and policies developed and implemented for the urban environment, are neither solely or even primarily focused on issues of population density relevant to school activities, school management, or teacher preparation. As discussed by Watson (2011), the word urban is employed as a proxy for the socio-cultural, racial, and economic qualities and conditions associated with cities. In the United States (U.S.), many urban contexts possess a higher than average poverty level, a substantial portion of residents are racially, culturally, or linguistically diverse, an immigrant population, and a crime rate that, while it has decreased historically, is of concern for many (Frey, 2019; Grawert & Kimble, 2019; Parker et al., 2018; Wheaton et al., 2021). The U.S. urban context thus reflects the confluence and complexity of the many social issues, challenges, and tensions of a multicultural democracy made up of a wide spectrum of individuals with varying beliefs and life experiences (Purcell, 2013). Of note is that many individuals in urban settings possess differential access to social goods on the basis of their own racial/cultural/national identities and/or their socio-economic status (American Psychological Association, 2017; Gourevitch & Greene, 2018).

As such, the urban context challenges teachers to provide meaningful, relevant, and effective learning experiences to the diverse students in their classrooms. Many urban students possess funds of knowledge that do not align with the norms and customs of U.S. schools (Rodriguez, 2013). In addition, the economic struggles confronted by many urban students and their families inhibits the ability to reap the full benefits of school instruction (Milner, 2015). While these difficulties highlight pedagogical tensions present in the work of urban teachers, structural and systemic issues further diminish the possibilities for U.S. urban students to partake in transformative educational experiences.

Urban schools have a rate of teacher turnover that is higher than those in rural or suburban settings (Simon & Johnson, 2015). It is difficult to retain teachers, and classrooms might be staffed with substitute teachers who do not possess requisite credentials. This, in conjunction with funding that is often insufficient for adequate school supplies and materials, curricula that fails to reflect the diversity of the local community, and large class sizes negatively impact the schooling of urban students and the work of urban teachers (Chingos & Blagg, 2017; Dee & West, 2011; Dyches, 2017). Additionally, urban settings have a higher percentage of transient students and many who have experienced interrupted schooling (Sparks, 2016). These variables, along with a history of de jure racial segregation (Rothstein, 2015), have contributed to inequitable learning conditions in many urban schools. Given the concentration of racial minorities, immigrants, and people living in poverty, the current status quo in many U.S. urban schools serves to reproduce cycles of inequity and furthers the socio-political marginalization of the communities and individuals therein (Weiner & Jerome, 2016).

Insight of how the urban context and urban school systems and structures mitigate academic achievement is critical if urban teachers are to support their P-12 students' learning, mastery of the curriculum, and academic standards. Moreover, working in culturally, linguistically, and socio-economically diverse settings necessitates that teachers possess the skills to differentiate instruction to meet the needs of all their students (Tomlinson, 2017). Given the diversity in urban settings, it is not unusual for teachers to teach students that possess a breadth of life experiences, varying degrees of familiarity with mainstream U.S. culture and school norms, proficiency in mainstream English, and preparedness to take up grade level work (Fenner, 2014; Villegas et al., 2018). On account that the U.S. teacher demographic continues to be predominantly White, middle-class women who are monolingual speakers of English lacking substantive experiences with culturally and linguistically diverse individuals (Martin, 2016; Villegas & Lucas, 2002), it is imperative that urban teachers (who work with some of the most diverse, marginalized, and underprivileged students in the U.S.), possess affirmative, inclusive, and growth-oriented mindsets, attitudes, and dispositions (Martin & Spencer, 2020a; Strom et al., 2018). Without such an orientation, it is unlikely that urban teachers will be able to enact differentiated and culturally affirmative pedagogical practices or advocate for and on behalf of their students.

Urban teaching, therefore, extends beyond the aims of schooling to prepare students for citizenship or for the workforce. Serving an urban community as a teacher is, in essence, a call to advance equity and social justice. It means enacting one's pedagogical practices with the aim to stop the reproduction of the status quo contextual conditions characteristic of urban students' lives, and instead enable possibilities for individual and collective social transformation. To borrow from Freire (1970), urban teachers must engage in problem-posing education and dialogic teaching and learning as means of reshaping the world as is towards a more equitable and socially just society.

The dispositional and epistemological orientation adopted by many teacher education programs, teacher educators, and education researchers has taken up this call towards advancing equitable and socially just learning contexts as a professional obligation and responsibility (Mills & Ballantyne, 2016; Zygmunt & Clark, 2016). Theoretical and conceptual frameworks for teaching diverse students (Ladson-Billings, 1994; Villegas & Lucas, 2002), students in poverty (Gorski, 2017), and pedagogical strategies to make content accessible to all learners (Garguilo & Metcalf, 2016) have been a consistent element in teacher education coursework, preservice field experiences, and teacher professional development (Cochran-Smith et al., 2015; Cochran-Smith & Villegas, 2015). These frameworks, coupled with learning opportunities that enable preservice teachers to critically analyze, appraise, and evaluate pedagogical activity, academic content, and the structures of schooling have the capacity to promote the development of a teacher workforce that is more readily able to meet the needs of diverse urban students.

Yet, despite such efforts and the social justice oriented values espoused by many colleges of education, and more specifically teacher education programs, learning conditions, curriculum, and instruction are still too often inequitable in urban schools. To be sure, teacher education programs and colleges of education do not bear full responsibility for the multiple inequities in urban schools. However, teacher education programs are tasked to prepare teacher candidates to teach all children and young adults. Most especially for those that hold social justice as a core value, it is paramount that teacher education programs provides quality, in-depth, and powerful learning experiences that support preservice and inservice teachers to thrive (and not just survive) when teaching in urban schools (Strom & Martin, 2013, 2016). While the research literature has chronicled the effects of poli-cies in urban schools (Hollins, 2019), preservice teacher initiatives and school reform efforts (Scott & Holme, 2016), quantitative analyses of urban student perfor-mance (Chingos, 2018; Katherine, 2017) and the challenges confronted by teachers in urban schools (Martin, 2019; Strom & Martin, 2017), less is known about the actual teacher education practices employed by teacher educators, with a commit-ment to social justice, who are preparing teachers to teach in urban schools.

This volume, *Self-Studies in Urban Teacher Education: Preparing U.S. Teachers to Advance Equity and Social Justice*, expands and builds upon the knowledge base in the teacher education scholarly literature. The empirical inquiries gathered in this collection provide examples of teacher educators and teachers in diverse contexts with a commitment to preparing teachers to teach in U.S. urban schools. The inqui-ries reflect that urban teacher education does not solely occur in urban institutions of higher education. Indeed, preparing teachers for urban and city schools is taken up by teacher educators in rural and suburban contexts as well. Thus, the responsi-bility for attending to educational equity and social justice issues in relation to the urban context is a shared responsibility among all teacher educators. The self-studies contained herein provide critical insights, detailed and nuanced accounts, and rigorous analyses by teachers and teacher educators who work with teachers candidates and practicing teachers, and how these endeavors contribute to and inform teacher education. The self-study of teacher education practices (S-STEP) is a unique methodology. Given that in S-STEP the researchers/teacher educators themselves are the units of analysis, the chapters provide possibilities in teacher education for urban education and are exemplars for the kinds of inquiries teacher educators can conduct to improve their own professional practices.

1.1 S-STEP as an Entry Point for Urban Teacher Education

Inquiries centered on the teaching practices, identities, and experiences of teacher educators and teachers in urban schools have productively employed self-study methodology in prior publications. These works demonstrate that self-study is a powerful and compelling methodology that urban teacher educators and teachers can utilize to not only enhance their own professional practice, but also to contribute to the knowledge base on teaching and learning. Indeed, as with the self-studies collected in this volume, many of the teachers and teacher educators in previous self-studies were focused on gaining insight of how their professional endeavors could contribute towards facilitating equity and social justice.

For example, in their 2006 publication, Kroll and Breaur explored literacy prac-tices from a critical perspective with an awareness of how racism mitigates the learning experiences of diverse students, particularly in urban schools. Focused on more fully understanding their professional practices and how these supported pre-service teachers with the insight that they would need to teach diverse students in a racist society, the authors recognized the imperative of knowing themselves and their own values, who their students were, and how curriculum and instruction could be used to facilitate representative and inclusive pedagogical experiences. Being aware of one's own biases as teacher educators, the funds of knowledge teacher candidates bring to the classroom, and the perspectives and topics taken up in class were foundational towards this aim.

Other teacher educators engaged in self-studies with related aims. Lang and Siry's (2008) study also focused on preparing teacher candidates for diverse contexts. The authors, former urban elementary school teachers themselves, recognized the need for sustained learning opportunities for all teachers, that diversity issues need to be attended to explicitly, and the importance of critical dialogue. The value of engaging in professional practices as a teacher educator from this social justice orientation is echoed in other works as well (e.g., Hamilton & Pinnegar, 2015; Laboskey, 2004; Martin, 2020; Taylor et al., 2014). Still, other teacher educators have explored conceptual frameworks, such as culturally responsive teaching, as a lens to analyze and make meaning of their work (e.g., Constable et al., 2008; Nicol & Korteweg, 2010). Thinking with and enacting pedagogical practices aligned with culturally responsive teaching suggests that teacher educators need to adapt to their students' learning needs; in addition, there is a need for teachers (and teacher educators) of the same cultural/racial backgrounds and identities as those that they are teaching. Given the student diversity in the urban context, it is critical to support a teacher workforce that reflects this diversity, and in turn, a teacher educator workforce as well. In both Constable et al.'s (2008) work and Nicol and Korteweg's (2010), the collaborative process of unpacking and exploring these themes was central to their methodological approach.

The efficacy of collaboration, a topic of much investigation in self-study research, is also highlighted in those studies related to urban schooling. Cooper and Gronseth (2020) collaborated to learn how their values were enacted and reflected in their paired teacher education courses in an urban teacher education program. Ragoonaden and Bullock (2014) collaborated to explore the notion of boundary crossing between urban and rural institutional settings, and Martin and Spencer's (2020b) collaboration attended to the ways that changes in geographic setting (from urban to suburban) over a period of a few years shaped their enactment of teaching and their identities as teacher educators. These studies demonstrate that not only is trust key to conducting collaborative self-studies, but that the mutual learning that emerges from this form of inquiry can productively inform and contribute to future teaching practices. In a related set of studies, teacher educators collaborated with teachers (e.g., Freidus, 2000; LaBoskey & Richert, 2015). As with the collaborations among teacher educators, collaborations between teachers and teacher educators were joint learning experiences where each individual gained an enhanced appreciation of their own work as well as that of their self-study colleague. Indeed, these inquiries cast light on the efficacy of collaborative endeavors to more fully discern the challenges and opportunities of the urban context for teachers and students.

In contrast to these collaborations with teacher educators, some P-12 educators have employed self-study methods to explore their work as urban teachers. The self-studies by Byrd (2015), Jones (2015) and Miller (2015) were each by urban elementary school teachers who sought to facilitate more equitable learning experiences for their students. These teachers utilized self-study methodology to identify how academic content can be presented to urban students in culturally relevant ways, the power and importance of inspiring a love of reading, and the affordances of analyzing moments of instructions and attending to the details of one's pedagogy. Strom and Martin's (2013) self-study similarly reflects these tenets and the effects of neoliberal systems on the experiences of an urban teacher.

The self-study literature highlights how the work of teaching and teacher education is not conducted in isolation; rather, interactions and engagement with others is central to processes of teaching and learning. Kitchen's (2005) conceptualization of relational teacher education underscores the connectedness (and the imperative to attend to the connectedness) between and amongst teachers, teacher educators, and students. Self-study researchers focused on the urban context have also emphasized connectedness. Building relationships with preservice teachers and inservice educators is central in the work by Hansen et al. (2014), Taylor et al. (2014), and Martin (2020). These self-studies demonstrate the complexities in relationship building, the need for nuanced insight of the settings, systems, and bureaucracies that teachers work in, the ethic of supporting teachers as lifelong learners, and that teacher educators themselves must continue their own lifelong learning.

The relational dimension of teacher education may serve as a facet of one's teacher educator identity. Identity and the understanding of self in the urban setting was the subject of self-studies by Brown and Benken (2006), Craig (2006), Muchmore (2008) and Martin (2018). Brown and Benken (2006) attended to how working on a professional development endeavor with urban teachers informed their understanding on the development of a context-driven professional identity. Craig's (2006) exploration on her entry into an urban school setting in the era of urban school reform led her to recognize the need to assume a "working-with" position and identity, rather than as an expert with the teachers she worked with. Muchmore's (2008) identity and understanding of professional self as a teacher educator was negotiated in the process of his run for school board, and Martin (2018) learned that his own teacher educator identity was mutable and shifted through his engagement with the graduate inservice urban teachers he taught. The lived experience, be it entry into the urban setting, seeking a position (and thus, an identity) in an urban setting other than that of teacher educator, and the day to day interactions with urban students and teachers were all entry points towards understanding oneself, one's teaching, and consequently one's future work.

However, the work of teacher educators often encompasses engagement with non-traditional routes towards teaching licensure for teacher candidates. A number of states in the U.S. have allowed for alternative pathways, or routes, as options for individuals interested in obtaining a teacher license. While many of these programs are university-based, some are not. Many of these options for licensure were approved by state governmental entities in order to diversify the teacher workforce and increase the number of qualified teachers in urban schools. Alternate route programs were the focus in self-studies by Graham (2006) and Peterman and Marquez-Zenkov (2002). The tensions, challenges, and struggles to implement powerful learning experiences and gain the support of multiple stakeholders in these programs were discussed as challenges that needed to be worked through. Tensions were also explored by Taylor et al. (2014), who surmised that their own graduate urban teacher residency program was a "third space" between the university and the school setting where the role of teacher, teacher educator, mentor and mentee were reimagined and renegotiated. Such renegotiation is also highlighted by Martin (2020) who reported on the tensions inherent in discussing controversial topics with inservice teacher graduate students and the pedagogical approaches for navigating such circumstances.

Clearly, the self-study of teaching and teacher education practices provides fertile ground upon which teachers and teacher educators can attend to and explore the multiple dimensions of their work and identities in relation to urban teacher education and urban schools. Furthermore, the conceptual grounding and social justice orientation that much of this literature is rooted in suggests the political and pedagogical efficacy inherent in self-study research. This work can be deployed by teacher educators who seek to advance equitable and socially just schools and, by extension, a socially just and equitable society. This volume serves as a foundational text that can be utilized by education researchers, teacher educators, teachers, and others with a vested interest in enabling urban education to be characterized by excellence in teaching and learning. Novices and seasoned self-study researchers alike will find the studies collected in this volume as powerful entry-points to consider possibilities for urban teacher education and urban schools. Urban education researchers will find the accounts provided by the authors as insider perspectives on the efforts and initiatives of those preparing teachers for urban schools. Certainly, teacher educators in diverse contexts work to prepare teachers to teach in urban schools. Engaging in this professional practice necessitates a willingness to not only reflect, but to also analyze and critically appraise one's efforts and how one's teaching practices align with one's values. The authors in this volume have taken up this challenge, and the methodology of self-study inquiry, and the scholarship on urban teacher education, are better because of it.

1.2   Self-Studies in U.S. Urban Teacher Education

The self-studies in this volume reflect the work of teacher educators and teachers across the United States. The authors, who come from multiple, diverse contexts, are unified in their commitment to advance equity and social justice through their teaching practices and through their self-study research endeavors. They represent scholars at multiple points across the professional continuum and demonstrate how, despite differing years of professional experience in education and teacher education, each employed S-STEP as a powerful, transformative, and illuminating methodology. The volume is divided into four parts. The first part is "Preparing Teacher Educators and Teachers for Urban Education Contexts". The opening Chap. 2 by Taylor and colleagues reports on a critical feminist community consisting of a social justice oriented teacher educator, teachers, and future teacher educators. Through the lens of co/autoethnography, the authors critically analyze their experiences, meaning-making, and reflections throughout the summer of 2020, a tumultuous period marked by the Covid-19 pandemic and the waves of Black Lives Matter activism. Grappling with the socio-political challenges of the time, the authors highlight the need for authentic communities among teachers and teacher educators, and the need to attend to (and care for) the holistic self when taking up social justice work. As such, the chapter provides keen insights towards adopting such an ethic in the work of urban teacher educators and urban teachers.

In the following Chap. 3, Haniford and Sánchaz also take up their understanding of teaching for social justice. They explore the relevance of place, specifically New Mexico, as a cartographic analytic to identify contextualized pedagogical forms of modeling instruction that are grounded in the uniqueness and history of their locality. The chapter serves as an exemplar of self-study research between a teacher educator and practicing secondary education social studies teacher who collaborated as critical friends. Drawing upon the history of New Mexico and their own life experiences, the authors consider the implications of time, space, and place in their teaching with the aim to advance equity through their pedagogy. Ultimately, the work reveals that the tensions, struggles, questions, and opportunities that teacher educators take up in the preparation of candidates to teach in urban contexts is not limited to institutions of higher education in city or urban settings.

The Chap. 4 by Edge and Vipperman also took up the theme of exploring teaching for equity and the preparation of teachers for diverse urban classrooms. This collaborative self-study examined the authors' work in teacher education and in the teaching of urban elementary classroom students. Together, Edge and Vipperman investigated how they made their teaching practices, and the aims of their teaching practices, visible and meaningful to their students. Centered on preparing teachers to teach in urban schools, the chapter provides an insider perspective by those who have taught in urban schools themselves.

The second part of the volume, "Race, Culture, and Urban Teacher Education", explores racial and cultural positionalities in relation to education in the urban setting. The Chap. 5 by Hannon and colleagues reflects how biography, life experiences, and past professional practices are informed by the racial identities and cultural characteristics of the educational setting. The chapter reports on the authors' experiences as five Black educators in an urban high school. The self-study chronicles their conversations, narratives, and quandaries on the processes through which they worked in their own classrooms, turned to each other for collegial and personal support, and sought to bring their identities, wholly and fully, as Black teachers to their work. The chapter serves as a vital and unique contribution to self-study research and education research in general; it centers the voices of Black, urban educators who critically analyze how they navigated complex bureaucratic, institutional systems and structures that all too often served to uphold and perpetuate racial oppression and injustice. Indubitably, the chapter's pedagogical insights, principles for resiliency in urban teaching, and analysis of urban education are powerful considerations not only for the authors themselves, but for the broader teacher education and education research community.

To be sure, the enactment of equity-oriented and critically conscious pedagogical principles can be challenging. In teacher education, it calls upon a teacher educator to skillfully engage teacher candidates in complex, difficult, and often uncomfortable conversations about social injustices, prejudice, discrimination, and the historical legacy of institutional racism in the United States. Peercy and Sharkey's (Chap. 6) self-study sheds light on the challenges of taking this up in teacher education coursework. The critical friends explored the ways that racism was addressed in Peercy's pedagogy through examples drawn from her teaching experiences. This powerful self-study serves as a compelling example of vulnerability in self-study research. The authors center critical friendship and self-study as instrumental towards gaining awareness of White complicity in pedagogical activity and engage in in-depth, critical, and honest reflections and analyses to conceptualize future teaching practices attentive to social justice issues in their work.

Part three of the volume, "The Academic Content Areas and Urban Teacher Education", attends to the advancement of content knowledge for urban students through the practices of teacher educators. In the part's first chapter, Burrell (Chap. 7) utilizes an insider perspective to explore how pedagogy can be leveraged by students' experiences to promote inclusion in the urban elementary science classroom. Her work employs culturally responsive teaching as a lens to consider how science teacher education can respond to the needs of preparing future educators for urban schools. The analysis of her initiatives in her own classroom highlights the saliency of culturally responsive teaching, and addresses the need for detailed, in depth accounts of how the teaching of science as a content area and science methods can incorporate the cultural identities and experiences of urban youth.

In the following Chap. 8, Pough and Willey explored teaching elementary mathematics methods and utilized narrative data as a means of gaining critical insights of their own teaching practices for the preparation of urban elementary math teachers. This collaborative self-study contributes to the literature on the benefits of teacher educators mutually exploring their teaching practices. For Pough and Willey, exploring their pedagogy emerged not only as a means of preparing the future urban teacher workforce to successfully teach academic content, but also as a means to foster transformative learning experiences for urban students.

The fourth part of the volume, "Rethinking the Boundaries of Online, Rural, and Urban Teacher Education" sets out to complicate normative constructions of where teacher preparation for urban schools takes place. In the part's first chapter, Morretini (Chap. 9) takes up identity as a salient construct in relation to online teaching as explored through self-study. Morretini investigated her professional teacher educator identity as a relational role and drew from the framework for relational teacher education. As the instructor of a course focused on urban and inclusive education, she investigated the shift to online, remote teaching during the Covid-19 pandemic and attended to the ways that her identity as a relational teacher educator was enacted throughout this period of time. Utilizing the principles of intimate scholarship and drawing from life-history self-study, she provides in-depth, nuanced, and critically analyzed vignettes of her online teaching practices with the aim of preparing critically conscious future educators.

In the following Chap. 10, Rice and Casteñon explore the possibilities of working alongside with and learning from teachers. Their collaborative self-study crossed the boundaries between urban and rural teacher education and school contexts. The authors adopted the concept of intra-action to showcase how the emergence of teaching practice and pedagogical activity surface through the joint activities of multiple elements across time and space. Rice and Casteñon's work signals possibilities for future self-study research through the use of an innovative conceptual lens and reflects the possibilities for teacher educators when emergent theoretical frameworks and concepts are utilized. The authors of this self-study demonstrate the value and efficacy of taking up constructs that compel one to think in new ways.

The volume concludes with Martin and Mill's (Chap. 11) self-study, an inquiry that sought to gain insight of the parallels and differences in urban and rural teacher education and school settings. The authors employed new materialism as a theoretical framework and centered materiality as the nexus of their investigation. Drawing from the notion of affect, the authors analyzed the shaping effects of material resources, how these produced affective responses, and the implications and possibilities of this for their own teaching practices and identities as teacher educators. The work calls attention to the relevance and need to more fully consider the material world and the role of the non-human as an agentic actor in pedagogical activity and in the production of teacher educator identities.

Ultimately, this volume demonstrates the salience of the self-study research in urban teacher education and the imperative for teacher educators and education professionals to utilize self-study methodology to facilitate justice-oriented and equitable schooling systems. Such work is challenging and rigorous. Yet, if teacher educators are to engage in ethical practice and inquiry, it is necessary to attend to issues of equity and social justice in one's pedagogy and scholarship. This can enable opportunities and avenues for inclusive schooling systems that can attend to the academic needs of today's students.

References

American Psychological Association. (2017). *Ethnic and racial minorities and socioeconomic status*. https://www.apa.org/pi/ses/resources/publications/minorities
Brown, N. & Benken, B. (2006). So when do we teach mathematics? Grappling through a troubling dilemma. In D. L. Tidwell, L. M. Fitzgerald, & M. L. Heston (Eds.), *Journeys of hope: Risking self-study in a diverse world*. Proceedings of the fifth international conference on Self-study of teacher education practices (pp. 41–45).
Byrd, B. (2015). Good readers get smart: Reading orientations in a second-grade classroom. *Studying Teacher Education, 11*(2), 124–142. https://doi.org/10.1080/17425964.2015.1045772

Chingos, M. M. (2018, May 24). *What can NAEP tell us about how much U.S. children are learning?* Brookings Institute. https://www.brookings.edu/research/what-can-naep-tell-us-about-how-much-us-children-are-learning/

Chingos, M. M., & Blagg, K. (2017, May). *Do poor kids get their fair share of school funding?* The Urban Institute. https://www.urban.org/sites/default/files/publication/90586/school_funding_brief.pdf

Cochran-Smith, M., & Villegas, A. M. (2015). Framing teacher preparation research: An overview of the field, part 1. *Journal of Teacher Education, 66*(2), 109–121. https://doi.org/10.1177/0022487114549072

Cochran-Smith, M., Villegas, A. M., Abrams, L., Chavez-Moreno, L., Mills, T., & Stern, R. (2015). Framing teacher preparation research: An overview of the field, part 2. *Journal of Teacher Education, 66*(1), 7–20. https://doi.org/10.1177/0022487114558268

Constable, S., Weiss, A., Fayne, H. Ryan, P., & Ortquist-Ahrens, L. (2008). Connections and boundaries: Exploring culturally responsive pedagogy in our own classrooms. In M. L. Heston, D. L. Tidwell, K. K. East, & L. M. Fitzgerald (Eds.), *Pathways to change in teacher education: Dialogue, diversity, and self-study.* Proceedings of the seventh international conference on Self-study of teacher education practices (pp. 72–76).

Cooper, J. M., & Gronseth, S. L. (2020). Pedagogical tapestries: Paired-course collaboration and course design for authentic student learning. In C. Edge, A. Cameron-Standerford, & B. Bergh (Eds.), *Textiles and tapestries: Self-study for envisioning new ways of knowing.* EdTech Books. https://equitypress.org/textiles_tapestries_self_study/chapter_21

Craig, C. (2006). Change, changing, and being changed: A self-study of a teacher educator's becoming real in the throes of urban school reform. *Studying Teacher Education, 2*(1), 105–116. https://doi.org/10.1080/17425960600557538

Dee, T. S., & West, M. R. (2011). The non-cognitive returns to class size. *Educational Evaluation and Policy Analysis, 33*(1), 23–46. https://doi.org/10.3102/0162373710392370

Dyches, J. (2017). Shaking off Shakespeare: A white teacher, urban students, and the meditating powers of a canonical-counter curriculum. *The Urban Review, 49*(2), 300–325. https://doi.org/10.1007/s11256-017-0402-4

Fenner, D. S. (2014). *Advocating for English learners: A guide for educators.* Corwin.

Freidus, H. (2000). Narrative research and teacher education A quest for new insights. In J. Loughran & T. Russell (Eds.), *Exploring myths and legends of teacher education.* Proceedings of the third international conference on Self-study of teacher education practices (pp. 80–84).

Freire, P. (1970). *Pedagogy of the oppressed.* Seabury Press.

Frey, W. H. (2019, April 22). *As Americans spread out, immigration plays a crucial role in local population growth.* Brookings Institute. https://www.brookings.edu/research/as-americans-spread-out-immigration-plays-a-crucial-role-in-local-population-growth/

Garguilo, R. M., & Metcalf, D. (2016). *Teaching in today's inclusive classrooms: A universal design for learning approach* (3rd ed.). Cengage Learning.

Gorski, P. (2017). *Reaching and teaching students in poverty: Strategies for erasing the opportunity gap* (2nd ed.). Teachers College Press.

Gourevitch, R., & Greene, S. (2018, February 27). *Racial segregation is a stubborn feature of our nation's history, but it does not have to be our future.* Urban Institute. Retrieved from https://www.urban.org/urban-wire/racial-segregation-stubborn-feature-our-nations-history-it-doesnt-have-be-our-future

Graham, B. (2006). Meeting at LEAPS: Building relationships to build a program. In D. L. Tidwell, L. M. Fitzgerald, & M. L. Heston (Eds.), *Journeys of hope: Risking self-study in a diverse world.* Proceedings of the fifth international conference on Self-study of teacher education practices (pp. 98–102).

Grawert, A., & Kimble, C. (2019, December 18). *Takeaways from 2019 crime data in major American cities.* Brennan Center for Justice. https://www.brennancenter.org/our-work/analysis-opinion/takeaways-2019-crime-data-major-american-cities

Hamilton, M. L., & Pinnegar, S. (2015). Considering the role of self-study of teaching and teacher education practices research in transforming urban classrooms. *Studying Teacher Education, 11*(2), 180–190. https://doi.org/10.1080/17425964.2015.1045775

Hansen, A., Danilchick, A., & Hill, C. (2014). Possibilities for deepening mentor-mentee relationships through self-study communities of practice. In D. Garbett, & A. Ovens (Eds.), *Changing practices for changing times: Past, present, and future possibilities for self-study research.* Proceedings of the tenth international conference on Self-study of teacher education practices (pp. 115–117).

Hollins, E. R. (2019). *Teaching to transform urban schools and communities: Powerful pedagogy in practice.* Routledge.

Jones, K. E. (2015). Implementing academic choice: A self-study in evolving pedagogy. *Studying Teacher Education, 11*(2), 143–163. https://doi.org/10.1080/17425964.2015.1045773

Katherine, K. (2017). *Trends in NAEP scores among 17-year olds in the era of accountability* (Unpublished doctoral dissertation). Indiana State University.

Kitchen, J. (2005). Conveying respect and empathy: Becoming a relational teacher educator. *Studying Teacher Education, 1*(2), 197–207. https://doi.org/10.1080/17425960500288374

Kroll, L. R., & Breuer, F. B. (2006). Learning to teach reading: Preparing teachers for urban contexts. In L. M. Fitzgerald, M. L. Heston, & D. L. Tidwell (Eds.), *Collaborations and community: Pushing boundaries through self-study.* Proceedings of the sixth international conference on Self-study of teacher education practices (pp. 161–164).

Laboskey, V. (2004). "To be or not to be": Social justice teacher identity formation and transformation. In D. Tidwell, L. M. Fitzgerald, & M. L. Heston (Eds.), *Journeys of hope: Risking self-study in a diverse world.* Proceedings of the fifth international conference on Self-study of teacher education practices (pp. 174–177).

Laboskey, V. K., & Richert, A. E. (2015). Self-study as a means for urban teachers to transform academics. *Studying Teacher Education, 11*(2), 164–179. https://doi.org/10.1080/1742596 4.2015.1045774

Ladson-Billings, G. (1994). *The dreamkeepers: Successful teachers of African American children.* Jossey-Bass.

Lang, D. E., & Siry, C. (2008). Diversity as a context for inquiry-based preservice teacher learning and teaching in elementary school settings: A self-study in teacher education practices. In M. L. Heston, D. L. Tidwell, K. K. East, & L. M. Fitzgerald (Eds.), *Pathways to change in teacher education: Dialogue, diversity, and self-study.* Proceedings of the seventh international conference on Self-study of teacher education practices (pp. 213–217).

Martin, A. D. (2016). *The professional identities of mainstream teachers of English learners: A discourse analysis* (Unpublished doctoral dissertation). Montclair State University.

Martin, A. D. (2018). Professional identities and pedagogical practices: A self-study on the "becomings" of a teacher educator and teachers. In A. Ovens & D. Garbett (Eds.), *Pushing boundaries and crossing borders: Self-study as a means for knowing pedagogy* (pp. 263–269). S-STEP.

Martin, A. D. (2019). The agentic capacities of mundane objects for educational equity: Narratives of material entanglements in a culturally diverse urban classroom. *Educational Research for Social Change, 8*(1), 86–100. https://doi.org/10.17159/2221-4070/2018/v8i1a6

Martin, A. D. (2020). Tensions and caring in teacher education: A self-study on teaching in difficult moments. *Studying Teacher Education: A Journal of Self-study of Teacher Education Practices, 16*(3), 306–323. https://doi.org/10.1080/17425964.2020.1783527

Martin, A. D., & Spencer, T. (2020a). Children's literature, culturally responsive teaching, and teacher identity: An action research inquiry in teacher education. *Action in Teacher Education, 42*(4), 387–404. https://doi.org/10.1080/01626620.2019.1710728

Martin, A. D., & Spencer, T. (2020b). Teaching across time and space: A collaborative self-study of teacher educator identity and critical practices. In C. Edge, A. Cameron-Standerford, & B. Bergh (Eds.), *Textiles and tapestries: Self-study for envisioning new ways of knowing.* EdTech Books. https://edtechbooks.org/textiles_tapestries_self_study/chapter_27

Merriam-Webster. (n.d.). *Urban.* https://www.merriam-webster.com/dictionary/urban

Miller, R. (2015). Learning to love reading: A self-study on fostering students' reading motivation in small groups. *Studying Teacher Education, 11*(2), 103–123. https://doi.org/10.1080/17425964.2015.1045771

Mills, C., & Ballantyne, J. (2016). Social justice and teacher education: A systematic review of empirical work in the field. *Journal of Teacher Education, 67*(4), 263–276. https://doi.org/10.1177/0022487116660152

Milner, H. R. (2015). *Rac(e)ing to class: Confronting poverty and race in schools and classrooms.* Harvard Education Press.

Muchmore, J. (2008). Running for the local school board-and finishing last: A story of opposing narratives. In M. L. Heston, D. L. Tidwell, K. K. East, & L. M. Fitzgerald (Eds.), *Pathways to change in teacher education: Dialogue, diversity, and self-study.* Proceedings of the seventh international conference on Self-study of teacher education practices (pp. 243–247).

Nicol, C., & Korteweg. (2010). Braiding teacher lives into relation: The steps and dilemmas of culturally responsive teacher education in Canada. In L. B. Erickson, J. R. Young, & S. Pinnegar (Eds.), *Navigating the public and private: Negotiating the diverse landscape of teacher education.* Proceedings of the eighth international conference on Self-study of teacher education practices (pp. 183–187).

Parker, K., Horowitz, J. M., Brown, A., Fry, R., Cohn, D., Igielnik, R. (2018, May 22). *Demographic and economic trends in urban, suburban, and rural communities.* Pew Research Center. https://www.pewresearch.org/social-trends/2018/05/22/demographic-and-economic-trends-in-urban-suburban-and-rural-communities/

Peterman, F., & Marquez-Zenkov, K. (2002). Resiliency and resistance in partnering to prepare urban teachers. In C. Kosnik, A. Freese, & A. P. Samaras (Eds.), *Making a difference in teacher education through self-study.* Proceedings of the fourth international conference on Self-study of teacher education practices (pp. 84–90).

Purcell, M. (2013). The right to the city: The struggle for democracy in the urban public realm. *Policy & Politics, 41*(3), 311–327. https://doi.org/10.1332/030557312X655639

Ragoonaden, K., & Bullock, S. (2014). Challenging our pedagogies of teacher education: Crossing boundaries through collaborative self-study. In D. Garbett, & A. Ovens (Eds.), *Changing practices for changing times: Past, present, and future possibilities for self-study research.* Proceedings of the tenth international conference on Self-study of teacher education practices (pp. 171–173).

Rodriguez, G. M. (2013). Power and agency in education: Exploring the pedagogical dimensions of funds of knowledge. *Review of Research in Education, 37*(1), 87–120. https://doi.org/10.3102/0091732X12462686

Rothstein, R. (2015). The racial achievement gap, segregated schools, and segregated neighborhoods: A constitutional insult. *Race and Social Problems, 7*, 21–30. https://doi.org/10.1007/s12552-014-9134-1

Scott, J., & Holme, J. J. (2016). The political economy of market-based educational policies: Race and reform in urban school districts 1915-2016. *Review of Research in Education, 40*(1), 250–297. https://doi.org/10.3102/0091732X16681001

Simon, N. S., & Johnson, S. M. (2015). Teacher turn-over in high poverty schools: What we know and can do. *Teachers College Record, 117*(3), 1–36. https://www.tcrecord.org/Content.asp?ContentId=17810

Sparks, S. D. (2016, August 11). Student mobility: How it affects learning. *Education Week.* http://68.77.48.18/RandD/Education%20Week/Student%20Mobility%20-%20How%20It%20Affects%20Learning.pdf

Strom, K. J., & Martin, A. D. (2013). Putting philosophy to work in the classroom: Using rhizomatics to deterritorialize neoliberal thought and practice. *Studying Teacher Education: A Journal of Self-study of Teacher Education Practices, 9*(3), 219–235. https://doi.org/10.1080/17425964.2013.830970

Strom, K. J., & Martin, A. D. (2016). Pursuing lines of flight: Equity-based preservice teacher learning in first-year teaching. *Policy Futures in Education, 14*(2), 252–273. https://doi.org/10.1177/1478210315615475

Strom, K. J., & Martin, A. D. (2017). *Becoming-teacher: A rhizomatic look at first-year teaching.* Brill/Sense Publishers.

Strom, K. J., Martin, A. D., & Villegas, A. M. (2018). Clinging to the edge of chaos: The emergence of novice teacher practice. *Teachers College Record, 120*(7), 1–32.

Taylor, M., Klein, E. J., & Abrams, L. (2014). Tensions of reimagining our roles as teacher educators in a third space: Revisiting a co/autoethnography through a faculty lens. *Studying Teacher Education, 10*(1), 3–19. https://doi.org/10.1080/17425964.2013.866549

Tomlinson, C. A. (2017). *How to differentiate instruction in academically diverse classrooms* (3rd ed.). ASCD Press.

Villegas, A. M., & Lucas, T. (2002). *Educating culturally responsive teachers: A coherent approach.* State University of New York Press.

Villegas, A. M., Saiz de la Mora, K., Martin, A. D., & Mills, T. (2018). The preparation and development of mainstream teachers for English language learners: Review of empirical research. *The Educational Forum, 82*(2), 138–155. https://doi.org/10.1080/00131725.2018.1420850

Watson, D. (2011). What do you mean when you say urban? Speaking honestly about race and students. *Rethinking Schools, 26*(1), 48–50.

Weiner, L., & Jerome, D. (2016). *Urban teaching: The essentials* (3rd ed.). Teachers College Press.

Wheaton, L., Giannarelli, L., & Dehry, I. (2021, July). 2021 Poverty projections: *Assessing the Impact of benefits and stimulus measures.* Urban Institute. Retrieved from https://www.urban.org/sites/default/files/publication/104603/2021-poverty-projections_0_0.pdf.

Zygmunt, E., & Clark, P. (2016). *Transforming teacher education for social justice.* Teachers College Press.

Adrian D. Martin, Ph.D., is a faculty member in the College of Education at New Jersey City University. Dr. Martin's scholarly agenda attends to equity, social justice, inclusion in education and, more specifically, in teacher education. Grounding his research in diverse theoretical and conceptual frameworks, Dr. Martin engages with multiple methodologies to explore the work of teacher educators, critical pedagogies, and teacher preparation. An active member of the American Educational Research Association (AERA) Self-Study of Teacher Education Practices (S-STEP) special interest group, he served as the 2019–2021 program co-chair. Dr. Martin's research has been published in multiple peer-reviewed journals, including *Action in Teacher Education, Studying Teacher Education, Teachers College Record*, and *International Journal of Qualitative Studies in Education*.

Part I
Preparing Teacher Educators and Teachers for Urban Education Contexts

Chapter 2
Collectively Caring: Co-Creating a Critical Feminist Community of Teacher Educators

Monica Taylor, Jennifer Fernandes, Necole Jadick, Lisa V. Kenny, Kelly Lormand, Kate Meza Fernandez, Erin Pomponio, Laurie Summer, Meredith Valentine, Katie F. Whitley, and Jameelah R. Wright

Abstract As we become teacher educators, what is our responsibility to those marginalized, invisible, and voiceless: children and teachers in our schools and communities, our preservice teachers, and ourselves as teacher educators? What kind of authentic feminist learning community supports doctoral students to be social justice activists? We are a group of doctoral students, a doctoral teaching assistant, and a professor who participated together in an elective called *Critical Feminisms: Disrupting the Patriarchy in Teaching and Teacher Education*, during the summer of 2020, a tumultuous time in the thick of a pandemic and also amidst another wave of Black Lives Matter activism in the face of the murders of Breonna Taylor, George Floyd, and Ahmaud Arbery. Our collaborative co/autoethnographic self-study focuses on the attributes of our authentic feminist community that helped us become teacher educator activists. Some themes we discuss include: bringing our whole self, mind, body, emotions, into activist work; the power of collective vulnerability and shared uncertainty; and the need for authentic community to buoy activism. This self-study is important because it centers on the kind of care necessary for the well-being of teacher educators as they find their voices, modes of activism, and agency.

Keywords Feminist pedagogy · Community · Co/autoethnography · Care · Intersectional

M. Taylor (✉) · J. Fernandes · N. Jadick · L. V. Kenny · K. Lormand · K. M. Fernandez · E. Pomponio · L. Summer · M. Valentine · K. F. Whitley · J. R. Wright
Montclair State University, Montclair, NJ, USA
e-mail: taylorm@montclair.edu

A. D. Martin (ed.), *Self-Studies in Urban Teacher Education*, Self-Study of Teaching and Teacher Education Practices 25,
https://doi.org/10.1007/978-981-19-5430-6_2

The Fool is a card of new beginnings, opportunity, and potential. Just like the young man, you are at the outset of your journey, standing at the cliff's edge, and about to take your first step into the unknown. Even though you don't know exactly where you are going, you are being called to commit yourself and follow your heart, no matter how crazy this leap of faith might seem to you. (Biddy Tarot, n.d.)

The self-study community has always worried about injustice, but the current political climate has heightened the need for explicit attention to addressing social justice issues in P–16 settings (Taylor & Diamond, 2020). In the United States (U.S.) in particular, the rights of all people who are othered are threatened: children, those of color, women, non-binary people, the LGBTQ community, the poor, speakers of English as a second language, immigrants, non-Christians, and people with disabilities. In urban schools, these threats are magnified by systemic factors such as poverty, limited resources, underfunding, overcrowding, and teacher attrition (Milner, 2006). In addition, deficit views of students and their parents are commonly used to explain the achievement gaps present in urban schools. When these oppressions are examined through an intersectional feminist lens, the impact feels insurmountable. Our self-study considered: as we become teacher educators, what is our responsibility to those who are marginalized, invisible, and voiceless such as children and young people in our schools, the teachers who work with them, our schools, families, and communities, our preservice teachers, and ourselves as teacher educators? What kind of authentic feminist learning community supports and nurtures doctoral students to be racial justice activists? How can we advocate and empower those who lack agency?

We are a group of doctoral students, a doctoral teaching assistant, and a professor who participated together in a doctoral elective, *Critical Feminisms: Disrupting the Patriarchy in Teaching and Teacher Education*, during the summer of 2020, a particularly tumultuous time in the thick of a pandemic and also amidst another wave of Black Lives Matter activism in the face of the murders of Breonna Taylor, Ahmaud Arbery, and George Floyd. During this unsettling time, our class community, constructed over Zoom, collaboratively designed a course that included a critically feminist theoretical foundation, nurtured an environment that provided emotional and intellectual support, and bridged theory with practice as we navigated between our discussions of texts and actions that we could take on the ground outside of class. We committed to reflecting on our responsibility to fight sexism, heteronormativity, and racism. Adopting an intersectional feminist lens, as many of our self-study colleagues have in the past (Cortez-Castro, 2016; McNeil, 2011; Skerrett, 2006), we created a space where we could examine our positionality in the face of racial injustice with honesty and vulnerability.

2.1 Co/Autoethnographic Self-Study

Our collaborative co/autoethnographic self-study focused on describing the attributes of our authentic community that helped us become teacher educator activists. We used co/autoethnography as a self-study feminist research methodology that takes autoethnography, "a form of self-representation that complicates cultural norms by seeing autobiography as implicated in larger cultural processes" (Taylor & Coia, 2006, p. 278), and moves it beyond the singular to the plural. We chose this methodology "because it explicitly values relationships and collaboration" (Taylor & Coia, 2020, p. 571) and it enabled us to come to know through the interweaving of our stories and dialogue so that validity, insight, and analysis all emerged as we reflected together. We wrote "into each others' lives" (Coia & Taylor, 2007, p. 26), allowing our identities to be blurred as educators, co-learners, friends, and humans.

Once the course was completed, we brainstormed prompts to which we all responded in a shared online document on Google Drive. This supported us in generating narratives of our experiences. We read our narratives and reflections individually and then coded them for emerging themes using the constant comparative method (Glaser & Straus, 1967). We collectively reviewed the themes and analytically collapsed those that seemed narrow or repetitive. Six months later, we met over Zoom to conduct a second round of dialogic reflection about the course. We transcribed the dialogue and then individually mined the transcript for emerging patterns. Collectively, we put together a list of themes and to illustrate them, we added examples from our written reflections and Zoom transcript. Via email we discussed the format for this chapter. We divided up the task of writing and each of us authored different portions. We then collaboratively edited the chapter. We believe that this feminist co/autoethnographic process clearly mirrored the ways in which the course was facilitated and therefore made the most sense for our self-study.

Similarly, rather than constructing this chapter in an academically traditional manner, we present our co/autoethnography through collective and individual voices (e.g., Martin & Taylor, 2019; Taylor & Klein, 2018), interweaving our reflections about our experiences in the course with theory, research, and analysis. Our chapter tells the story of our course, and, in particular describes the context in which our community developed, its unique features, our experiences of participating in a feminist community, and finally, how these experiences impacted our work as teacher educators for racial justice. Some themes we discuss include: (a) navigating a context of unknowability, (b) creating a fluidity of power, (c) bringing our whole selves to and recognizing them in the classroom, (d) caring for one another to birth courage and quell fear, (e) allowing for discomfort to open our hearts and minds, and (f) finding our activist voices.

2.2   Co-Creations of Our Critical Feminist Learning Community

Sections of our chapter begin with the description of a tarot card, illustrating the mind/body/soul journey on which we embarked together. As the Biddy Tarot Card site stated, "The Major Arcana Tarot cards represent the life lessons, karmic influences and the big archetypal themes that are influencing your life and your soul's journey to enlightenment" (Biddy Tarot, n.d., para 1). The Fool, a major arcana card, illustrates how our self-study was a new beginning in our journey to interrogate our own assumptions and biases as we pushed ourselves beyond thought and into action.

Our community became a space where we could "check on" one another, the educators who were so often neglected or ignored during this tumultuous time. This self-study is an important and unique contribution to the field because it centers on the kind of care necessary for the well-being of teacher educators in the process of what Greene (Inside the Academy, ASU, 2010), as an existentialist, would call "still becoming," as they find their voices, modes of activism, and agency rather than a more typical checklist of actions. For urban teacher education, our work provides useful insight into how we might create spaces that support and cultivate the voices of educators of color. Such educators often enter the white[1]-dominated field of P–16 teaching having a lived experience of discrimination along with the pedagogical and social awareness of the inequities plaguing urban schooling, the need for teachers to combat these, and most importantly, a sense of critical hope (Borrero, 2011). We welcome readers to engage with our story bringing their hearts and minds and perhaps catch a glimpse of something new from within.

2.2.1 Our Unknowable Context

> The Hanged Man calls you to release the old mental models and behavioral patterns that no longer serve you so you can see your world from a new perspective and embrace new opportunities that would have otherwise been hidden from you if you didn't hit the brakes. (Biddy Tarot, n.d.)

In the spring of 2020, the world changed because of the Covid-19 pandemic. The initial two-week shutdown turned into a prolonged period of uncertainty, turmoil, and loss. As educators, we are accustomed to building and nurturing relationships with our students, and so much of that nurturing is contingent upon us being physically present with them—reading their body language, observing their social interactions, and engaging with their daily lives. We lost this proximal access to our students, leaving us to search for ways of sustaining our relationships through technology. We worried about our students and how this forced social isolation would affect them emotionally.

The context of our feminist class was defined as intersectional, not in a merely academic sense, but also in the personal ways in which the intensity of the shared cultural, historical, and global moments we were living through brought us together. In order to live this out collectively, our feminism needed to be as intersectional as the group itself. This became apparent in the very first class session as we discussed *Feminists: What were they thinking,* a 2018 documentary we watched for our initial

---

[1] We have deliberately chosen not to capitalize the term white as a political statement disrupting the status and privilege of Whiteness.

meeting. While the white women in our group shared feelings of connection to the women interviewed in the documentary who mirrored their own lives, the Black women and women of color pointed to the limitations created when feminist works center the lived experiences and activism of white women.

In the conversations during the class and in the self-study group reflections afterward, the white members expressed a common tension between wanting to shift away from the traditions and blind spots of white feminism and being cognizant of one's own whiteness and the desire to not be centered accordingly. All of us wanted to make space for our Black, Indigenous, People of Color (BIPOC) sisters, our queer brothers and sisters, and other marginalized individuals in our class, using the privileges we each possessed to position ourselves as co-conspirators. We continually revisited this tension to ensure that in our work together, we were not unintentionally othering members of our class community.

We also collectively engaged in expanding our conceptions of knowing, taking an intersectional stance. Feminist theorists and queer theorists call for the validation of ways of knowing that fall outside traditional academic hierarchies. Marinucci (2010) acknowledged that both feminism and queer theory have within them a history of racism and classism, adding that the acknowledgement of those biases "serve[s] as a reminder of how important it is to filter ideas through multiple disciplinary and personal screens" (p. 107) in order to push back against oppression and the "logic of domination" that drives the dominant hierarchical structures embedded in the systems in which we operate. In contextualizing our specific group, it is important to note that we came together, not merely as a group of feminists, but in the context of a class in which students were interested in engaging in the study of feminist theory. Even though we were 2 months into pandemic lockdowns when our course began, Monica (the course instructor) and Kelly (the doctoral teaching assistant) could not have anticipated the unique circumstances that would mark our time together from May 21st to June 25th of 2020. Although we knew we were navigating turbulent times as we began our course, after only our first meeting, the tides turned yet again with the breaking news of the murder or George Floyd, which followed the murders of Breonna Taylor and Ahmaud Aubrey whose deaths had occurred months earlier, and the subsequent emotion, public outcry, and protesting that followed in the midst of the COVID-19 pandemic.

The foundation on which Monica and Kelly built our course—one that drew from feminist, engaged pedagogies—quickly drew us together, forging the bond that led us to write this chapter. Although feminist theorists resist fixed definitions, they share commonalities including focus on social change and equity, multiplicity and questioning, disrupting binaries and power structures, and reflection, which, in turn, influence the feminist classroom (Britzman, 1995; Forrest & Rosenberg, 1997; hooks, 1994; McCusker, 2017). The feminist pedagogy Monica and Kelly co-constructed with us was one,

> in which everyone's views and questions [were] heard and responded to. One in which everyone receive[d] opportunities to work through their thoughts and … one in which every student [was] treated equally regardless of age, race, gender, sexuality, nationality, religion, size, etc. (Pallapothu, 2018, para 3).

In the open sharing of our views and questions, our multiple ways of seeing emerged.

This focus on multiplicity and diverse ways of knowing informed the development of our class community into a "space" where we could work through the complex thoughts and emotions that pervaded the tumultuous time during which our course took place. Gilligan's (2013) feminist ethics of care reflected this orientation as well, considering emotional knowledge as a valid and rich resource for understanding and challenging the patriarchal dominance of rational thought over all. Within this ethic of care stance, responsive relationships in which emotions "join with reason" are viewed as yielding a far more nuanced understanding of how humans interact with others in the world as well as within specific contexts. Teachers preparing to work in urban schools can benefit from these nuanced understandings of themselves and the specific challenges they will face in an urban school context. Gilligan's (2013) work emphasized the acts of listening and hearing others and reading the human world around us.

Like the Hanged Man, we were called to let go of old thought patterns around feminism, particularly those that position feminism as primarily concerned with social mobility or women. For those of us who identify as white women, we saw a clear connection between this ethics of care stance and our own critical examination of our positionality as so much of the harm done by white feminists lies in our centering gender to the detriment of other marginalized facets of identity. We moved consciously and fluidly through the theory and practice of our work and our engagement with what was culturally, socially, and politically happening around us. The emotional impact of our experiences were undeniable, and rather than omit them from our work, we embraced Gilligan's ethics of care (2013) and established emotion as an additional way of knowing in our work.

2.2.2   Fluidity of Power

> After a period of pause and reflection with the Hanged Man, the Death card symbolises the end of a major phase or aspect of your life that you realise is no longer serving you, opening up the possibility of something far more valuable and essential. You must close one door to open another. (Biddy Tarot, n.d.)

An important aspect of the structure of the class and building our feminist learning community was the fluidity of power, a tenet of feminist pedagogy that challenges hierarchies of power and the status quo (McCusker, 2017). Disrupting the inherent power dynamic that exists in every classroom, including the roles and responsibilities placed on the teacher-student relationship (Rymes, 2016), was the first indication that we would be learning in a different way and in a different space. A common theme of our shared reflections described the learning environment as a more democratic, free, and negotiated space than most of us had ever experienced. In our community, building relationships was the first priority and students' voices were elevated from the start. Monica and Kelly exemplified Freire's (1998/2005) notion of teachers learning with and from students with love, courage, and humility.

Their relationship to the class and each other modeled the fluidity of power. In our Zoom Reflective Session after the course concluded, Necole (a doctoral student) reflected on "the blurred lines of the hierarchy" and not being able to come up with a word or phrase to "do justice" to the collaborative co-teaching model that Monica and Kelly presented. Kelly described it as, "Feminist teachers should be thoughtful and purposeful with how they attempt to share power. Sharing power is something you do actively, consciously, and recursively over time" (Zoom Reflective Session, April, 2021). This reminds us that we have to be cautious about simplistic explanations of power sharing (Gore, 2003). Throughout the semester, as we worked as co-constructors and broke down the barriers between us, what we rebuilt in place of the status quo was infinitely better. Erin (a doctoral student) suggested the following about our class community by quoting from Davis (1997) that, "Human interaction is thus cast in terms of a complex choreography … rather than coordinated actions or competing voices" (p. 370). Erin continued by stating,

> Instead, we created a harmony born out of vulnerability and shared purpose. Our group leaned into empowering pedagogy which did not 'dissolve the authority of power of the instructor' but did help to 'move from power as domination to power as creative energy' (Shrewsbury, 1993, cited in Gore, 2003, p. 342). (Zoom Reflective Session, April, 2021)

Throughout our class, creative energy was apparent in the activities and activism in which we participated and the fluidity of shared power gave all participants the space to experiment, learn, and grow. While traditional power relations are an oppressive force in urban classrooms, understanding and mitigating the effects of hierarchical power dynamics can improve the chances of students and teachers being successful in urban settings (Milner, 2006).

The symbolic death of the normative student-teacher dynamic created the opportunity for the more valuable and essential personal connections we were able to forge in our feminist class environment. Rather than settling into the normative, hierarchical roles pervasive in P–16 settings, we strove for vulnerability, wholeness, and connection. We enacted risks within our individual and collective learning, drawing connections between the academic and the personal, and allowing our intellectual and professional growth to be deeply entwined with the embodied, relational, and emotional aspects of ourselves. These opportunities to resist patriarchal models of teaching and learning gave us practice at how we could, simultaneously, facilitate such sharing of power within our urban and suburban school settings. During a global pandemic, and a time when the U.S. was visibly grappling with racial, economic, and political injustice, we were cultivating feminist ways of teaching and learning. Our feminist teacher-learning community taught us as we learned, and aided us in reflecting about our students, our families, and the larger communities in ways that embraced the whole, the personal, and the complex, varied levels of our dynamic, ever-changing identities. We found new ways to engage with learners, to assess and build upon learning, and to relate with students, parents, colleagues and administrators. Sometimes this growth led us to choose particular forms of content to teach. Sometimes we put aside the content to meet learners where they were, and address what was meaningful to them, in the here-and-now.

2.2.3 Emotions, Mind, and Body: Recognizing Ourselves in the Class

Sitting at the threshold of the conscious and subconscious mind, the High Priestess has an innate ability to travel between these realms effortlessly. She teaches you that the world is not always as it seems and more profound influences are often at play. She ushers you through the thin veil of awareness, offering you a deep, intuitive understanding of the Universe and a heightened awareness of secret or hidden information. (Biddy Tarot, n.d.)

Traditionally, educators singularly determine a specific set of content and knowledge deemed important to teach. But what happens when a professor creates a space where she positions herself as a learner alongside her students? When students are invited to co-construct what is valued in the curriculum, they feel valued and begin to recognize themselves in the coursework. By intentionally sharing power with students in the course, Monica and Kelly fostered a rich learning experience that engaged us as learners to build upon our personal prior knowledge and interests. For example, as the mom of a Black son and the teacher of preschool-aged Black boys, Jameelah (a doctoral student) came to our Critical Feminisms course deeply invested in how the school-to-prison pipeline impacts the lives of Black boys. Through the blurred lines of power in our course dynamics, she not only saw herself and her passions in the coursework, but she came to learn about a tangential, yet related nuance, of how the school-to-prison pipeline affects Black girls as she discovered Black Girlhood Studies. As with many of us, the course was able to shape Jameelah's burgeoning interests in ways that she never imagined.

As students, when our whole selves were recognized, appreciated, and welcomed into the conversation as valued forms of knowledge, our lived experiences were present, and honored, as if seeing ourselves in the mirror. Erin reflected,

The freedom and encouragement to be ourselves and bring ourselves, to question with support and kindness, to experiment, explore, be angry, be sad and be joyful allowed us to recognize new parts of ourselves and, seeing others going through the same experience, provided a way to see ourselves in others, deepening our own sense and recognition of self. (Zoom Reflective Session, April, 2021)

Similarly, when one person introduced a topic to the collective group of learners, we were given a glimpse into the window of their reality.

Kate, who self-identifies as a mixed-race international doctoral student, expressed the invigoration she felt as she saw herself in the curriculum. This was counter to other course constructions in that our course opened the door to knowledge outside the traditional American norm. Kate emphasized, "It was not another place where my experience was absent" (Zoom Reflective Session, April, 2021). Instead, the multiplicity of our diverse experiences was valued within a compassionate space for us to take risks and share deeply held beliefs, concerns, and values without judgment. During her time in the U.S. she had seen an underrepresentation of her own lived experiences and identity in courses and assigned readings, texts which are often not focused on the experiences of people outside the U.S. (Zeichner, 2010). Our perspectives, multiple identities, and cultural backgrounds encouraged our engagement with discourse that pushed us as a caring community to better understand one another as complex beings whose differences could be supported for one another's growth as individuals.

Through the use of a metaphorical canvas, paint, and paintbrush, we were invited to bring our whole selves to the learning experience which unveiled previously unimagined possibilities. Erin posited:

> There's a difference between looking in a mirror and expecting to see your reflection, the same reflection you've seen since you've been alive, and the kind of reflection I came to recognize in the class…It was like rather than the mirror/window metaphor that is sometimes used when talking about students "seeing themselves" in their classrooms, we were given a canvas, paint, and a paintbrush to recognize ourselves as we painted and reacted to the class. (Zoom Reflective Session, April, 2021)

For some of us, we began to see ourselves in new ways, as Jameelah who wrote in her reflection, "We discovered some things about ourselves that we were able to share and present in our final project. Some people were in tears because they were revealing these very intimate parts of themselves that they discovered in this class" (April, 2021).

Since our class curriculum was interpersonally co-constructed, many of us felt changed and were able to have, as Erin reflected, a new "emergent recognition of myself 'becoming' throughout the class" (Zoom Reflective Session, April 2021). As educators, all of us appreciated the value of the mantra "practice what you preach." Kate shared her impressions as to why these outcomes were revealed when she explained,

> We enacted what we as teachers always are told to do in our classrooms; to include the experiences and cultures of our students. We did that. We did it because we were allowed that freedom to do it, and we did it for ourselves. (Zoom Reflective Session, April, 2021)

Holding up our own lived experiences in the context of the class community we co-constructed, we highlighted the power of bringing our personal knowledge into the classroom, which pushed us to examine how consistently the students we work with in our varied school contexts have the opportunity to feel the same connection to their curriculum and learning experiences. In urban schools where teachers can expect greater student diversity but less representation in the curriculum and academic content, valuing personal knowledge and lived experiences is more challenging but also more necessary (Milner, 2006).

2.2.4 Care Births Courage

> The Empress signifies a strong connection with our femininity. Femininity translates in many ways–elegance, sensuality, fertility, creative expression, nurturing–and is necessary for creating balance in both men and women. (Biddy Tarot, n.d.)

Within our feminist community, we enacted trust and care in ways that embraced our individual and collective wholeness and complexities. During a time of profound uncertainty, the time we took to engage in "chit chat" established stability and caring, a place we could count on in our twice weekly class sessions. We learned, together, that "small talk" is anything but small. The fraught sociopolitical context, the repeated assault on Black lives, and the transformation of our teaching and personal experiences, due to the pandemic, continually filtered into all aspects of our conversations. We cried, laughed, read, protested, raged, wrote, and listened as we ached with questions, as we struggled and processed, individually and collectively. We met remotely, but *we* were not remote. Our class was a place that held space for us all, and held room for all of our selves to enter, to be, and to manifest our truth.

Forgasz and Clemans (2014) observed that teachers who enact care-centered pedagogy, by intentionally valuing emotional and embodied experiences, enable students to engage with feminist ways of constructing knowledge. Urban students in particular can benefit from care-centered pedagogy and its tenet of teaching to the *whole* person, as they are so often disparaged simply because of their cultural and linguistic identities and are thus positioned as less-than or partial. In our class, Monica and Kelly used their teacher leader roles to center relationship building and freedom, providing a safe haven for us to express ourselves genuinely (hooks, 1994). Together, Monica and Kelly allowed space for and affirmed our desire to seek emotional understandings of ourselves and each other, and we were afforded time, before and during class, to connect relationally. These practices supported us in melding our academic, personal, political, and professional selves, and cultivated our ability to value ourselves and each other more fully. These forms of feminist pedagogy added to the rich understandings and connections we developed between academic content and lived experiences.

2.2.5   Discomfort: Hearts Broken and Minds Open

> After a Tower experience, you will grow stronger, wiser and more resilient as you develop a new perspective on life you did not even know existed. These moments are necessary for your spiritual growth and enlightenment, and truth and honesty will bring about a positive change, even if you experience pain and anxiety throughout the process. (Biddy Tarot, n.d.)

Paradoxically, the emphasis on care and connection allowed us to have the courage to embark on a journey of challenging ourselves and each other (Kishimoto & Mwangi, 2009). As we learned about each other as whole people, we grew in our awareness of the multiple perspectives and diverse, intersectional identities that we embodied. These relationships, as much as the content with which we engaged, cultivated courage as we examined our personal biases, privilege, and areas of unknowing. We encouraged ourselves and each other to stretch–as we listened, made space, expanded learning boundaries, and rethought what we once took as truth.

Our care for each other held the door for us to experience trust. Trust in our community's capacity to hold space for our diverse ways of being and doing. Trust that we could abide in disagreement, and within contradictory and fluid perspectives (hooks, 1994). We discovered that there was room to misstep, to make mistakes, to feel a wide variety of emotions, and to be supported as we corrected or adjusted. Trust emboldened us to ask questions that, in other spaces, we may have shied away from because of the ways those questions could tie us in knots. Care, trust, and community allowed our bubbles to be pierced, and our perspectives challenged. Our comfort gave birth to discomfort, and our discomfort prompted a reckoning (Ohito, 2016).

This class, both historically and culturally, was grounded in a particular place and time. We were called, at an embodied and emotional level, to see, without looking away. We had watched as a white man with a badge and a gun pressed his knee into George Floyd's neck, publicly murdering him. As activists demanded that we "say her name" we thought about Breonna Taylor, killed in her own home by police. The context of our class was defined as intersectional, not in a merely academic way, but in the intensity of these shared cultural moments through which we were living. For the white feminists among us, it was a call to see, with open eyes, hearts, and minds, our complicity with white, masculine, ableist, and capitalist forms of oppression.

As our classmates of color shared anger, pain, passion, fear, and political possibilities for creating justice, the white feminists among us confronted our internalized "respectability politics" (Kendall, 2020, p. 93). Kendall (2020) used respectability politics to describe how white people invalidate the legitimate resistance responses that people of color express. When people of color show emotion, particularly anger, or articulate ideas that defy dominant cultural norms, white people deem these acts as lacking in "respectability." In reality, these acts of resistance challenge white norms and power structures, and are thus, met with reactions that reproduce marginalization.

Ahmed (2017) noted that white women often frame BIPOC women as "the problem" because they raise uncomfortable truths. As BIPOC women in our class raised their voices to call for defunding the police, or to name and resist colonial practices within education and society, the white feminists among us were challenged to scrutinize our ideas and our practices. What assumptions had white feminists constructed about "safety" that we needed to challenge (Kishimoto & Mwangi, 2009)? When white feminists felt tempted to center white, hegemonic voices and perspectives, could we lean into our intense, complex feelings, breathe, and commit to hearing the other beautiful, strong, worthy voices among us? Could they challenge their own conditioned privilege, and ensure that everyone felt valued and heard? This was the reckoning, an opportunity to harness our feminist work to resist injustice and oppression, even within ourselves, so that we might avoid reproducing the status quo (McCusker, 2017).

As Taylor and Diamond (2020) wrote, "We react to these times as 'robust, full human beings' (Cullors & Burke, 2018) with a mixture of emotion, anger, joy, sadness, frustration, and love" (p. 511). Who were "we"? There were many moments of our whole group where we worked and learned as a community. But real learning is messy, and there was a fluidity between how we moved from whole-community to varied, fluctuating collaborations and relationships among the members within that community.

The work was not always fun. The ideas were neither pretty nor abstract. In moments, we experienced genuine, raw struggle. Old wounds from past traumas reopened. We reached out to each other. We called. We texted. We cried. Separately, we sat on porches, on chairs, on pillows, on hard floors, and worked to abide with our full, complicated experiences as we strove to see through new eyes. We stretched beyond our comfort zones. In moments, we turned away, numbed and distracted ourselves, and paused. We showed up again, dove into projects that contradicted what we thought we had known. As classmates shared their projects, passions, and activism, diverse cultural knowings were affirmed and afforded space and worth. We listened, and rethought structures we took for granted: police forces, prison systems, and, yes, schools. We slowed ourselves, even as we buzzed with confusion or reactivity. How might we uncover greater awareness, as women, as educators, as allies, as co-conspirators? What could we discover and where might our insights lead us? We carved out a space where the towers within us and outside of us could be torn down and reconstructed, and in the aftermath of these Tower experiences, our drive, now necessary and urgent, emerged.

2.2.6   Need to Act, Need to React

> The Justice card represents justice, fairness, truth and the law. You are being called to account for your actions and will be judged accordingly... A level of compassion and understanding accompany Justice, and although you may have done something you regret, this card suggests that you will be treated fairly and without bias. Be ready to take responsibility for your actions and stand accountable for the ensuing consequences. (Biddy Tarot, n.d.)

Once we had committed ourselves to seeing, we discovered that we could not un-see. We could not tap out, in our professional work, in our personal lives, or in our politics. Rather, we needed to act and to react. Our collective inability to un-see what was in front of us gave way to a perspective that called us to act in a felt unity, regardless of whether or not we physically came to act together. Within class, we shared upcoming protests and marches. We all had different ways of engaging with advocacy at that moment in time. When protests were student-organized, we were reminded of WHY we were doing this work: to make schools more equitable and openly reflective of all student identities.

It was very important to the group that we were not just talking the talk, but taking action. As Laurie (a doctoral student) reflected, "It was a time when we were all turning our gaze in the same direction" (Doctoral Reflection Session, April, 2021). Attending to what we collectively saw through our feminist lens gave rise to a feeling of urgency, a sense within the group that we the collective and I the individual had to do something. So the class became a place to share ways to be activists. For example, one district organized a widely attended march specifically for educators. Some of us could not stay away and attended in solidarity with those with Black or Brown skin, who were directly impacted and did not have the luxury to stay home, whose bodies were endangered more by racism than by a deadly virus; some of us were more reluctant because of the pandemic and the fears about safety in a large crowd. Regardless, no one was judged based on their individual expression of activism. Some activism took the form of conscious decisions in our professional spaces or classrooms. Katie reached out to administrators and asked if she could start a faculty social justice discussion group in her school. Kelly shared how her already established teacher inquiry group had recommitted itself to doing anti-racist work. Another student in the class (a school administrator), created a shelf of culturally competent texts for her fellow educators. Through this class we became advocates for ourselves, our colleagues, and our students. Katie reflected, "It isn't that I didn't push for change before—I'm sure we all did in our own ways—but I've found myself more confident about directly disrupting power structures because I'd had the space to work out my thinking around disrupting with all of you" (Zoom Reflective Session, April, 2021).

In the time since our class ended, we have explored the various ways we feel transformed by the experiences we shared within our learning community. Our teaching practices, our interactions with colleagues, and even our interactions with friends have shifted. The moments of tension, where we examined our own assumptions and limited understandings, have led to ongoing reflection and discussion and changes in our beliefs and our behaviors. Our deep immersion into diverse ways of being and doing have allowed for a blossoming that is bearing fruit beyond the timeline of our class.

There is an emergent recognition of self, a self that is becoming, and an ability to see self in other, and other in self. We seek out books, films, articles, and conversations that prompt us to contextualize history and culture outside of our own limited perspectives. As we continue to bloom and fall, take seed, root, and reemerge, we grow in strength and in vibrancy, not forgetting what it felt like to turn our gaze together towards a moment of unforgettable injustice. In our schools, we raise our voices, harness our agency, and demonstrate more confidence as we seek to disrupt power. From the reckoning of the Justice card, we continue to seek fairness for ourselves and others. We ask ourselves, "What should we do here? How do we proceed? How am I complicit?" Our participation within our intersectional, feminist community, served as an act of resistance. We continue to experience the ripples from this shared moment in time, and carry it forward, wondering where it will take us, as we ground ourselves in relationship with one another.

2.3 Being a Feminist Educator in P–16 Classrooms

Transforming learning in urban schools has often focused on students from a deficit lens and placed the onus for change on improving test scores and closing the achievement gap. In our thinking about practical aspects of teaching that lead to transformative learning experiences that may be beneficial to urban teachers and teacher educators, feminist teaching practices invite learners to find meaning in their lives, through community and in solidarity; to question preconceived notions; to examine the world through alternate lenses and develop new and evolving understandings; and to genuinely appreciate and embrace multiple ways of knowing and being in the world. More specifically, below we offer some ways that P–16 educator in urban contexts may introduce feminist practices in their everyday teaching and learning. hooks (1994) argued that, for teachers to successfully support learners in taking risks within the classrooms, educators must model that risk-taking, by making themselves vulnerable, and by demonstrating their vulnerability within the classroom. Feminist pedagogy has the potential to facilitate this kind of meaningful learning within urban and suburban schools, by rethinking how power is shared among educators and learners, honoring multiple ways of knowing and being, and engaging the complex, varied, and fluid identities that contribute to learning communities.

2.3.1 Empower Students Individually and Collectively

Although empowering students in the classroom might look different across P–16 grade levels, all teachers and students can negotiate the class curriculum together as a learning community. At the early childhood and elementary levels, teachers can co-create class expectations and understandings. At the middle school through college levels (including urban teacher education), educators can foster more collaborative relationships with their students by encouraging shared leadership in activities and discussions, fostering collaboration on stories, poems, posters, and presentations. They can collectively develop learning tools, select readings, propose discussion topics, and provide caring feedback to others. All of these actions give agency to learners in creating how they express themselves.

In this sense, feminist teachers and teacher educators can be thoughtful and purposeful with how they attempt to share power with their students. Gore (2003) argued that teachers should reflect on the way power dynamics operate in their classrooms. However, "in attempts to empower others we need to acknowledge that our agency has limits, that we might 'get it wrong' in assuming we know what would be empowering for others, and that no matter what our aims or how we go about 'empowering,' our efforts will be partial and inconsistent" (p. 340). Feminist teachers must always balance attempting to "get it right" with knowing that we might "get it wrong." That involves being vulnerable, not all-knowing, taking risks, and openly acknowledging mistakes or missteps. Modeling that vulnerability and honesty encourages students to do the same.

2.3.2 Legitimize Students' Multiple Ways of Knowing

Feminist practices hold space for multiple learning experiences (Marinucci, 2010), legitimizing students' numerous ways of knowing. Students are invited to deliberately explore emotions, making them reflect and critically interrogate their realities. In doing so, students begin to realize that thinking involves both the intellectual as well as the affective and the relational. Welcoming diverse means of expression encourages students to expand how they represent their learning and newly constructed knowledge to include audio visuals, literature, and art. By expressing themselves through a wide range of media, students (including preservice teachers) can deeply engage in fluid and reflective learning processes that are centered around critical dialogues rather than finished products.

A feminist teacher opens conversations where there is no right or wrong answer—where everyone feels safe enough to say their truths and be heard. They facilitate dialogue that is not focused on winning or losing but on having spaces for multiple ways of existing. That type of practice requires an initial communal agreement of rules focused on but not limited to respect, care, and solidarity. In an urban teacher education setting where most of teachers experience a demographic divide between themselves and their students (Borrero, 2011), solidarity is at the heart of healing and moving forward as a collective force against systemic injustice.

2.3.3 Engage Students' Whole Selves in the Curriculum

Classrooms should be places where learners can feel comfortable bringing their whole selves and their whole persona: personal, academic, familiar, communal, and past and present (Taylor & Coia, 2020). Teachers and teacher educators must tend to the whole individual, the whole being, the whole self. The Covid-19 pandemic has exposed that the social and emotional lives of learners must be acknowledged, addressed, and tended to in classrooms.

Learners' intersectional identities must be accounted for in the development of classroom curriculum. In typical urban and suburban school settings, some kinds of identities, and some ways of constructing knowledge—some ways of being in the world—are privileged, because they conform to the school culture. Much of school is built on individual achievement and competition. Yet, if we center the idea that all participants in our community have worth and value, if we center community over competition, and care over all else, we begin to build a new way of "doing school" in these spaces.

These shifts may bring tension and discomfort, but these tensions and discomforts should be recognized and discussed; never avoided, ignored, or swept under a rug. They are opportunities to reflect, as they are part of our unexplored selves.

Students' life experiences have value, and should be valued. Teachers and teacher educators can encourage their students to incorporate personal experiences into their learning via journal entries, vignettes, autobiographies, and identity maps to help ensure that all members of the classroom community feel seen and heard in the curriculum.

2.4 Conclusion

> When the World card appears in a Tarot reading, you are glowing with a sense of wholeness, achievement, fulfilment and completion. A long-term project, period of study, relationship or career has come full circle, and you are now reveling in the sense of closure and accomplishment. (Biddy Tarot, n.d.)

The World Tarot card represents our sense of wholeness for having fully embodied a feminist pedagogy that allowed us to grow as educators and human beings with some closure through the writing of this chapter. However, we know this is not the end; we are thinking about what journey comes next—where is our next Fool card?

Our path is circular; from the experience taking this class, to now writing about this class, somewhere down the road, the opportunity to reconstruct and co-construct similar possibilities await. By guiding our work with insights of the Tarot, we found important themes in our own collective journey that punctuated our reflections with moments of life's cycles–further illuminating the spiraling and recursive path that emerged from our class's experience. This learning experience produced in us a desire to give back to our teaching community and share with others what we have learned. We are committed to making the world a better place because we understand that everything is connected. We are all connected.

References

Ahmed, S. (2017). *Living a feminist life*. Duke University Press.

Biddy Tarot. (n.d.). *The major arcana*. https://www.biddytarot.com/tarot-card-meanings/major-arcana/

Borrero, N. (2011). Entering teaching for and with love: Visions of pre-service urban teachers. *Journal of Urban Learning, Teaching, and Research, 7*, 18–26. http://jultr.online/index.php/jultr/issue/view/6/19

Britzman, D. P. (1995). Is there a queer pedagogy? Or, stop reading straight. *Educational Theory, 45*(2), 151–165.

Coia, L., & Taylor, M. (2007). From the inside out and from the outside in: Co/autoethnography as a means of professional renewal. In C. Kosnik, C. Beck, A. R. Freese, & A. P. Samaras (Eds.), *Making a difference in teacher education through self-study: Studies of personal, professional, and program renewal* (pp. 19–33). Kluwer Press.

Cortez-Castro, D. H. (2016). Vivencias (lived experiences) of a feminist Chicana as praxis: A testimonio of straddling between multiple worlds. In J. Kitchen, D. Tidwell, & L. Fitzgerald (Eds.), *Self-study and diversity: Vol 2. Inclusive education for a diverse world* (pp. 39–54). Sense Publishers.

Cullors, P., & Burke, T. (2018). *Patrisse Cullors and Tarana Burke: Anger, activism and action.* Elle. https://www.elle.com/culture/career-politics/a19180106/patrisse-cullors-tarana-burke-black-lives-matter-metoo-activism/.

Davis, B. (1997). Listening for differences: An evolving conception of mathematics teaching. *Journal for Research in Mathematics Education, 28*(3), 355–376. https://www.jstor.org/stable/749785

Demetrakas, J. (2018). *Feminists: What were they thinking.* Netflix.

Forgasz, R., & Clemans, A. (2014). Feeling: Feminist? A self-study of emotion as a feminist epistemology in education practice. In M. Taylor & L. Coia (Eds.), *Gender, feminism, and queer theory in the self-study of teacher education practices* (pp. 61–75). Springer.

Forrest, L., & Rosenberg, F. (1997). A review of the feminist pedagogy literature: The neglected child of feminist psychology. *Applied & Preventive Psychology, 6,* 179–192.

Freire, P. (1998/2005). *Teachers as cultural workers: Letters to those who dare teach* (Expanded Edn.). Westview Press.

Gilligan, C. (2013, April 18). Resisting justice: A feminist ethics of care. *Josep Egozcue lectures.* Victor Grifols Foundation for Bioethics, Barcelona.

Glaser, B. G., & Straus, A. S. (1967). *The discovery of grounded theory: Strategies for qualitative research.* Aldine De Gruyter.

Gore, J. (2003). What we can do for you! What can "we" do for "you"?: Struggling over empowerment in critical and feminist pedagogy. In A. Darder, M. Baltodano, & R. D. Torres (Eds.), *The critical pedagogy reader* (pp. 331–348). Routledge Falmer.

hooks, b. (1994). *Teaching to transgress: Education as the practice of freedom.* Routledge.

Inside the Academy ASU. (2010). https://www.youtube.com/watch?v=30LytP3IaIE&t=57s

Kendall, M. (2020). *Hood feminism: Notes from the women that a movement forgot.* Viking.

Kishimoto, K. & Mwangi, M. (2009). Critiquing the rhetoric of "safety" in feminist pedagogy: Women of color offering an account of ourselves. *Feminist Teacher, 19*(2), 87–102. https://muse.jhu.edu/article/262816

Marinucci, M. (2010). *Feminism is queer: The intimate connection between queer and feminist theory.* Zed Books.

Martin, A., & Taylor, M. (2019). An intergenerational self-study of narrative reflections on literature, gender, and LGBTQ identities. In A. D. Martin & J. K. Strom (Eds.), *Exploring gender and LGBTQ issues in K12 and teacher education: A rainbow assemblage* (pp. 163–182). Information Age Publishing.

McCusker, G. (2017). A feminist teacher's account of her attempts to achieve the goals of feminist pedagogy. *Gender and Education, 29*(4), 445–460. https://doi.org/10.1080/0954025 3.2017.1290220

McNeil, B. (2011). Charting a way forward: Intersections of race and space in establishing identity as an African-Canadian teacher educator. *Studying Teacher Education, 8*(1), 69–85. https://doi.org/10.1080/17425964.2011.591137

Milner, R. H. (2006). Preservice teachers' learning about cultural and racial diversity: Implications for urban education. *Urban Education, 41,* 343–375. https://doi.org/10.1177/0042085906289709

Ohito, E. O. (2016). Making the emperor's new clothes visible in anti-racist teacher education: Enacting a pedagogy of discomfort with white preservice teachers. *Equity & Excellence in Education, 49*(4), 454–467. https://doi.org/10.1080/10665684.2016.1226104

Pallapothu, V. (2018). *What does a feminist classroom look like?* Medium. https://medium.com/the-red-elephant-foundation/what-does-a-feminist-classroom-look-like-af073dac3dc9

Rymes, B. (2016). *Classroom discourse analysis: A tool for critical reflection* (2nd ed.). Taylor & Francis.

Shrewsbury, C. M. (1993). What is feminist pedagogy? *Women's Studies Quarterly, 3 & 4*, 8–16.

Skerrett, A. (2006). Looking inward: The impact of race, ethnicity, gender, and social class background on teaching sociocultural theory in education. *Studying Teacher Education, 2*(2), 183–200. https://doi.org/10.1080/17425960600983213

Taylor, M., & Coia, L. (2006). Complicating our identities as urban teachers: A co/autoethnography. In J. Kincheloe, P. Anderson, K. Rose, D. Griffith, & K. Hayes (Eds.), *Urban education: An encyclopedia* (pp. 273–281). Greenwood Press.

Taylor, M., & Coia, L. (2020). Co/autoethnography as a feminist methodology: A retrospective. In J. Kitchen, M. Berry, S. M. Bullock, M. Taylor, A. Crowe, H. Guojonsdottir, & L. Thomas (Eds.), *2nd international handbook of self-study of teaching and teacher education practices* (Springer International Handbooks of Education) (2nd ed., pp. 565–610). Springer.

Taylor, M., & Diamond, M. (2020). The role of self-study in teaching and teacher education for social justice. In J. Kitchen, M. Berry, H. Guojonsdottir, S. M. Bullock, M. Taylor, & A. R. Crowe (Eds.), *2nd international handbook of self-study of teaching and teacher education practice* (Springer International Handbooks of Education) (2nd ed., pp. 509–544). Springer.

Taylor, M., & Klein, E. J. (2018). Tending to ourselves, tending to each other: Nurturing feminist friendships to manage academic lives. In N. Lemon & S. McDonough (Eds.), *Mindfulness in the academy: Practices and perspectives from scholars* (pp. 99–111). Springer.

Zeichner, K. (2010). Rethinking the connections between campus courses and field experiences in college-and university-based teacher education. *Journal of Teacher Education, 61*(1–2), 89–99. https://doi.org/10.1177/0022487109347671

Monica Taylor, Ph.D., is the Director of Gender, Sexuality, and Women's Studies and a feminist professor and social justice advocate in the Department of Educational Foundations. She also is Academic Co-Editor of The Educational Forum. She writes about feminist pedagogy, self-study, LGBTQ+ inclusive practices, teaching for social justice, and teacher leadership. She recently co-edited *The 2nd International Handbook of Self-Study of Teaching and Teacher Education Practices* and is currently writing a book, *Our bodies tell the story: Using co/autoethnography to disrupt the patriarchy in our lives and in our classroom.* She serves on the Board of Planned Parenthood of Metro NJ and volunteers as an advocate for asylum seekers as well as for voter protection. Her commitments to fighting sexism, heteronormativity, and racism manifest in all aspects of her life.

Jennifer Fernandes, M.A., has taught mathematics in secondary education in urban districts for the past eight years. She holds a Bachelor's degree in Mathematics with a concentration in Education and a Master's degree in Educational Leadership from Montclair State University. She is currently continuing her studies as a doctoral candidate in Teacher Education and Teacher Development at Montclair State University. Closing the opportunity gap in mathematics education drives her passion to be an educator. This has influenced her research interests in our cultural understanding of mathematics and inequity in mathematics curriculum and assessments. Her commitment for high-quality instruction for all students is guided by this research.

Necole Jadick, M.A., has been an elementary school principal for nearly a decade. Prior to becoming an administrator, she taught fourth grade for ten years in urban and suburban districts. She holds a Bachelor's degree in Theatre from the University of Virginia, a Master's degree in Individualized Study from New York University, and a Master's degree in Educational Leadership from Montclair State University. She is currently a doctoral candidate in Teacher Education and Teacher Development at Montclair State University. Her primary area of research is intersectional feminist leadership, and she is currently examining her gendered experiences as a woman in educational administration via autoethnography.

Lisa Kenny, M.A., is a secondary English teacher with over twenty years of experience. She teaches AP Literature at a large high school in central New Jersey and serves as a member of the school's Diversity, Equity, and Inclusion Committee. She earned a Bachelor of Arts in English with Teacher Certification from Montclair State University in 2000, a Master of Arts in English Education from Teachers College, Columbia University in 2006, and is currently pursuing a doctoral degree in Teacher Education and Teacher Development at Montclair State University. Her research interests include antiracist English practices, racial literacy, and feminist pedagogy.

Kelly Lormand, Ph.D., has been teaching high school English for 17 years. She co-wrote the A.P. English language and composition curriculum focused on social justice, power, identity, and equity. In addition to teaching at the high school level, she is an adjunct professor in Gender, Sexuality, and Women's Studies at Montclair State University. With a group of secondary educators and colleagues, she founded a social justice professional learning community committed to dismantling racism, sexism, classism, and other forms of oppression. Her research focuses on queering feminist pedagogy, self-study, collaboration, and teacher activism. She recently defended her dissertation, *Queering feminist facilitation: A culture circle discusses gender & sexuality*, and earned a Ph.D. in Teacher Education and Teacher Development.

Kate Meza Fernandez, M.A., was born and raised in Villa El Salvador, an urban coastal district in Lima, Peru. Through a combination of inclusive city policy and effective community mobilization at the neighborhood's inception, Villa El Salvador, Kate's beloved place of birth, transformed itself from a squatter settlement to a well-organized and flourishing neighborhood. This is how growing up, Kate learned how community and reciprocal care are critical to producing transforming changes that benefit all, as is seen throughout this collective article, created in sisterhood by a powerful village of women. Kate is a senior EFL teacher in Peru with experience coaching elementary teachers in rural and urban schools. Before becoming an international doctoral candidate in the Teacher Education and Teacher Development Program at Montclair State University (MSU), Kate earned a Master's in Educational Leadership (MA) at MSU.

Erin Pomponio, M.A.T., is a middle school mathematics teacher of students with disabilities in northern New Jersey and a current doctoral student in mathematics education at Montclair State University. She leverages her background in music, fine arts, and veterinary medicine to bring a unique perspective to her teaching and research. Her current interests include embodied cognition and feminist pedagogies and their intersection with creativity and qualitative mathematical learning and teaching at the elementary level. Erin holds a Bachelor's degree in fine arts from The College of New Jersey, an associate degree in applied science from Bergen Community College, and a Master's degree in teaching from Montclair State University.

Laurie Summer, M.S., is a school-based speech language pathologist, who lives and works in Northern New Jersey. She earned her Bachelor degree at Queens College University and her Master's degree at Hunter College University. Through her doctoral studies within the Teacher Education Teacher Development program at Montclair State University, Laurie has developed commitments to social justice within education. Her particular areas of interest, at this time, include feminist pedagogy, cultivating inclusion for all learners, and feminist disability studies. Laurie is one of several co-authors of the chapter, "Disability and Inclusive education: Changing perspectives" within the book, *Understanding glocal contexts: What every novice teacher needs to know*. As a poet, Laurie has enjoyed publication in small presses and anthologies. Laurie shares her life with her two sons, Benjamin and Preston, her partner, Don, their mini-poodle, Chance, and their cats, Filbert and Rockford.

Meredith Valentine, M.A., is a doctoral candidate in Teacher Education and Teacher Development at Montclair State University. She holds a Bachelor's in Elementary Education and a Master's in Early Childhood Education with a focus in Curriculum and Instruction. As a former elementary classroom teacher for nearly two decades, she values practical, experiential knowledge of teachers as a way of knowing. Her research interests include the role of teachers in disrupting systemic racial and class inequities in their classrooms, schools, and communities.

Katie Whitley, M.A., has been teaching English and theater arts for fourteen years and is an adjunct professor in the Writing Studies Department at Montclair State University. She also recently signed on as co-editor of the *New Jersey English Journal*. Katie has a B.F.A. in Acting from the University of Maryland Baltimore County and a Master's in Contemporary Literary Studies from Goldsmiths University of London. As a doctoral candidate at Montclair State University, she is committed to feminist research and is currently writing about feminist disability studies, self-study, and teachers' conceptions of literacy.

Jameelah R. Wright, M.A., is the Head Teacher and Assistant Director of Three Stages Academy in East Orange, New Jersey, and the founder of The Urban Flower Project, a professional development organization for Early Childhood Educators. Jameelah earned her B.A. in Sociology from Douglass College at Rutgers University-New Brunswick, and her M.A. in Reading Specialization from Kean University. She is a doctoral candidate in the Teacher Education and Teacher Development program at Montclair State University. Her research interests include informal professional learning, equity in gifted education, and Black Girlhood Studies.

Chapter 3
Tourist Teachers and Layers of Colonization: Lessons from New Mexico

Laura C. Haniford and Rebecca M. Sánchez

Abstract In this self-study, two teacher educators explore what it means to develop a critical pedagogy of place in New Mexico—a place with a history of layers of colonization and a population with rich and enduring connections to the land. Through dialogue, the two authors describe how they came to define and understand the trap of the tourist teacher, as well as what is required to overcome this trap and teach in community. The findings presented in this chapter have implications for urban teachers and teacher educators working with students from communities different from their own. Throughout our reflective processes we weave together the way critical place-based theories and approaches have transformed and contributed to our experience, and we explore what it means to develop a critical pedagogy of place in New Mexico from our respective social and historical positions. We invite others to consider the challenges inherent in their specific places for socially just teacher education and explore how educators at all levels might build on the knowledge of localized communities within urban contexts.

Keywords Critical place based teacher education · Tourist teacher education · New Mexico querencia

3.1 Tourist Teachers and Layers of Colonization: Lessons from New Mexico

This is a different manuscript than the one we originally envisioned writing. Originally Laura thought that a review of artifacts from her teaching practice would tell her something about the impact living and working in New Mexico has had on her teaching for social justice. When she embarked on the analysis, she did not see

L. C. Haniford (✉) · R. M. Sánchez
University of New Mexico, Albuquerque, NM, USA
e-mail: haniford@unm.edu

what she expected in her syllabi, written statements of teaching, and other teaching documents. She felt changed as a person and as a teacher educator from her time here, and yet the readily available materials did not show evidence of difference. Looking back, this is not surprising because it took the process of engaging in this inquiry to articulate the ways her thinking has changed. For both of us, the changes to practice (discussed later in the paper) come as a result of the work represented here.

In this chapter, we explore what it means to teach in communities different from the ones in which we were raised. How do educators at all levels develop the connections to place and communities necessary for true socially just teaching to occur? What gets in the way of developing these connections? Even in urban areas when teachers and students are from the same city, they are often not from the same communities. This matters because, "Anybody who has spent a significant amount of time in an urban school quickly learns how perceptive students are of those who are not from 'there'" (Sutters, 2016, p. 14).

As with most issues in education, what we describe coming to know are best characterized as dilemmas (Cuban, 2001) or tensions (Berry, 2007). By that we mean there are no clear-cut, easy answers to the challenges we pose. Instead, we recognize the hard work involved in becoming a part of a place in ways that add to our pedagogy. Throughout our reflective processes we weave together the way critical place-based theories and approaches have transformed and contributed to our experience, and we explore what it means to develop a critical pedagogy of place in New Mexico from our respective social and historical positions. We invite others to consider the challenges inherent in their specific places for socially just teacher education. How do we as teacher educators, teacher candidates, teachers, and K-12 students build on the knowledge of localized communities within urban contexts? What assumptions might we make in urban contexts about understanding the places our students come from and what we share in common?

The context for this work is the Teacher Education, Educational Leadership and Policy department at the University of New Mexico, situated in Albuquerque, the largest city in New Mexico. Albuquerque is an urban context, but as with most cities, where one lives in Albuquerque has consequences and implications for teaching and learning. New Mexico is a predominantly rural state, with a population of just over two million. There are 23 Native American sovereign nations within the state's boundaries; and the capital of Santa Fe was founded as a Spanish colonial city on Pueblo land in 1610, a full decade before pilgrims landed at Plymouth Rock. Preparing teachers to teach in New Mexico requires a nuanced understanding of history and place, particularly if you are an outsider.

Laura is a White woman who grew up in the midwestern United States, and attended very racially and socioeconomically segregated schools. She participated in a program offered by her teacher preparation institution that placed her in a school on the Navajo reservation for her student teaching experience. She then taught middle school in New Mexico and in her home state of Indiana before attending graduate school where she studied educational foundations and policy, focusing on how to prepare teacher candidates to teach diverse students. A critical pedagogy of place (Gruenwald, 2003), and culturally rooted pedagogy (Sosa-Provencio et al., 2018) helped re-shape her theoretical perspectives about the role of place in teaching and teacher education.

Rebecca is a Chicana social studies educator from New Mexico. She comes from a long line of educators committed to improving access, opportunity and rich learning experiences for the children of New Mexico. The idea of New Mexico querencia (Arellano, 2007; Romero, 2020), connection to place and people, has shaped the way she approaches teacher education.

3.2 History and Place in New Mexico

In order to explore a critical pedagogy of place in New Mexico, we draw on literature articulating the importance of place in education. However, in order to understand how place and education function here, we begin with a brief history of the contested nature of homeland in New Mexico. We then review literature on place-based education, specifically a critical pedagogy of place (Gruenwald, 2003) before articulating the love of place grounded in New Mexico, known as querencia (Arellano, 2007; Romero, 2020).

3.2.1 Contested Homelands

New Mexico is a culturally distinct place with many groups having generational and even millennial connections to the land. Prior to European colonization, the place that is currently known as New Mexico was home to hundreds of Indigenous tribal groups, with many tribes settling along the Rio Grande. The Spanish began the colonization project in 1598, after initial expeditions as early as 1540 (Sánchez et al., 2013). The colonization of New Mexico was violent and brutal, characterized by the use of forced conversion, an encomienda system of slave labor, and other oppressive tactics. After years of enduring the violent tactics of the Spanish, the Pueblo Peoples[1] revolted in 1680 and successfully expelled the Spanish. This marked the only significant expulsion of European Colonizers in North America (Sando, 2005).

New Mexico was reconquered and recolonized by the Spanish in 1692. Terms of the reconquest established a new set of expectations. Over the next centuries and with Mexican Independence, many other Spanish settlement communities came to be known as *nuevo mexicano* communities. The population grew, and with the Camino Real de Tierra Adentro (the royal road connecting Mexico City to Santa Fe and beyond), a robust system of cultural, linguistic and commercial exchange

---

[1] In New Mexico, the Spanish referred to the sedentary Indigenous groups as Pueblos. In present day, the Pueblos of New Mexico are sovereign Indigenous nations.

occurred (Sánchez et al., 2013). Very real tensions, exertions of force, and violence continued to exist between Indigenous groups and the nuevo mexicanos. However, due to time and the geographic isolation of New Mexico, the people developed distinct land, agricultural and language communities. In 1848, New Mexico became part of the United States ushering in another round of colonization. New Mexico remained a territory for 62 years and in those years, while attempting to gain statehood, the national narrative about the people New Mexico was characterized by deficit perspectives, racism, and discrimination (Nieto-Phillips, 2004). This history of violence, accommodation, and connection to the land in spite of the layers of colonization, is ever-present in the hearts and minds of many in the state and shapes peoples' relationships to schools and to outsiders.

3.2.2   A New Mexican Critical Pedagogy of Place

> Education in "advanced" societies has long been characterized by the aim of transcending place, but there is a paradox in this aim. First, it is assumed that some identifiable universal truth underlies all knowledge and should guide all educational efforts; second, it is supposed that some group…has possession of this knowledge or the path to it…This, of course, was the great conceit of colonialism (Noddings, 2002, p. 157).

Seeking to replace traditional knowledge with "universal" knowledge is yet another form of colonization, as Noddings hints at in the quote above. The standardization movement is grounded in economic discourses, with the expressed aim being helping students compete in a global economy (Gruenwald, 2003). However, this focus on sameness and generalization has not improved the lives of children and families from the most marginalized communities and has not led to better teaching and teacher education. Because social action happens in specific places, we cannot call for collective action and social justice from a decontextualized place.

What is the appropriate response from teachers and teacher educators interested in decolonization and social justice efforts? A critical pedagogy of place argues the response is to start where you are—to focus on "the well-being of the social and ecological places people actually inhabit" (Gruenwald, 2003, p. 3). Gruenwald goes on to argue "A critical pedagogy of place, moreover, proposes two broad and interrelated objectives for the purpose of linking school and place-based experience to the larger landscape of cultural and ecological politics: decolonization and reinhabitation" (2003, p. 9). Reinhabitation means focusing on the place you live, and shaping educational practices and objectives around local issues and concerns. In this framework, decolonization calls for explicit recognition and naming of the injustices that exist (and have existed) in a particular place.

The history, geography, and cultural practices that have shaped New Mexico have resulted in a significant portion of the population having enduring connections to place. As such, New Mexico has long held its own place orientations (Sánchez, 2021). The reality of conflict and contestation over land has also influenced relationships and attitudes among the people of New Mexico. Yet, amid this contestation, there is a deep sense of belonging and a sense of homeland. The ideas of querencia and contested homelands offer a New Mexican lens from which to develop place-based pedagogies relevant to New Mexico. Querencia, a love of place, "is that which gives us a sense of place, that which anchors us to the land, that which makes us unique people" (Arellano, 2007, p. 50). Salmón (2012) describes querencia as a "blend of mental spaces not only including bioregionalism but also including emotional, spiritual, cultural, and ecological health. When people think of land, the concept is enmeshed with notions of cultural memory" (Salmón, 2012, p. 118). Just as culture cannot be separated from education, neither can place.

Pedagogically, querencia can invite us to seek out the "wisdom of the ancestors" (Anaya, 2020, p. xiv). As educators we must interrogate our claims to place and situate ourselves among a homeland cartography that is both contested and loved. Furthermore, we cannot disconnect educational practices from a "querida patria [beloved homeland], united in language, culture and history" (Anaya, 2020, p. xvi). Just as many in New Mexico have longstanding roots, we too (as teacher educators) need to establish ourselves and take stock of the surrounding ecology in order to avoid yet another iteration of colonization (however unintentional).

3.3 Methodology

Self-study methodologies recognize the contexualized nature of teaching, learning, and preparing teachers (e.g., Koster & van den Berg, 2014; Tidwell et al., 2012). Self-study has also consistently explored how to prepare teacher candidates to teach diverse student populations (e.g., Cutri & Whiting, 2015; Kitchen, 2020; Kitchen et al., 2016; LaBoskey, 2012; Whiting & Cutri, 2019). However, an area that is underexplored in self-study research is place-based education and its connection to social justice and urban education.

The study described in this chapter is a form of "intimate scholarship" (Hamilton & Pinnegar, 2015). That is, our coming to know in this work is grounded in relationship—our relationship to one another, our relationship to knowing, and our relationship to place. We utilized co/autoethnography (Taylor & Coia, 2006; Taylor & Coia, 2020) as a way to work together to build our understanding of the impact of place on our teaching and on our relationships with the communities within which we work. We recognize that our identities as teachers, teacher educators, women, and inhabitants of a particular place are fluid and constantly under construction (Britzman, 2003; Danielewicz, 2001; Haniford, 2005, 2010; Taylor & Coia, 2006, 2020). One of the ideas we explored in this research was how New Mexico as a specific and unique place is an additional partner in our co/autoethnography. As we dialogued with one another (both via video conferencing and in writing), we kept this place forefront in our minds. Of course this was different for each of us, but that was part of the choice to work together--Rebecca is a native New Mexican whose family has lived here for centuries. Laura grew up in the midwestern United States but has made New Mexico her home for over 15 years. Each of these positionalities were critical in our coming to know together.

We began by writing individual journals about our understanding of place and how New Mexico has impacted our teaching. We read one another's initial journals and raised questions, highlighting important concepts and ideas we wanted to explore further. Through our ongoing written dialogue, we identified three recurring themes important for understanding some of the issues with place-based teaching and teacher education that exist here in New Mexico. These three themes are: (1) layers of colonization; (2) tourist teachers and teacher educators; and (3) the importance of time and building trust. Within each of those themes, we have also identified tensions and dilemmas with which we are still grappling. Utilizing dialogue as "a way for developing understanding or insight that can guide or determine practice" (Guilfoyle et al., 2004, p. 1112), we sought not to uncover "truth," but to explore meaning.

Utilizing an online writing platform, we scheduled shared writing times where we wrote back and forth in real time. These written dialogues were intended to explore our understanding and experiences with the concepts listed above. We used different colored font to indicate authorship, and as time went on we dated later entries to try and capture the evolution of the dialogue. We met weekly via Zoom to discuss the process, our emerging interpretations, and to determine new writing prompts for exploration. During the Zoom meetings we also sought to clarify and explore clear points of tension, adding notes and clarification to the shared written dialogue document. For example, as we wrote about our experiences teaching in situations disconnected from place, we found ourselves returning again and again to the question, "What does it take for teacher education to be seen as trustworthy and as a part of the community?" As a result, we responded to that question, describing the experiences we have had that either contributed to the building of trust or diminished it.

We present our findings in the form of a dialogue to demonstrate both how we came to unearth some of these understandings, tensions, and dilemmas, but also to emphasize how open and unfinished our understandings are at this point. We are writing this chapter in the middle of a conversation, one that we are intentionally inviting others to take part in with us.

3.4 Findings

Although we listed three themes above, in this section we focus on two: tourist teachers and time and trust. We do so because the layers of colonization experienced here in New Mexico has led to these last two findings and because we have addressed the multiple layers of colonization in the section on contested homelands.

3.4.1   The Trap of the Tourist Teacher

We call this section the "trap" of the tourist teacher because we see this phenomena as one that is easy to fall into and one that is ultimately not conducive to long-lasting, sustained change for communities and schools. A tourist is a visitor. A tourist can also be a person who resides somewhere for an extended time, but does not establish meaningful connections with the people, history and culture of the area. As such, the sustained commitment and engagement *with* a community cannot exist. Some work has been done exploring the concepts of tourist and tourism within art education (e.g., Ballengee-Morris, 2002; Sutters, 2016). Ballengee-Morris articulated the ways tourism and souvenirs impact cultural crafts and can function as a colonizing force. She describes tourists as those who "seek to capture memories of their experiences and they are often motivated to buy souvenirs that remind them of those experiences" (2002, p. 235). Sutters (2016) draws on the conception of tourism to describe how field placements occur within teacher education. By placing teacher candidates in urban schools with which they have little familiarity, teacher education institutions (unintentionally) position these schools and the students within them as "foreign." "Like tourists, the teachers arrive at the ordained time and destination (far) only to return to their point of departure (home) to enjoy many of the luxuries that teachers can" (Sutters, 2016, p. 13). The souvenir(s) that teachers bring home are lines on their resume that they worked in an urban, underfunded school. We draw on these conceptions while also working to expand them to highlight the ways internalized perspectives treat some communities as "exotic" and "foreign" and our time within them as souvenir badges of honor we share with colleagues, family, and friends.

As we each began to interrogate our own relationships to place, pedagogy, and teacher education in New Mexico we shared our stories. We identified the way tourist education has operated in New Mexico and in our own professional development. In the reflective dialoguing process Laura wrote:

> Obviously the very first times I felt like a tourist teacher were on the reservation. When a student told me that Columbus had blue eyes. When students asked why I was there. When adults asked why I was there. I didn't know how to deal with it then because I kind of felt what they were trying to say to me. The bigger thing they were saying I guess. And I had such mixed feelings because I knew I was leaving.

This point, echoed an earlier observation, was included in the initial reflective essay:

> Even though I stated in multiple letters and reflections throughout the years that my time teaching in Shiprock and Tohatchi helped me to learn "the importance of connecting to the community you are serving, I discovered I could not do the job I wanted to do if I was not a part of the community. As an outsider (as I was on the reservation), I had to reach out and make connections. I asked many questions of many people, and learned how to listen to what parents and others in the community told me." But that was really very surface level at best. You can't connect to a community (especially a community that has experienced centuries of layered colonization) in any kind of meaningful way if you are only visiting that community for a year or two. I was a tourist, not a resident. Not a community member.

Unpacking the idea of tourist teacher became central to our own understanding about our commitments as teacher educators in this place. As a native New Mexican, Rebecca noted how in her career, she has seen tourist teachers come into New Mexican communities with a spirit of adventure and self-serving attitudes swaddled in altruistic motives. She defined tourist teacher in this way:

> To me, a teacher tourist is a person who is collecting life and teaching experiences at the expense of others. It's a drop-in model in which talented (sometimes!) people get to say they have done something, like: work with poor kids, work in underfunded schools, work in remote locations, work in inner cities, work with "at risk" people. For tourist teachers, the destination is never a permanent landing place where the time/energy/relationship building is about the community, rather there is this weird crediting that values the tourist. There is always another community to go to, for work, pleasure, and change-making on the quick. There is something glamorous (although superficial) for the tourist teacher, that people who are long-term committed to places do not enjoy.

Because layers of colonization have shaped New Mexico (Gómez, 2018), the tourist teacher, though often recruited by communities with teacher shortages, is a temporary solution and ultimately part of the larger colonization project. These teachers are not often trusted by the communities that hire them and because of the short-term nature of the teaching appointments, there are few opportunities for sustained and reciprocal engagement. This point was reinforced by Laura:

> When I came here for the first and even the second time I knew there were bigger issues at play but I didn't have the language or ideas for understanding what was going on. I knew the issues were bigger than me and that I wasn't helping anything, but I didn't understand how structurally things were created to perpetuate inequity. And how a steady stream of young people coming in and out doesn't change anything. It creates an illusion of help while actually perpetuating all of the problems. It's a quick "fix" instead of trying to look more long term. But I'm not at all placing any blame on the communities that are struggling. The quick fix is so needed in the moment.

Examining tourist teacher mentalities, we also realized the ways institutions in New Mexico exacerbate or promote tourist approaches based on the desire for larger systemic uniformity or the desire for quick results with local schools and districts. Rebecca noted how standardization forces teachers, even if local and community rooted, to adhere to externally driven constraints to shape teaching choices. In the dialogue she commented:

> This makes me think about how the structure of schools also sometimes positions teachers as tourists. I met with a group of cooperating teachers the other day and all they could talk about was what the new curriculum programs the district was going to adopt that they would have to do. As I told them what we do in the university social studies methods class they seemed very disconnected from their own ability to develop and implement their own curriculum. If the curriculum is always externally driven, and teachers have to actualize it, then there is a disconnect from the children and their communities.

These larger institutional structures and initiatives, though often well-intentioned, create separations between the teacher, the students and the community and they situate knowledge as coming from "outsiders." As Laura described:

But who has "the knowledge" that matters is a real sign of the waves of colonization and understanding this has helped me understand what I have heard time and again since living here—that this idea or that idea worked somewhere else but that doesn't mean it will work in New Mexico.

In teacher education, institutional practices also contribute to tourist teacher education models. Both of us have observed how weak partnerships, pseudo partnerships, and academic posturing have done real damage to our ability as individual faculty members to actualize place oriented teacher education. The dialogue that follows emerged in our written conversations and demonstrates the sort of back and forth that occurred when we wrote together in real time.

Laura: When I got here to Albuquerque [ABQ] and University of New Mexico [UNM], I was told that one of the things I was now responsible for was running the cooperating teacher [CT] meetings with all CTs twice a semester. CTs were being paid a lot at that time. Like $1500 or something in secondary ed. So we could expect them to attend these meetings. But I remember feeling this huge wall of distrust and frustration the first several times I ran these meetings. But again, they were trainings. The way I dealt with it at the time was twofold. One, I remember really clearly telling all the teachers that I wasn't going anywhere. And that was true! The way I tried to handle it internally was by making those trainings something I could live with. I tried to construct them as more equitable—as more of a sense of working together and less of me the "expert" telling them what they needed to do. It's funny though, because there were some teachers who really resisted that. They wanted it to be a training and they wanted to be unhappy about it.

Rebecca: When I started at UNM in 2005 I had a similar experience. The dean had just decided to place cohorts of teacher candidates at partner schools...but she chose to place like 18–25 at one school... Interestingly enough, almost every teacher had a student teacher whether they wanted one or not, so there was some resistance with that. Even though I wanted to build relationships and work with the two schools we were partnering with, the forced nature of the collaboration went against my instincts and values.

Laura: I feel like a tourist teacher when I am positioned as an "expert" and asked to just present. That isn't teaching to me. That is positioning me.

Rebecca: I feel like a tourist teacher in those instances as well. But, when we are just told by our department chairs and deans, to do things with schools or communities I also feel like a tourist...so every time I went to the "partner" school I felt like the relationship was forced.

Laura: Huh, so there seems to be an element of leadership and leadership decisions that create/force tourist teacher positionings. I mean, you kind of can't help it if you're asked to "teach" like 75–100 cooperating teachers all at the same time. And, if you didn't make the decisions that created the partnerships or expectations.

Through our online dialogue, we were able to define the ways particular programs create tourist teachers (e.g., Teach for America), and also the ways that our own programs have created initiatives that made us feel positioned as tourists here in Albuquerque and surrounding communities.

3.4.1.1 Implications for Assignments

Because we are teacher educators committed to "walking our talk" (Hamilton & Pinnegar, 1998, p. 239), we turned our attention to the ways some of our assignments might unintentionally reinforce the trap of the tourist teacher for our students. For example, each of us does some form of a community mapping activity with our students. In Rebecca's case, the community mapping work is embedded in a larger project called TECLA[2] that she is a part of at one local elementary school. Both of us have tinkered and adapted the assignment over time, ultimately directing students to focus on asset mapping, rather than simply describing the challenges a particular community faces. But we each questioned the ways the assignment might continue to position students as tourists.

> Laura: Are there ways in which we set our students up to be tourist teachers? For example, the community mapping project over the years I'm sure has functioned in a touristy way. I'm happier with the changes I made to it this year as a result of the pandemic. But just talking about and developing this concept in the past couple of weeks has me thinking about assignments and the work we ask students to do.
>
> Rebecca: I think community mapping has the potential to be a tourist event, however, what if it's framed as asset mapping with focused attention on how the community supports its residents? I guess I see a purpose in the mapping if it becomes part of the longer year-long conversation with the teacher candidates. In TECLA, the community walk is facilitated by parents and family members from the school and it is followed by a conversation with the families. The teacher candidates get a sense of the community from those who live there. One of the interesting things with the TECLA community walk is that the parents identify sources of strength and challenge.
>
> Laura: I don't remember if I wrote above about how I changed it this year. Instead of having them be tourists in a community (although I wouldn't have called it that even in the fall), I had students ask the focal student they were working with for another assignment to describe their different communities and the people, places, and institutions that support those communities. And then we looked across everyone's assignments to see the richness of communities represented. It also helped us to not essentialize anyone. And I didn't get weird presentations about police, or grocery stores, or Walmarts.
>
> Rebecca: One thing I noticed when the mothers started guiding the community walk is that they highlighted more challenges than were revealed when we did the asset mapping. One of the things with the asset assignment was to of course avoid deficit thinking, and so, some of the challenges of the community weren't mentioned for fear of deficiting [having deficit perspectives]. So in another way, it was kind of like that rose-colored glasses tourist trap. The mothers have real concerns about certain parts of their community. It's like the gaze. Who gets to hold the camera and what gets focused on. When members of the community get to show, and describe, it's a different gaze. Makes me wonder what it would be like if the teacher candidates complete the assignment or a version of it on their own and then go on the walk with the mothers…
>
> Laura: I've also thought about having students start by mapping their own communities. However they define it. So they view it through their insider lens first before they do something similar to the communities surrounding their placement school.

---

[2] TECLA is an acronym for the Teacher Education Collaborative in Language Diversity and Arts Integration. It is an undergraduate licensure pathway. The community walk as part of the teacher education experience was conceptualized by a colleague and TECLA collaborator.

As stated above, this conversation is ongoing. We do know that identifying the concept of tourist teachers has changed the way we look at the assignments we ask teacher education students to complete and how we establish and maintain collaborations with schools and communities. We now also have language to help us articulate misgivings when administrators ask us to do things that position us as tourists in our communities.

As we continued discussing the trap of the tourist teacher and teacher educator, we began to consider ways to sidestep this trap and worked to pinpoint times we have successfully resisted acting or being positioned as a tourist teacher, as well as what conditions make it possible to engage in a critical pedagogy of place in New Mexico. Ultimately, we determined that trust, time, and intentional relationship building are essential.

3.4.2   Time and Trust

Because a tourist is always visiting, avoiding this trap requires sustained time and commitment. For communities who have experienced layers of colonization, further perpetuated by years of short term teachers who come and go, trust is built slowly, over years of shared work. As with any long term relationship, the work is not always easy or smooth.

> Rebecca: I think time and trust are so interrelated. When we started TECLA we were working at La Montanita because a number of us had connections at that school. I think we are on our third principal (maybe fourth) and with each one there are new rules, different levels of interest and engagement from the principals. We have often thought of leaving the school, to find a place where the leader is a more interested partner, however, we continue to think about how much time we have been there. I think there is something about staying, even when the ideologies shift and the work becomes more difficult to achieve. I think often teacher education programs come and go and we leave school communities without much thought. In our particular context, the school leadership turnover doesn't help and I don't think our partners often analyze their side of the trust relationship.

In dialogue we examined how the perpetual underfunding of education continues to undermine trust and relationship building. For example, in our context much of the innovative teacher education work has been supported with external funds. Laura has been working consistently with a colleague to transform the relationship between her program and a local high school, one that has suffered from years of tourist teacher education practices.

> Laura: And part of the reason we're thinking long and hard about grant funding is that we're trying to build something not dependent on money. The money allows you to do big things but when the money goes away, the changes aren't sustainable. But the other problem is that it can't be about the two of us. We have to put in institutional structures and agreements in order to make sure the work continues even if (heaven forbid) something happened to one of us.

But ultimately, it is more than just funding that impacts the relationships we build with communities and schools, as Rebecca described:

> I also think there is something about having a core set of practices that we engage in when working with community partners. For example, sometimes it is our own leadership who undermines the work with partners, then, it's not only about funding but about the institutional type of supports that contribute to the work. In teacher prep it has to do with scheduling, staffing, etc.

Teaching load (and what "counts" as teaching), research productivity expectations (and what "counts" as research), hiring practices, and departmental politics all impact how we (as individuals and as representatives of the university) are seen by communities and schools.

But time is not enough to develop the type of trust we are seeking in our place-based pedagogy. In one of our online dialogue sessions, we explored what needs to happen in between time and trust.

> Laura: What is between time and trust should be learning. I have felt here more than anywhere else I have lived that there has to be a pattern of you showing up again and again. But you have to show up ready to listen, ready to learn, and ready to work alongside.
>
> Rebecca: Between time and trust...effort, cycles of reflection, action. I think part of establishing trust has to do with as you say, showing up and following through. It's important to have real experiences with people in the partnership...the teachers, the custodians, the parents. I also think laughter and kindness are important, so is empathy. Maybe in between time and trust is reciprocity, where everyone is learning and exchanging.

In our work both separately and together, we note how authenticity has promoted positive relationships with our students and the extended community. Rather than showing up as "experts" or "academics", we engage as ourselves.

> Rebecca: I think that is a real danger for teacher education. In trying to legitimize our work, by relying on academic theories, we sometimes move past the actual work. I'm not suggesting we simplify everything or be focused on technocratic training approaches, but there is something in the posturing that distances us from communities.
>
> Laura: What are the choices we make in teaching? In relating to and working with the communities surrounding the university. What words do we choose to use in speaking about teaching? Are they esoteric or understandable? I mean, it's even sometimes do we walk around while teaching or sit behind a desk that separates us from students? Do we position ourselves as working with people on shared issues and challenges or do we just provide little nuggets of brilliance from afar?

Others have written about the low status of teacher education in universities and the ways teacher education is habitually marginalized even within colleges of education (e.g., Labaree, 2004; Rice et al., 2015). The lack of status can cause even well-intentioned teacher educators to fall into the trap of tourists, relying too heavily on their own "expertise" when engaging with communities. As we have briefly discussed here, even our smallest choices can position us either as tourists or as fellow community members, working with others to improve the education of the students of New Mexico—our students.

3.5 Discussion and Implications

In this chapter, we have focused on what we see as a trap that gets in the way of socially just teacher education, as well as our thoughts about how to avoid that trap. In this section, we document some of the tensions inherent in our dialogue. As Berry (2007) describes them, tensions in teacher education result from attempts to "manage complex and conflicting pedagogical and personal demands within their work as teachers of prospective teachers" (p. 119). We also consider how the tensions impact preparing teachers in urban contexts, including those made up of distinct communities with specific histories and differing needs.

As discussed above, we believe the trap of the tourist teacher (and teacher educator) is a real threat to sustained change in schools and communities. However, we also acknowledge that some communities face real teacher shortages that cannot be easily filled. But who gains and who loses when teaching in a community is short term and a resume builder? Laura was changed profoundly by her time teaching on the Navajo reservation, and yet she has long grappled with whether what she gained was worth what the students lost from having yet another temporary White teacher.

One way of breaking the cycle of the tourist teacher is to establish roots in a place. As any gardener will tell you, establishing roots takes more than time. Querencia informs us that learning the history of a place, adopting a sense of care about the environment and others, and listening to the stories of the people who call the place home can root us (Anaya, 2020; Arellano, 2012; Romero, 2020). In our own discussions we have talked about how dialogue, listening, and building relationships can support urban communities. While we both know we have been tourists in different ways, we also have learned that humanizing experiences with those from the community such as our students and others in schools, can foster place-based connections. We have also come to understand that true listening is complex and involves more than just providing someone else the space to talk. Listening involves negotiation, reciprocal learning, and letting go of our egos and the need to be seen as experts. As teacher educators, when we model deep listening, we demonstrate to future teachers one way to connect to community, whether urban, suburban, or rural, in order to better serve diverse learners.

The need for negotiation and reciprocal learning is another tension identified through our work. In their analysis of culturally rooted pedagogy, Sosa-Provencio et al. (2018) explained that in decisions about young people and education, "any educational framework within marginalized communities must be led by those communities" (p. 6). Actualizing this vision takes work, and it means that as teacher educators we have to understand the aspirations of each community while also sharing our own knowledge and concerns. For example, when Rebecca was a bilingual third grade teacher, many of the parents at the school wanted their children in English only classrooms because they were very committed to their children learning English. Through dialogue, the bilingual teachers shared their knowledge about literacy learning, the value of bilingualism, and language acquisition and addressed misconceptions about bilingual programs. In the end, the families came to see how bilingual education would support their children in both their home languages and English. But this took time, "listening with grace" (Hammond, 2015, p. 78), and respectful negotiation.

Ultimately, we worry about the ability of teacher education to take the necessary time and care in developing critical place-based pedagogies in the current higher education environment. Exceptionally lean budgets force colleges to increase class sizes and teaching loads in ways that do not result in the kind of teaching and learning we aspire to (Madeloni, 2014). They also create the circumstances for grant money to be viewed as necessary for survival, even when that funding may perpetuate the trap of the tourist teacher. Framing the challenges in education as "crises" forces people to look for quick fixes. Outside grant funding promises transformative changes; but when the money ends, all too often those changes are unsustainable.

3.6   Conclusion

As teacher educators, we see a need for vigilance. The trap of the tourist teacher is seductive. It gives us something to talk about that positions us as worldly, altruistic and capable of solving complex problems by our mere presence. Part of our journey in this inquiry has been to recognize when we ourselves fall victim to becoming tourists, even in our own community. Some of this is rooted in our own desire to be part of genuine change, but there are other enticing motives that must be constantly examined.

So many mandates and external accountability forces work to separate us from community and the place-based orientations that align with our values. We now have a framework to help us make decisions. When we decide on a project, a teaching assignment, or service work, what motivates our decision making? Is it part of our ongoing work, grounded in community and real relationships? Or, are we motivated by the lines we can add to our CVs and the positive attention we might receive from colleagues? These are difficult questions to ask, but any teacher or teacher educator committed to equity and social justice in urban education must have the courage and clear sightedness to ask and answer these questions truthfully.

The work documented here has given us new lenses with which to view our own work. We now have the language to help ensure the choices we make in our classes and in local schools and communities are aligned with our values. When we embrace the idea of place in teaching, and as being part of a place, we are less reliant on outside versions of ourselves, our academic credentials don't show up to do the work, we do, as humans. When we engage in teacher education with and for the community the end goal is nontransactional. Our own efforts are guided by equity and not ego. We are part of this community and what happens for students here matters for us. To truly transform education, we must see young people not as "other peoples' children" (Delpit, 2006), but as members of our communities. With time, energy and patience, we too, can belong. We share a future. Romero discusses this when he says his querencia is, "Where I am understood by those who know me without explanations or footnotes for what I say, think or feel (2020, p. 2).

References

Anaya, R. (2020). Querencia, mi patria chica. In V. Fonseca-Chávez, L. Romero, & L. Herrera (Eds.), *Querencia: Reflections on the New Mexico homeland* (pp. xiii–xxii). University of New Mexico Press.

Arellano, J. (2007). *Taos: Where two cultures met four hundred years ago*. Grantmakers in the Arts.

Arellano, J. (2012). La Cuenca y la querencia: The watershed and the sense of place in the Merced and Acequia landscape. In J. Loeffler & C. Loeffler (Eds.), *Thinking like a watershed: Voices from the west*. University of New Mexico Press.

Ballengee-Morris, C. (2002). Cultures for sale: Perspectives on colonialism and self-determination and the relationship to authenticity and tourism. *Studies in Art Education, 43*(3), 232–245. https://doi.org/10.1080/00393541.2002.11651721

Berry, A. (2007). Reconceptualizing teacher educator knowledge as tensions: Exploring the tension between valuing and reconstructing experience. *Studying Teacher Education, 3*(2), 117–134. https://doi.org/10.1080/17425960701656510

Britzman, D. (2003). *Practice makes practice: A critical study of learning to teach*. University of New York Press.

Cuban, L. (2001). *How can I fix it? Finding solutions and managing dilemmas: An educator's road map*. Teachers College Press.

Cutri, R. M., & Whiting, E. F. (2015). The emotional work of discomfort and vulnerability in multicultural teacher education. *Teachers and Teaching, 21*(8), 1010–1025. https://doi.org/10.108 0/13540602.2015.1005869

Danielewicz, J. (2001). *Teaching selves: Identity, pedagogy, and teacher education*. State University of New York Press.

Delpit, L. (2006). *Other people's children: Cultural conflict in the classroom*. The New Press.

Gómez, L. E. (2018). *Manifest destinies: The making of the Mexican American race* (2nd ed.). New York University Press.

Gruenwald, D. A. (2003). The best of both worlds: A critical pedagogy of place. *Educational Researcher, 32*(4), 3–12. https://www.jstor.org/stable/3700002

Guilfoyle, K., Hamilton, M. L., Pinnegar, S., & Placier, P. (2004). The epistemological dimensions and dynamics of professional dialogue in self-study. In J. J. Loughren, M. L. Hamilton, V. K. LaBoskey, & T. Russell (Eds.), *International handbook of self-study of teaching and teacher education practices* (pp. 1109–1167). Kluwer Academic Publishers.

Hamilton, M. L., & Pinnegar, S. (1998). Conclusion: The value and promise of self-study. In M. L. Hamilton (Ed.), *Reconceptualizing teaching practice: Self-study in teacher education* (pp. 235–246). Routledge.

Hamilton, M. L., & Pinnegar, S. (2015). *Knowing, becoming, doing as teacher educators: Identity, intimate scholarship, inquiry*. Emerald Group Publishing.

Hammond, Z. (2015). *Culturally responsive teaching and the brain: Promoting authentic engagement and rigor among culturally and linguistically diverse students*. Corwin.

Haniford, L. (2005). *Becoming an English teacher: Positioning discourses and professional identities* (Unpublished doctoral dissertation). University of Michigan.

Haniford, L. (2010). Tracing one teacher candidates' discursive identity work. *Teaching and Teacher Education, 26*, 987–996. https://doi.org/10.1016/j.tate.2009.10.041

Kitchen, J. (2020). Attending to the concerns of teacher candidates in a social justice course: A self-study of a teacher educator. *Studying Teacher Education, 16*(1), 6–25. https://doi.org/1 0.1080/17425964.2019.1691134

Kitchen, J., Tidwell, D., & Fitzgerald, L. (2016). *Self-study and diversity II: Inclusive teacher education for a diverse world*. Sense Publishers.

Koster, B., & van den Berg, B. (2014). Increasing professional self-understanding: Self-study research by teachers with the help of biography, core reflection and dialogue. *Studying Teacher Education, 10*(1), 86–100. https://doi.org/10.1080/17425964.2013.866083

Labaree, D. F. (2004). *The trouble with ed schools*. Yale University Press.

LaBoskey, V. (2012). The ghost of social justice education future: How the words of graduates contribute to self-transformation. *Studying Teacher Education, 8*(3), 227–244. https://doi.org/1 0.1080/17425964.2012.720929

Madeloni, B. (2014). From a whisper to a scream: Ethics and resistance in the age of neoliberalism. *Learning and Teaching, 1*, 79–91. https://doi.org/10.3167/latiss.2014.070106

Nieto-Phillips, J. M. (2004). *The language of blood : The making of Spanish-American identity in New Mexico, 1880s–1930s*. University of New Mexico Press.

Noddings, N. (2002). *Starting at home: Caring and social policy*. University of California Press.

Rice, M. F., Newberry, M., Whiting, E., Cutri, R., & Pinnegar, S. (2015). Learning from experiences of non-personhood: A self-study of teacher educator identities. *Studying Teacher Education, 11*(1), 16–31. https://doi.org/10.1080/17425964.2015.1013024

Romero, L. (2020). Mi querencia: A connection to place. In V. Fonseca-Chávez, L. Romero, & L. Herrera (Eds.), *Querencia: Reflections on the New Mexico homeland* (pp. 1–12). University of New Mexico Press.

Salmón, E. (2012). *Eating the landscape: American Indian stories of food, identity, and resilience*. The University of Arizona Press.

Sánchez, R. (2021). Sites as storied texts, querencias, and contested homelands: Exploring the place orientations of New Mexico in a teacher workshop. In M. Rice & A. Dallacqua (Eds.), *Luminous literacies: Stories of growth and renewal from the land of enchantment* (pp. 15–28). Emerald.

Sánchez, J. P., Spude, R. L. S., & Gómez, A. (2013). *New Mexico: A history*. University of Oklahoma Press.

Sando, J. (2005). The Pueblo revolt. In J. Sando & H. Agoyo (Eds.), *Po'pay: Leader of the first American revolution* (pp. 5–54). Clear Light Publishing.

Sosa-Provencio, M., Sheahan, A., Desai, S., & Secatero, S. (2018). Tenets of body-soul rooted pedagogy: Teaching for critical consciousness, nourished resistance, and healing. *Critical Studies in Education., 61*(3), 345–362. https://doi.org/10.1080/17508487.2018.1445653

Sutters, J. P. (2016). Disrupting the tourist paradigm in teacher education: The urban art classroom as a globalized site of travel, transience, and transaction. *The Journal of Social Theory in Art Education, 36*, 9–19. https://scholarscompass.vcu.edu/jstae/vol36/iss1/3/

Taylor, M., & Coia, L. (2006). Complicating our identities as urban teachers: A co/autoethnography. In J. L. Kincheloe, K. Hayes, K. Rose, & P. M. Anderson (Eds.), *The Praeger handbook of urban education* (pp. 273–282). Greenwood Press.

Taylor, M., & Coia, L. (2020). Co/autoethnography as a feminist methodology. In J. Kitchen, A. Berry, S. M. Bullock, A. R. Crowe, & M. Taylor (Eds.), *International handbook of self-study of teaching and teacher education practices, second edition* (pp. 565–588). Springer.

Tidwell, D., Farrell, J., Brown, N., Taylor, M., Coia, L., Abihanna, R., Abrams, L., Dacey, C., Dauplaise, J., & Strom, K. (2012). Presidential session: The transformative nature of self-study. In J. Young, L. Erickson, & S. Pinnegar (Eds.), *Extending inquiry communities: Illuminating teacher education through self-study* (pp. 15–16).

Whiting, E. F., & Cutri, R. M. (2019). Teacher candidates' responses to examining personal privilege: Nuanced understandings of the discourse of individualism in multicultural education. *Frontiers in Education, 4*(111), 1–8. https://doi.org/10.3389/feduc.2019.00111

Laura C. Haniford, Ph.D., is an Associate Professor of Secondary Education in the Teacher Education, Educational Leadership and Policy department at the University of New Mexico. Her background is in educational foundations and teacher learning and development. She teaches courses in secondary education and in teacher action research. Dr. Haniford's research focuses on teacher education, the self-study of her own practice, and preparing new teachers to teach in ways that advance equity and social justice.

Rebecca M. Sánchez, Ph.D., is a Professor in the Department of Teacher Education, Educational Leadership, and Policy at the University of New Mexico. She teaches courses in Social Studies Education, Social Justice Education, and Curriculum Development. She seeks to expose students and teachers to both the place-based social studies of New Mexico and the history that is over-looked in the national narrative of American history. Dr. Sánchez is involved in research focusing on historical topics, teacher activism in a high-stakes environment, translating research to the arts, and meaningful arts integration for language learning and social justice.

Chapter 4
How Do We Praxis? Becoming Teachers of Diverse Learners in Urban Environments

Christi U. Edge and Chelsie Vipperman

Abstract In this chapter, a teacher educator and a beginning teacher explore and examine the enactment of *praxis* from multiple perspectives, over time, and in the space of a rural teacher education program seeking to prepare candidates to teach in city schools. Through the lens of narrative self-study, we first explore our lived experiences contributing to how we each formed understandings of teaching diverse learners. Next, we examine tensions and turning points in our understandings and enactment of teaching practices in the context of a longitudinal inquiry into teacher candidates' accounts of *becoming* teachers of diverse learners in a field-based rural teacher education program. Emerging insights from our collaborative self-study of teaching practices include reading our lived experiences, re-seeing them through juxtaposition, and illuminating the relationship between becoming and praxis to address ways teacher educators and teachers can make these processes visible to self and others for the purposes of advancing equity and social justice. Implications include making meaning from lived experience as continuous becoming.

Keywords Collaborative self-study · Narrative self-study · Rural teacher education · Urban teaching · Reading experience · Equity and social justice

Teacher learning that improves teaching practice requires new knowledge and skills, and also new ways of thinking and of seeing oneself. As a teacher becomes a more confident knowledge constructor, they learn through *praxis,* trying new practices while seeking to understand how and why those practices work or do not work, becoming more deliberate and attentive to their instructional decisions (Cohen, 2011) as they learn new ways to think about and carry out their work. Teachers with

C. U. Edge (✉) · C. Vipperman
Northern Michigan University, Marquette, MI, USA
e-mail: cedge@nmu.edu

© The Author(s), under exclusive license to Springer Nature Singapore Pte Ltd. 2022
A. D. Martin (ed.), *Self-Studies in Urban Teacher Education*, Self-Study of Teaching and Teacher Education Practices 25,
https://doi.org/10.1007/978-981-19-5430-6_4

a well-developed sense of agency build theory grounded in classroom practice (Bruner, 1986). Through inquiry, they actively formulate questions of importance to them, direct their own investigations, and communicate their newly constructed ideas, improving their practice in the process (Liston & Zeichner, 1991). Rather than a finite, linear progression of improvement over time, teacher learning is dynamic. The Transactional Theory of Reading and Writing (TTRW) (Rosenblatt, 1978/1994, 1994, 2005) applied to teaching and learning events (e.g., Edge, 2011, 2022; Edge et al., 2016, 2022b; Edge & Olan, 2020) is a Theory of Transactional Teaching and Learning (TTL). TTL suggests learning occurs when people consider, discuss, and inquire into problems and issues of significance to them (Dewey & Bentley, 1949; Edge, 2022; Rosenblatt, 1978/1994, 2005). Enacting these theories, the goal of professional learning for educators would be that they become constructivist thinkers and knowers who engage in continuous meaning-making through reading and writing their own experiences, sharing their interpretations, and expanding those interpretations within a trusted community with the intent of improving their teaching practices.

In 2011, I (Christi) accepted a position at a rural, teaching-focused university in the Midwestern United States. I sensed one challenge I was expected to address in my teaching was to prepare prospective teachers (PTs) to be equipped to teach *all* learners in *all* settings, including the many urban/city schools in our state in need of teachers. As a former classroom teacher, I had worked in two large, diverse, high school settings; as a doctoral student, I taught, placed, and supervised PTs in methods courses and practicum settings in urban and urban fringe school settings. On some level, I utilized these experiential resources to help me teach and prepare PTs in my new rural teacher education setting; still, I knew candidates needed to learn through their own experiences. Based on my early experiences teaching PTs during my doctoral program and findings from a longitudinal study of two students through their methods courses and into their first 3 years of teaching (Edge, 2011, 2022), I taught PTs to keep and to use a Praxis Notebook (PN) with the intention of helping them attend to and reflect on their process of becoming a teacher.

In 2014, I (Chelsie) was a Freshman Fellow (i.e., a first-year, undergraduate student who works with a faculty member for 3–4 h per week to learn about research and practice scholarship) and secondary English education major who worked with Christi to analyze data from a study focused on understanding the process of transitioning from being a student to being a teacher during PTs' methods coursework and early practicum experiences. Over the course of two semesters (2014–2015), we met weekly to analyze PTs' statements about becoming teachers. Three years later (2017), I became a student in one of Christi's classes, taking the same methods courses I once studied as a researcher. During my full-time student teaching semester (2018), I returned to work with Christi as a part-time, undergraduate research assistant.

Over time, our research meetings and interactions together included dynamic and meaningful discussions about teaching and resulted in ongoing reflection. Opportunities to (re)frame our own teaching experiences emerged in response to research data we were analyzing and discussing together, especially as Chelsie completed her full-time student teaching experience, grappled with navigating multiple offers to teach in urban/city schools, and as she prepared to accept her first appointment as a teacher in an urban, high-needs setting on the opposite side of the United States. Now, as a teacher educator in a rural teacher education program and a fourth-year teacher who graduated from that rural program, we share a concern for preparing teachers. We are conscious of how school settings, mandates, and the challenges of commencing a teaching career are (some) additional aspects that further complicate (even obfuscate) working with diverse learners. We worry about teacher retention statistics and the individuals we know who quit teaching. Given the rising number of out-of-state, urban school districts recruiting from teacher education program settings such as ours, we seek to develop and share insights that may contribute to teacher education, beginning teachers, and to advancing equity and social justice.

This chapter aims to contribute to self-study of teaching and teacher education practices (S-STTEP) literature by exploring our process of becoming and praxis relative to teaching diverse learners. We asked, "How do we praxis?" Drawing from Freire (1970), we conceptualize and define praxis as the dynamic interaction of theory and practice. Framed by a TTRW (Rosenblatt, 2005) praxis is a meaning-making event. This includes action, reflection, and discussion for transformation and informing action (Freire, 1970). Drawing from Deleuze and Guattari (1987), we conceptualize becoming as open, ongoing, processes of ever-expanding understandings and ever-emerging selves in ever-emerging contexts.

We draw from, yet background, Chelsie's experience studying her own learning process in a PN in Christi's classes, and Christi's 15 years of experience guiding PTs to utilize PNs. In this shared yet diversely experienced space, PNs were a kind of field notebook for collecting in-process observations, reflections, wonderings, and artifacts from learning and teaching experiences. Christi informally taught PTs to read, interpret and reflect on PN artifacts, responding to them as texts (Draper et al., 2010; Edge, 2011, 2022) composed in the process of learning and developing as professionals, in particular contexts and moments in time with the intention of helping PTs attend to and reflect on their process of becoming a teacher. We had studied PTs' learning processes before and after Chelsie was a student in Christi's classes; what might we learn from studying our own experiences learning to teach in urban environments? How might our inquiry help us to teach for equity and social justice? As Lyttle (2013) proposes, "Teaching involves the intentional forming and reforming of frameworks for understanding and enacting practice" (p. xvii). Self-study researchers "are focused on the nexus between public and private, theory and practice, research and pedagogy, self and other" (LaBoskey, 2004, p. 818). In this self-study study, we aimed to explore our own process of praxis in relation to our shared context of a rural teacher education program and our individual experiences with diverse learners in urban environments. "Self-study is about the learning from experience that is embedded within teachers' creating new experiences for themselves and those whom they teach" (Russell, 1998, p. 6). Through self-study, we aimed to engage in praxis for purposes of exploring and challenging our assumptions, for improving our practices, and for enabling transformation for teacher preparation as an outcome of praxis at the collective level (Schulte, 2016).

4.1 Theoretical Framework

Teaching and learning are complex processes. To address intersecting aspects of knowledge, identity, and practice in teaching for social justice, we draw from multiple perspectives that, together, help to meaningfully frame the complexities of praxis and becoming. Viewed as mutually informing, complementary, and nonlinear, we attend to praxis and becoming prismatically through processual, experiential, and relational ontological perspectives.

We situated our inquiry in a transactional paradigm (Dewey & Bentley, 1949), adopting the epistemological stance that humans are active meaning makers who share an ecological relationship with their environment. Informed by the TTRW (Rosenblatt 1978/1994, 1994), TTL (Edge, 2022; Edge et al., 2022a), a narrative view of experience (e.g., Clandinin & Connelly, 2000), and feminist communication theory (e.g., Colflesh, 1996), we positioned ourselves as active meaning makers who could nurture reflections and discourse grounded in complex teaching environments, who could read and make meaning from our lived experiences as we create new understandings of our practice (e.g., Bergh et al., 2018; Edge, 2022; Edge et al., 2016, 2022b; Edge & Olan, 2020, 2021).

Through TTRW and TTL, we see becoming and praxis as connected and mutually informing one another; our understandings, identities, practices, and environments are works ever in progress. We are ever-engaged in reading and composing internal and external communicative signs or texts in multiple contexts. We agree with other teacher educators who are self-study of practice researchers (e.g., Barak, 2015; Hordvik et al., 2021; Ovens et al., 2016; Pinnegar et al., 2020; Strom & Martin, 2013), that becoming teacher/teacher educator are ongoing processes. Through the TTRW applied to teaching and learning (e.g., Edge, 2022; Edge et al., 2022b; Edge & Olan, 2020), we have come to see *becoming* as an assertion that teacher learning, practice, and identity are dynamic, relational, multiple, continuous, transactional events.

From our disciplinary knowledge and experiences with literature and the teaching of English language arts, we embrace a perspective that stories lived, and told, are a way of understanding experience (Clandinin, 2006; Clandinin & Connelly, 2000; Connelly & Clandinin, 1990, 2006; Edge, 2022). People communicate, relate, and experience through the stories they live and tell. In reading, composing, and studying stories with our students, we believe we can model and teach learners to experience and develop critical thinking skills, empathy, and community; this experiential space is the fertile soil for understanding and learning to advocate for self and others. Stories help humans organize experiences, make connections, discover, and express meanings. Story is the landscape within which teachers and teacher education researchers live, experience the world, make sense of, develop, and order knowledge (Edge, 2022; Elbaz, 1991; Webster & Mertova, 2007).

To facilitate our inquiry, we positioned ourselves as collaborative researchers who could tell and write the stories of our experiences. As critical friends working with S-STTEP, we frame the stories we live and tell as teacher researchers and communicate to self and others as mediums through which we learn from experience and generate new experiences—for ourselves and those we teach (Edge, 2022; Russell, 1998). One purpose of self-study research is to articulate and to refine one's professional expertise and understanding of teacher education practices (Vanassche & Kelchtermans, 2015). Another multifaceted purpose is to produce knowledge that can inform "the complex and ever-changing process of teaching" (Gatlin et al., 2002, p. 13) and generate understandings that can be shared with others (LaBoskey, 2004). "The knowledge developed in and through self-study cannot be disconnected from the complex reality it refers to, and is embedded in" (Vanassche & Kelchtermans, 2015, pp. 515–516). The rich contexts in which knowledge of teaching and teacher education are evoked or discovered through self-study research have potential to inform, in context-sensitive ways, the broader, multifaceted knowledge base as an ever-evolving, representation of our collective becoming and praxis.

4.2 Methodology

Through narrative self-study (Kitchen, 2009), we sought to explore and challenge our assumptions with the purpose of improving our understanding and practice of teaching (Bullough & Pinnegar, 2001) and for producing contextual understandings that can be shared with others. As Webster and Mertova (2007) write, "Narrative is well suited to addressing the complexities and subtleties of human experience in teaching and learning" (p. 1). Self-study methodology enables us to examine the stories we live and tell from "a particular perspective about the nature of reality and research—one of becoming teacher, teacher educator, and researcher" (Pinnegar et al., 2020, p. 100).

Kitchen (2009) explains "narrative inquiry is the study of how people make meaning from experience. Telling or collecting stories is the beginning of the process, but it is through the multi-dimensional exploration of these stories that narrative knowledge emerges" (p. 37). To explore our stories and the process of uncovering narrative knowledge of our teaching practices, we met weekly via Zoom over 3 months (May–August). Initially, we began by catching up on our lives, sharing our teaching experiences since our last shared research (Vipperman & Edge, 2015), and thoughtfully considering the context and purpose of our present inquiry. Following our first Zoom conversation, we each identified a critical event or tension from our lived experiences, then textualized the experience through narrative writing.

For a researcher, holistically studying critical events can be "an avenue to making sense of complex and human-centered information (Webster & Mertova, 2007 p. 77). Through writing, each of us situated her own selected critical event within its broader context, and wrote to construct an understanding (Richardson, 2000; Richardson & St. Pierre, 2005) of what we each thought was happening in the critical event studied. Next, we each orally shared the critical event within our (digital) "public homeplace" (Belenky et al., 1997, p. 13) that included our individual home offices and the Zoom platform. Using Zoom created an in-between space: between work and home, between past and present collaborations, roles, identities, a public homeplace (Belenky, 1996) where we could connect, explore ideas, learn together, and construct knowledge.

As critical friends and collaborative researchers, we sought to support and empower one another to learn from studying our professional practices through reflective thinking, interaction, and collaborative knowledge generation (e.g., Edge et al., 2022a; Edge & Olan, 2021; Richards & Fletcher, 2018; Schuck & Russell, 2005; Stolle et al., 2019). Our Zoom interactions offered the opportunity to foster individual and shared emerging understandings; we asked challenging questions, supported reframing of events, and were active participants in the S-STTEP professional learning experience. Our extended dialogue moved through time to juxtapose recent events, memories, and unfolding ideas in the present. Our meaning-making led us to return to and review the shared texts of our earlier research related to PTs' writings in PNs in juxtaposition to our own emerging insights. Our discourse was driven by an exploratory stance, and included wondering, asking questions, sharing inferences, making connections, and responding to individual and shared experiences. Our Zoom meetings were recorded and transcribed. Later sessions were utilized to study the Zoom recordings. Additional data included journal entries we each wrote between our meetings, notes jotted down during meetings, screen shots, and archival data related to our previous research (e.g., participants' writings, course documents, research memos, themes charts, drafts of writings or presentations).

To facilitate our meaning-making from reading and analyzing our narratives and our Zoom discussions, we used a flexible, collaborative, meaning-making protocol (Bergh et al., 2018; Edge et al., 2016, 2022a; Edge & Olan, 2021). We employed this for purposes of seeing and re-seeing our critical events from multiple orientations in relation to the narratives as data, as stories we lived and told, and for forming new understandings of practice (Loughran & Northfield, 1998) through reading, listening, speaking, and writing interactions. This protocol included: listening to each individual's narratives and jotting notes; taking turns saying what we heard or noticed while the other quietly took notes; taking turns offering speculative comments, connections, and wonderings; inviting each other to respond to comments or questions; offering additional details or insights sparked by listening to one another's comments; and writing take-aways after our sessions. We also wrote reflections and read relevant literature (e.g., Gutiérrez et al., 1999) between meetings. Individual take-away statements became a way to attend to the themes that developed from our collaborative self-study.

4.3   Outcomes

Outcomes from our inquiry include identifying and describing a process of becoming through praxis. Juxtaposing our individual spoken and written narratives, we discovered we were experiencing similar phenomena though different in language, context, and experiences reported. Themes describing the phenomenon of our praxis process include: (1) reading experience; (2) seeing and re-seeing through juxtaposition; and (3) new insights leading to action. Reading experience entailed "seeing" (recognizing, identifying, making visible) experiences and noting our thinking about those experiences. This happened in several ways—by speaking aloud the stories of our experiences, writing a narrative of the experience, orally reading the narrative to our critical friend (each other), and discussing the textualized experience together. Situating a praxis process within the context of S-STTEP and the broader teacher education literature helped us to recognize and embrace our own becomings in relation to praxis.

Through the multiple modes of composing and reading (talk, writing, reading written narratives and discussing them), we juxtaposed our experiences. We recognized similarities and differences within our own narratives, across time, by positioning our separate experiences side by side within the context of the study. Juxtaposing events helped us to make connections and to see and to embrace differences. Juxtaposing these experiences shifted our positionality, enabling us to take a more analytical or distanced perspective. The situation of the inquiry and collaborative nature of our self-study provided a frame through which we engaged in meaning-making events in the present. Together, we noticed details, asked questions, probed for additional details, and offered contextual details which helped us to individually and collaboratively see and re-see those experiences from our present focus of teaching and learning to teach diverse learners in urban environments. In other words, juxtaposition enabled us to see our experiences differently and to see ourselves differently in relation to our past, unfolding present, and anticipated future experiences.

From the act of juxtaposing, seeing and re-seeing our experiences, we identified a pattern of insights leading to new actions. This phenomenon was represented in written and verbalized "Ah-ha!" moments; the "Ah!" aspect captured insight, while the "ha!" communicated the direction of our attention and desired or actual actions. The insight propelled us toward action in relation to the insight. (Re)reading the experiences, we could see that our insights were directly connected to new action. If action is not accompanied with the insights, we assert it is not praxis, as actions enact praxis to create new experiences or meaning-making events, looping the process to generate a continuous act of becoming that includes identity, knowledge, positionality, and understanding of self, practice, and individual experiences. Seeing insights in relation to actions helped us to identify clear instances of becoming—in general as educators and specifically related to awareness of teaching for equity and social justice.

4.3.1 Becoming the Teacher in an Urban Environment: Chelsie's Narrative

I started my first semester of teaching as a student. I approached my lesson plans, classroom management, and engagement as a student would. It was not until the second semester of my first year that I could combine my experiences with my praxis to create meaningful learning experiences for my students.

The moment that I realized I made the cognitive transition from student to teacher occurred during the second semester of my first year teaching. Throughout my first semester, I was trying to fit the knowledge from my methods courses into my current reality. I focused on Bloom's Taxonomy and the way that I thought my students were supposed to learn. I was struggling to connect my students to this structure of learning. It was then that I realized that I needed to meet my students at their level before I could reach them. All of my students were at such diverse levels of language development and reading comprehension. As I started to learn more about my students, I was able to create groups and implement targeted lessons that facilitated their needs as learners.

At the beginning of that second semester, I started a learning unit about the novel *The Outsiders* with my Structured English Immersion (SEI) students, students who were non-native speakers of English. My advanced English language learners were making a graphic novel version for the less fluent English-speaking students in the classroom. I wanted to create a shared experience for all my students. After getting to know them, I discovered which students needed to be challenged and which students needed additional support. After listening to the first three chapters of the book together, the classroom was silent. I was worried that this was another lesson that my students could not connect to. While I passed out sticky notes for students to practice annotations, one student raised her hand. This may seem like a normal classroom practice, but this was a rare action in my class at that time. Students had a lot to say, but they never felt a reason to share things with me. A hand was only raised when a student needed to use the restroom, and even that was not always the case. As I called on the student, I realized that tears were streaming down her face. She explained how she could connect to the main character in the story because she had also lost her parents at a young age. As I processed this response, I was overwhelmed with emotion. Emotion from her experience and from her participation. She had something that she wanted to share with me. She recognized me as her teacher. As I started to direct the responses and conversations, another student not yet proficient in English brought me a Chromebook. He used the feature Google Translate to communicate that he was recently separated from his parents and understood how the character felt. Other students started participating. Students that refused to interact with each other were having discussions about their experiences and the content in the text. I was asking follow up questions and students were citing evidence to support their understanding. We shared laughs and tears that day. When the bell rang, the students did not rush out of the classroom. The learning continued. I was learning from my students, and they were learning from each other. That was the moment I became a teacher.

Reading and reflecting on this experience led to new insights on my teaching practice. This gave me the space to understand what was happening within my classroom and to see myself becoming a teacher.

4.3.2   Becoming Teacher Educator in Urban Environments: Christi's Narrative

After listening to Chelsie talk about her initial teaching experiences, I began to recall my own. In light of our conversation and the context of the study, I began re-seeing these events alongside Chelsie's experiences. In my journal, I wrote and later shared with Chelsie some early memories.

> I began my first teaching job on December 1, 1998, after Thanksgiving break, before my student teaching semester officially ended. Looking back, I jumped into a completely different world from student teaching or any that I had known as a learner myself. At a large, urban-fringe high school, I worked two weeks for free with a long-term substitute teacher officially on the books, until I had officially completed my university's semester. I don't think anything could have prepared me for the "first days of school" in this place.
>
> I remember readying the room [a portable classroom behind the school] the weekend before for my first day, adding decorative touches to make it feel more welcoming. Then, picking up the Sunday newspaper, I discovered Ricky, one of my first students, had been arrested for assaulting the substitute teacher the Friday before.
>
> Some unexpected early experiences included standing between two students who were suddenly ready to fight. Because there was no way to call for assistance, I had to wait for a student to run to the office and get help. Placing my whole body between, arms outstretched to hold steady a student holding her desk ready to throw it. A student, Jason, introducing himself to me, still a student in a Christian College on my first day as a Satanist…and somehow asking him a question and hearing him share a little of his world. In hearing, "Miss, we don't come to class. We just wanted to check you out. See what you're about."
>
> Due to the expanding student population, district boundary lines were redrawn and new schools created…to accommodate overcrowding...As a result, boundary lines for schools and neighborhoods were changing too. The initial clash of cultures…was evident in every way; fights and rivaling neighborhoods … some students enduring long bus rides, others walking from nearby neighborhoods, and some teens driving to school in cars I could never imagine affording… individual identities collided and somehow, we had to become a school together. Dr. B [the school leader]…anticipated these issues and really sought, through hundreds of little and big actions, to make us a school with a shared sense of pride from the start. (Journal Entry, May 13, 2021).

As these memories surfaced, I also identified an event in which I first felt like a teacher educator. In my journal I jotted:

> As a doctoral student, who was transitioning from teaching in this diverse district to becoming a teacher educator, I was the instructor of record in field-based, undergraduate methods courses, placing and supervising teacher candidates in urban and urban fringe classroom settings. I also served as a university supervisor to full-time student teachers completing their internship semester in a range of schools. Some were surrounded by high fences, security cameras, and metal detectors; others seemingly "appeared" amongst horse farms or orange orchards. (Journal Entry, May 13, 2021).

A critical event when I first felt like a teacher educator was identified as I made a connection in my own life narrative—from moving from teaching in urban schools to teaching prospective teachers as a doctoral teaching assistant who was the instructor in an urban fringe university.

> I remember recognizing practicum students didn't seem to know what to look for or how to think about what was happening in schools; they noticed superficial details and couldn't connect them in a meaningful way—like readers who could decode and read aloud okay but had no idea what the text was all about… Drawing from my experience teaching the reading class the semester before and again this semester with these PTs, I adapted, on the fly, the purpose of a reading strategy, and created some questions to guide us to make meaning in the moment. I remember thinking about my students—what they had been saying in our discussion, what they had written about before, what they were saying (and not) about the classrooms they had just been observing in, what was happening in the moment. I remember being right there in the flow of the event with them, like we were thinking and acting together—we were connected. The moment was powerful, and I think I first felt like a teacher educator then. I was using and repurposing my knowledge and experience, reading their needs, holding their words, our shared experiences, and an idea, an impression, a synthesized sense of what they were not yet understanding or able to yet see, yet somehow still communicating. I met them where they were, and the moment was harmonious, like instruments in an orchestra tuned together and holding a note, like the Ohm "aum" mantra sound, connected, all encompassing, energizing, the essence of our realities connected. (Journal Entry, May 31, 2021).

After (re)reading this experience and discussing it with Chelsie, I began to re-see myself in a state of becoming in relation to my students. At the time, that unplanned event was responsive, dynamic and generative in the connection between and across theory, experience, practice, identities and an openness to what could be and what we were in the process of becoming.

4.4   Discussion and Implications

Reading my (Christi's) experience with TTRW and TTL in mind, I see how my early experiences came to mind in response to and connection with what Chelsie shared. Our unfolding conversation was a text, evoking response, connections, and new meaning-making in the events of the present inquiry. I sought to understand, through the texts of my own experiences and empathizing with Chelsie around the difficulty of not only beginning teaching, but being in a situation that was even more challenging due to the many differences—some obvious others not. We were in classrooms and school settings different from those we were familiar with, including the classrooms in our own prior education. Although my first semester independently teaching a field-based methods course in the university setting and the event of first using a literacy strategy to help PTs think through field experiences is one I often thought about as an event that launched a line of research, I recalled these experiences very differently in our present study. In connection and juxtaposition to Chelsie's moment of first feeling like a teacher, I shifted the way I saw this event as a nodal moment (Tidwell, 2006). I identified it as a critical event (Webster & Mertova, 2007; Woods, 1993) or turning point (Bullock & Fletcher, 2017;

Bullock & Ritter, 2011) in my professional life story, as a meaning-making event when I first identified as a teacher educator. Repositioning the event to recognize it as becoming (Deleuze & Guattari, 1987) in the context of S-STTEP (e.g. Barak, 2015; Hordvik et al., 2021; Pinnegar et al., 2020; Strom & Martin, 2013) troubled the memory, complicated it, and created consciousness of a more complex whole (Freire, 1970). From the intersecting meaning-making events of the past and present, prismatic possibilities grew crystalline, creating both fixed and fluid openings from which I could inquire into my own praxis process in relation to others, then and now.

Though teaching for equity and social justice was present and saturated my textualized event of becoming a teacher educator, I now recognize, like my PTs who were trying to make sense of classroom events, I had (then) skittered at the surface level of how my insights and actions could form and transform learning for self and others. Learning from praxis, reading my own experiences through connections to theory and through the additional space of collaborative inquiry, and from juxtaposing my own experiences in relation to those of a critical friend distanced me from my lived experience enough to *see* my lived experiences. Textualizing a lived experience, I could "step in" to the text of that memory, move through it the context of the present, weaving insights afforded by the juxtaposition of time, experiences, and discourse with Chelsie, and make new meaning in the present. Stretching this critical event out to see its texture, to trace the metaphorical threads woven into it, is to see how teaching for social justice and becoming both include making meaning and using funds of knowledge and language, and the existing environment as curricular resources for re-seeing self and others. Curriculum is not simply the "stuff" jammed down the pipeline of mandates and standards; any classroom environment, any meaning-making event, can be a curricular-rich space for educative experience (Dewey, 1938; Rosenblatt, 1978/1994, 2005). To teach for equity and social justice in city schools is, in part, to embrace and frame events happening right where one is, to question, imagine into events, and seek to discover *how* and *why* and *what if* alongside and in relationship to diverse learners. The rich knowledge, experiences, languages, and identities of our learners are fertile landscapes intersecting in and through the classroom environment we share.

Referencing Freiere's call to see literacy as a relationship of learners in the world (Freire & Macedo, 1987), Ziemke and Muhtaris (2020) write about the power of stories and the need to consider literacy beyond words on a page to that of "reading the world; a juxtaposition of text and context. We cannot understand or use what we read, without comprehending the people, events, social movements, and inequalities that impact us" (1). Teaching and learning dynamically, transaction-ally, ecologically, and relationally includes co-authoring (Olan & Edge, 2019) or co-making curriculum with students in classroom events. Relational meaning-making in a classroom affords the opportunity to juxtapose texts and contexts by inviting individual's worlds and words. Diverse learners transform curriculum (Banks & Banks, 2004) by bringing to the teaching-learning meaning-making event, their knowledge and experience, wonderings, and observations. When educators attend to a learner's language as "pregnant" with meaning from their reading the world (Freire & Macedo, 1987, p. 35), teachers juxtapose the student's world-filled language with their own linguistic-experiential reservoir (Rosenblatt, 1978/1994). Through language (spoken, written, gestured, depicted, etc.) worlds come alongside one another. The juxtapositions of teacher-learner, learner-learner, learner-curriculum worlds forming-interacting-transacting-transforming in and through classroom events create prismatic opportunities for transforming the curriculum, one another, and the environment itself. Teachers and learners reading and responding to communicative signs in the classroom environment, make meaning in the ever-unfolding landscape of classroom events.

Praxis is a layered process. As I (Chelsie) recalled theory, creating lesson plans, and navigating the everyday tasks of teaching in a (new) school setting, I see them happening within the surface development of praxis. Understanding how to fit these elements into the reality of a classroom requires the transformation of past praxis into present action. Hattie (2015) explains that "Surface learning privileges knowing facts, ideas, and content, whereas deeper learning privileges knowing relations and connections between ideas and extending these ideas to other contexts" (p. 80). S-STTEP created the space to read my own experiences and learn beneath the surface. I recognized and identified my tension and wondering as rooted in knowing that I could recognize and recall what I learned about teaching and for teaching, yet still needing to figure out how to turn it into action for helping my specific students and their learning needs.

In my teacher preparation and student teaching, I had praxis experiences, and I needed to connect the *how* and *why* of praxis then to the *how* and *why* of praxis during the first year of teaching. Referencing Roth (2002), Robertine (2013) wrote, "...I will carry the lessons I have learned from these observations as a reminder that obtaining a teaching position is not the end of the journey but rather the beginning" (10). Now, in my fourth year of teaching, I can re-see becoming a teacher as a complex, continuous process (Hordvik et al., 2020; Martin, 2018). Even the notion of praxis transforms from something in a notebook or something that happened in particular classrooms into a continuous process across contexts. Learning from teaching is continuing praxis versus fractured practice—for purposes of equity and learning with diverse learners, and offers ways that I can repurpose my knowledge to help my students with what they are ready to learn.

In my teacher education practices, I (Christi) had sought to help PTs study their own learning process and to discover in the context of our classroom community the diversities present in and mediated by experience. Through S-STTEP, I considered my own identity, learning, and teaching experiences in urban environments. Self-study helped me to identify and embrace the complexities of learning and becoming, of becoming more mindful of equity and social justice education practices (Martin, 2018). Early in our study I wondered aloud to Chelsie in a moment of wobble (Fecho, 2011), "How do I model what prospective teachers have not yet experienced?" Studying my early teaching experiences in relation to Chelsie's and seeing my praxis process in multiple contexts over time help me to identify that the process of becoming is not "simply linear" happening over time and because of "more" experience; it is not an input-output, stimulus-response, reaction paradigm. Rather, becoming is, in time, through experience, within relationships and across contexts. Writing, discussing, and analyzing past events created present praxis events through which my identity, learning, and commitment to equity and social justice also *became*. As a result, I turned my attention again to the ontological and practical. Experience is event, a meaning-making event. Individuals read communicative signs in the world around them and make meanings. Meanings made may take the physical form of poems and scientific reports (Rosenblatt, 1978/1994), and meanings become identity, curriculum, relationships, and new events—opportunities for expanding knowledge, improving practice, deepening understanding, becoming equity-minded and socially just. Making meaning is a continual process of becoming (Bakhtin, 1981). Lived experiences are events, texts that are multifaceted, complex, imbued with meaning, language, and culture. These stories are rich spaces and resources for helping PTs develop agency, awareness, and skills for drawing from their own learners' reservoirs of knowledge, experiences, and languages to read and write the world.

Our learning has not ended or concluded; rather, we pause to metaphorically look back, embrace the present, and lean toward future possibilities. In hindsight, it is clear that our experiences and wonderings have changed our positionality in relation to our inquiry—to the research experience, to one another, and to our life worlds (Webster & Mertova, 2007). The challenge of forging our self-study inquiry and research event and juxtaposing our experience with existing literature (e.g., Dewey, 1938; Kitchen, 2005; Pinnegar et al., 2020; Strom & Martin, 2017) helped to illuminate:

- a relationship between praxis and becoming
- making meaning as becoming
- becoming as an ontological, reciprocal, and relational process
- experience as event and text, read and composed by self and others in multifaceted contexts

Enacting and studying our enactment of praxis enabled us to relate to our learners and one another, continue to process and learn from our previous collaborative research experiences, and mediated our own becoming through the present, S-STTEP, meaning-making event. With heightened awareness, responsibility, and urgency we (re)see our teaching practices as events in which we and our diverse learners "perceive critically *the way they exist* in the world *with which* and *in which* they find themselves; they come to see the world not as a static reality, but as reality in process, in transformation" (Freire, 1970, p. 71, original emphasis).

References

Bakhtin, M. M. (1981). *The dialogic imagination: Four essays by M. M. Bakhtin*. Austin University of Texas Press.

Banks, J. A., & Banks, C. A. M. (2004). *Multicultural education: Issues and perspectives*. Wiley.

Barak, J. (2015). Augmented becoming: Personal reflections on collaborative experience. *Studying Teacher Education, 11*(1), 49–63. https://doi.org/10.1080/17425964.2015.1013027

Belenky, M. (1996). Public homeplaces: Nurturing the development of people, families and communities. In N. Goldberger, J. Tarule, B. Clinchy, & M. Belenky (Eds.), *Knowledge, difference, and power* (pp. 393–430) Basic.

Belenky, M., Bond, L., & Weinstock, J. (1997). *A tradition that has no name*. Basic.

Bergh, B., Edge, C., & Cameron-Standerford, A. (2018). Reframing our use of visual literacy through academic diversity: A cross-disciplinary collaborative self-study. In J. Sharkey & M. M. Peercy (Eds.), *Self-study of language and literacy teacher education practices across culturally and linguistically diverse contexts* (pp. 115–142). Emerald.

Bruner, J. (1986). *Actual minds, possible worlds*. Harvard University Press.

Bullock, S. M., & Fletcher, T. (2017). Teaching about teaching using technology: Using embodiment to interpret online pedagogies of teacher education. In D. Garbett & A. Ovens (Eds.), *Being self-study researchers in a digital world* (pp. 33–46). Springer.

Bullock, S. M., & Ritter, J. K. (2011). Exploring the transition to academia through collaborative self-study. *Studying Teacher Education, 7*(2), 171–181. https://doi.org/10.1080/1742596 4.2011.591173

Bullough, R. V., & Pinnegar, S. (2001). Guidelines for quality in autobiographical forms of self-study research. *Educational Researcher, 30*(3), 13–21. https://doi.org/10.3102/0013189x030003013

Clandinin, D. J. (2006). Narrative inquiry: A methodology for studying lived experience. *Research Studies in Music Education, 27*, 44–54. https://doi.org/10.1177/1321103X060270010301

Clandinin, D. J., & Connelly, F. M. (2000). *Narrative inquiry: Experience and story in qualitative research*. Jossey-Bass.

Cohen, D. K. (2011). *Teaching and its predicaments*. Harvard University Press.

Colflesh, N. A. (1996). *Piece-making: The relationships between women's lives and the patterns and variations that emerge in their talk about school leadership* (Unpublished doctoral dissertation). Michigan State University.

Connelly, F. M., & Clandinin, D. J. (1990). Stories of experience and narrative inquiry. *Educational Researcher, 19*(5), 2–14. https://doi.org/10.3102/0013189X019005002

Connelly, F. M., & Clandinin, D. J. (2006). Narrative inquiry. In J. L. Green, G. Camilli, P. B. Elmore, A. Skukauskaite, & E. Grace (Eds.), *Handbook of complementary methods in education research* (pp. 477–487). American Educational Research Association.

Deleuze, G., & Guattari, F. (1987). *Capitalism and schizophrenia: A thousand plateaus*. University of Minnesota Press.

Dewey, J. (1938). *Experience and education*. Simon & Schuster.

Dewey, J., & Bentley, A. F. (1949). *Knowing and the known*. Beacon.

Draper, R. J., Broomhead, P., Jensen, A. P., Nokes, J. D., & Siebert, D. (Eds.). (2010). *(Re)imagining content-area literacy instruction*. Teachers College Press.

Edge, C. U., (2011). *Making meaning with "readers" and "texts": A narrative inquiry into two beginning English teachers' meaning making from classroom events* (Unpublished doctoral dissertation). University of South Florida.

Edge, C. U. (2022). *Making meaning with readers and texts: Beginning teachers' meaning-making from classroom events*. Emerald.

Edge, C. U., & Olan, E. L. (2020). Reading, literacy, and English language arts teacher education: Making meaning from self-studies of teacher education practices. In J. Kitchen, A. Berry, S. Bullock, A. Crowe, H. Guðjónsdóttir, J. Kitchen, & M. Taylor (Eds.), *International handbook for self-study of teaching and teacher education* (2nd ed., pp. 779–821). Springer. https://doi.org/10.1007/978-981-13-6880-6_27

Edge, C. U., & Olan, E. (2021). Learning to breathe again: Found poems and critical friendship as methodological tools in self-study of teaching practices. *Studying Teacher Education, 17*(2), 228–252. https://doi.org/10.1080/17425964.2021.1910807

Edge, C., Bergh, B., & Cameron-Standerford, A. (2016). *Critically reading lived experiences as texts: A four-year study of teacher education practices*. [Conference presentation]. American Educational Research Association Annual Meeting: Washington, DC, United States.

Edge, C. U., Cameron-Standerford, A., & Bergh, B. (2022a). Power-with: Strength to transform through collaborative self-study across spaces, places, and identities. In B. Butler & S. Bullock (Eds.), *Learning through collaboration in self-study: Communities of practice, critical friendship, and collaborative self-study* (pp. 171–184). Springer. https://doi.org/10.1007/978-981-16-2681-4_13

Edge, C., Monske, L., Boyer-Davis, S., VandenAvond, S., & Hamel, B. (2022b). Leading university change: A case study of meaning-making and implementing online learning quality standards. *American Journal of Distance Education, 36*(1), 53–69. https://doi.org/10.1080/08923647.2021.2005414

Elbaz, F. (1991). Research on teachers' knowledge: The evolution of a discourse. *Journal of Curriculum Studies, 23*(1), 1–9.

Fecho, B. (2011). *Teaching for the students: Habits of heart, mind, practice in the engaged classroom.* Teachers College Press.

Freire, P. (1970). *Pedagogy of the oppressed.* Continuum.

Freire, P., & Macedo, D. (1987). *Literacy: Reading the word and the world.* Routledge.

Gatlin, A., Peck, M., Aposhian, N., Hadley, S., & Porter, A. (2002). Looking again at insider knowledge: A relational approach to knowledge production and assessment. *Journal of Teacher Education, 53*(4), 303–315. https://doi.org/10.1177/0022487102053004003

Gutiérrez, K. D., Baquedano-López, P., & Tejeda, C. (1999). Rethinking diversity: Hybridity and hybrid language practices in the third space. *Mind, Culture, and Activity, 26*, 286–303. https://doi.org/10.1080/10749039909524733

Hattie, J. (2015). The applicability of visible learning to higher education. *Scholarship of Teaching and Learning in Psychology, 1*(1), 71–91. https://psycnet.apa.org/doi/10.1037/stl0000021

Hordvik, M., Fletcher, T., Haugen, A. L., Møller, L., & Engebretsen, B. (2021). Using collaborative self-study and rhizomatics to explore the ongoing nature of becoming teacher educators. *Teaching and Teacher Education*, 103318. https://doi.org/10.1016/j.tate.2021.103318

Hordvik, M., MacPhail, A., & Ronglan, L. T. (2020). Developing a pedagogy of teacher education using self-study: A rhizomatic examination of negotiating learning and practice. *Teaching and Teacher Education*, 102969. https://doi.org/10.1016/j.tate.2019.102969

Kitchen, J. (2005). Conveying respect and empathy: Becoming a relational teacher educator. *Studying Teacher Education, 1*(2), 195–207. https://doi.org/10.1080/17425960500288374

Kitchen, J. (2009). Passages: Improving teacher education through narrative self-study. In L. Fitzgerald, M. Heston, & D. Tidwell (Eds.), *Research for the self-study of practice* (pp. 35–51). Springer. https://doi.org/10.1007/978-1-4020-9514-6_3

LaBoskey, V. K. (2004). The methodology of self-study and its theoretical underpinnings. In J. J. Loughran, M. L. Hamilton, V. K. LaBoskey, & T. Russell (Eds.), *International handbook of self-study of teaching and teacher education practices* (pp. 817–869). Kluwer Academic Publishers.

Liston, D. P., & Zeichner, K. M. (1991). *Teacher education and the social conditions of schooling.* Routledge.

Loughran, J. J., & Northfield, J. (1998). A framework for the development of self-study practices. In M. L. Hamilton (Ed.), *Reconceptualizing teaching practices: Self-study in teacher education* (pp. 7–18). Falmer Press.

Lyttle, S. L. (2013). Foreword: The critical literacies of teaching. In C. Kosnik, J. Rowsell, P. Williamson, R. Simon, & C. Beck (Eds.), *Literacy teacher educators: Preparing teachers for a changing world* (pp. xv–xix). Sense Publishers.

Martin, A. D. (2018). Professional identities and pedagogical practices: A self-study on the "becomings" of a teacher educator and teachers. In D. Garbett & A. Ovens (Eds.), *Pushing boundaries and crossing borders: Self-study as a means for researching pedagogy* (pp. 263–269). Self-Study of Teacher Education Practices.

Olan, E. L., & Edge, C. (2019). Collaborative meaning-making and dialogic interactions in critical friends as co-authors. *Studying Teacher Education, 15*(1), 31–43. https://doi.org/10.1080/17425964.2019.1580011

Ovens, A., Strom, K., & Garbett, D. (2016). A rhizomatic reading of becoming teacher educator. In D. Garbett & A. Ovens (Eds.), *Enacting self-study as methodology for professional inquiry* (pp. 181–188). Self-Study of Teacher Education Practices.

Pinnegar, S., Hutchinson, D. A., & Hamilton, M. L. (2020). Role of positioning, identity and stance in becoming S-STEP researchers. In J. Kitchen, A. Berry, S. M. Bullock, A. R. Crow, M. Taylor, H. Guðjónsdóttir, & L. Thomas (Eds.), *International handbook of self-study of teaching and teacher education* (2nd ed., pp. 97–133). Springer. https://doi.org/10.1007/978-981-13-6880-6_4

Richards, K. A. R., & Fletcher, T. (2018). Learning to work together: Conceptualizing doctoral supervision as a critical friendship. *Sport, Education and Society, 37*, 225–231. https://doi.org/10.1080/13573322.2018.1554561

Richardson, L. (2000). Writing: A method of inquiry. In N. K. Denzin & Y. S. Lincoln (Eds.), *Handbook of qualitative research* (pp. 512–529). Sage.

Richardson, L., & St. Pierre, E. A. (2005). Writing: A method of inquiry. In N. K. Lincoln & Y. S. Lincoln (Eds.), *The sage handbook of qualitative research* (3rd ed., pp. 959–978). Sage.

Robertine, T. (2013). Continuous becoming: Fieldwork as a mutually transformative experience. In P. L. Thomas (Ed.), *Becoming and being a teacher: Confronting traditional norms to create new democratic realities* (pp. 3–11). Peter Lang.

Rosenblatt, L. M. (1978/1994). *The reader, the text, the poem: The transactional theory of the literary work*. SIU Press.

Rosenblatt, L. M. (1994). The transactional theory of reading and writing. In R. R. Ruddell, M. R. Ruddell, & H. Singer (Eds.), *Theoretical models and processes of reading* (4th ed., pp. 1057–1092) International Reading Association.

Rosenblatt, L. (2005). *Making meaning with texts: Selected essays*. Heinemann.

Roth, W. M. (2002). *Being and becoming in the classroom: Issues in curriculum theory, policy and research*. Ablex.

Russell, T. (1998). Introduction to part 1: Philosophical perspectives. In M. L. Hamilton (Ed.), *Reconceptualizing teaching practice: Self-study in teacher education* (pp. 5–6). Falmer Press.

Schuck, S., & Russell, T. (2005). Self-study, critical friendship, and the complexities of teacher education. *Studying Teacher Education, 1*(2), 107–121. https://doi.org/10.1080/17425960500288291

Schulte, A. K. (2016). Looking for my rural identity, finding community and place. In A. K. Schulte & B. Walker-Gibbs (Eds.), *Self-studies in rural teacher education* (pp. 17–36). Springer.

Stolle, E. P., Frambaugh-Kritzer, C., Freese, A., & Persson, A. (2019). Investigating critical friendship: Peeling back the layers. *Studying Teacher Education, 15*(1), 19–30. https://doi.org/10.1080/17425964.2019.1580010

Strom, K. J., & Martin, A. D. (2013). Putting philosophy to work in the classroom: Using rhizomatics to deterritorialize neoliberal thought and practice. *Studying Teacher Education, 9*(3), 219–235. https://doi.org/10.1080/17425964.2013.830970

Strom, K. J., & Martin, A. D. (2017). *Becoming-teacher: A rhizomatic look at first-year teaching*. Springer.

Tidwell, D. (2006). Nodal moments as a context for meaning. In D. Tidwell & L. Fitzgerald (Eds.), *Self-study and diversity* (pp. 267–285). Sense Publishers.

Vanassche, E., & Kelchtermans, G. (2015). The state of the art in self-study of teacher education practices: A systematic literature review. *Journal of Curriculum Studies, 47*(4), 508–528. https://doi.org/10.1080/00220272.2014.995712

Vipperman, C., & Edge, C., (2015, April). *Transition from student to teacher: A phenomenological study*. [Conference presentation.] 29th annual National Conference on undergraduate research: Cheeney, WA.

Webster, L., & Mertova, P. (2007). *Using narrative inquiry as a research method: An introduction to using critical event narrative analysis in research on learning and teaching*. Routledge.

Woods, P. (1993). Critical events in education. *British Journals of Sociology of Education, 14*, 355–371. https://doi.org/10.1080/0142569930140401

Ziemke, K., & Muhtaris, K. (2020). *Read the world: Rethinking literacy for empathy and action in a digital age*. Heinemann.

Christi U. Edge Ph.D., is a Professor in the School of Education at Northern Michigan University. She teaches graduate literacy and undergraduate methods courses and serves as the Scholar for Extended Learning and Community Engagement. Prior to academe, Christi taught high school English language arts and reading. Her research weaves together meaning-making, literacy, online teaching, narrative inquiry, and self-study of practice. Recent scholarship may be found in *Studying Teacher Education*, the *International Handbook for Self-Study of Teaching and Teacher Education*, *American Journal of Distance Education*, *Learning through Collaboration in Self-Study: Communities of Practice, Critical Friendship, and Collaborative Self-Study*, and *Textiles and Tapestries: Self-Study for Envisioning New Ways of Knowing*. Christi lives in Marquette, Michigan, USA, and enjoys adventuring with her husband, three children, and French bull-dog, Archie.

Chelsie Vipperman M.A., is a high school teacher who currently teaches at Hope High School Online. She teachers eleventh and twelfth grade English as well as a targeted instruction course for English Language students. She helps students in unique circumstances finish high school. As an educator, her approach to teaching takes the form of inquiry-based learning. Her goal is to cultivate a space for critical thinking. She recently earned her master's degree in Curriculum and Instruction from Grand Canyon University. Chelsie's research interests include teacher sustainability and retention, teacher evaluation systems, and the reflection, growth and development of educators. She currently lives in Cross Roads, Texas, and teaches on a remote platform.

Part II
Race, Culture, and Urban Teacher Education

Chapter 5
Teaching Black: Common Eyes All See the Same

LaChan V. Hannon, Lia M. Hannon, Monique S. Jenkins, Michael R. Jones, and Malcom A. Williams

Abstract Supporting Black urban educators in ways that are affirming and inclusive acknowledges the complexities of being both Black in America and an agent of the school system. For equity-minded Black educators who work to disrupt systemic racism in schools, the relationship between their racial and professional identities are often in conflict. That is, Black educators often have to reconcile that they were recipients of anti-Black education and are current actors in schools' assimilationist practices. This co/autoethnographic self-study privileges the voices of five Black teachers working in the same school and the actualization of their critical consciousness. The authors explored how they came to consistently bring their whole Black selves to the classroom and school setting. Drawing from the tenets of critical race theory of education and racial identity development in teaching, the authors operationalized what they call *teaching Black*. Through this lens, they interrogated their racialized navigation through the urban workplace to reveal the ways they created supportive and validating third-spaces to confront issues of anti-Blackness, abuses of power, and structural inequities for themselves, their colleagues, and most importantly their students. The chapter provides recommendations for creating and sustaining school practices that support pre-service teachers in urban teacher education and in-service Black teachers to more fully appreciate the cultural and racial community wealth they bring to their schools.

Keywords Black teacher identity development · Self-care

This chapter comes during a time of racial reckoning in America. It is happening in the streets, in schools, in work offices, in homes, and in so many more places. We are also living through a global pandemic which has separated families, friends, and teachers from students. Still, the digital technologies (e.g., Zoom, email) we have

L. V. Hannon (✉) · L. M. Hannon · M. S. Jenkins · M. R. Jones · M. A. Williams
Rutgers University, Newark, NJ, USA
e-mail: LHannon@getac.org

© The Author(s), under exclusive license to Springer Nature Singapore Pte Ltd. 2022
A. D. Martin (ed.), *Self-Studies in Urban Teacher Education*, Self-Study of Teaching and Teacher Education Practices 25,
https://doi.org/10.1007/978-981-19-5430-6_5

relied on to stay connected with one another have challenged us to provide support to each other in ways we did not even know we needed. We are five Black educators who engaged in a self-study as a joint sense-making endeavor with regard to the reconciliation of our racial and professional identities in the workplace (Pithouse-Morgan & Samaras, 2020). During the years 2009–2014, we all worked in the same urban vocational high school in the Northeastern United States (U.S.), and our singular and joint experiences exposed the tensions that exist between what it means to be Black in America and to be public-school teachers. In sharing our parallel narratives, we investigated what experiences influenced the development of our racialized professional identities as Black teachers. In our conversations, we addressed relevant constructs such as cultural dissonance, challenging the status quo, and Black teacher attrition (Chisanga & Meyiwa, 2019).

We recorded our online Zoom conversations, the first of which occurred the day after the murder of George Floyd, and the last 3 days after the 2020 U.S. presidential election (Martin, 2020). Through our conversations and the sharing of our experiences, we were able to make more transparent how and why we are not just colleagues, but friends as well. The comfort and criticality that we were able to show one another reiterated the need for teachers and teacher educators to have conversations and spaces such as the one we had created. This is even more relevant today as many states continue to pass legislation prohibiting schools from acknowledging racism, White supremacy, and the use of power and privilege to marginalize others (Sharma, 2022).

Through this work, we sought to define what *teaching Black* means for us as we developed as teachers. We desired to understand and explain the tensions in teaching Black and how we resolved those tensions (Kitchen & Brown, 2022). We learned that teaching Black is much more than any one person's individual contributions in their classroom. Teaching Black is the affirmation of truth for the edification of ourselves and students, as well as the confrontations that come with resisting whiteness. For us, teaching Black is less about what you do at work and more about sharing your life with your work.

Supporting Black urban educators in affirming ways acknowledges the complexities of being Black in America while also being an agent of the state (i.e., the school system); as such, this is an area of inquiry that merits more in-depth exploration and scholarly attention (Hannon, 2020). For equity-minded Black educators who work to disrupt systemic racism in schools, the relationship between racial and professional identities are often in conflict (Duncan, 2019). That is, Black educators often have to reconcile that they were recipients of anti-Black education and yet also current actors in schools' assimilationist practices (Lopez & Jean-Marie, 2021). Using co/autoethnography, a self-study methodology, (Taylor & Coia, 2009, 2020), we unpacked our separate and overlapping experiences about what it means to be a Black teacher in an urban-characteristic school (Milner, 2012). More specifically, we explored how we learned to bring our whole Black selves to the classroom (Hannon, 2019; Maloney, 2017) and the tensions this revealed. This self-study privileges our voices as five Black educators who worked in the same school and how our critical consciousness confronted school norms. We lean on the tenets of critical race theory of education (Ladson-Billings & Tate, 1995) and racial identity development in teaching (Hollins, 1999) to better understand our collective lived professional experiences of being Black educators in a high school that enrolls predominantly Black and Brown students.

This chapter is organized as follows. First, we situate this inquiry within the sociocultural framework of critical race theory in education (Ladson-Billings & Tate, 1995; Zamudio et al., 2010) and racial identity development in teaching (Hollins, 1999). Then, we discuss how co/autoethnography as methodology informed this self-study. Following this, we highlight the most salient themes that emerged from our analysis. We discuss our findings in relation to broader themes from our self-study and in relation to our conceptual frameworks. We provide recommendations on how to prepare teachers to work in urban schools and support Black teachers in ways that are affirming and encourage professional growth. We consider how to create and sustain culturally responsive school practices that support Black educators and the cultural community wealth we bring to our schools' environments (Yosso, 2005).

5.1 Theoretical Framework

For this study, we took our epistemological cues from two guiding theories, the sociocultural framework of critical race theory in education (Ladson-Billings & Tate, 1995; Zamudio et al., 2010) and racial identity development in teaching (Hollins, 1999). Critical race theory in education provides a lens to discuss the intersectionality of race and property in schooling. In essence, critical race theory positions education itself as property. Access to equitable schooling and a quality education is leveraged and obtained more easily by some social and racial groups (e.g., White middle/upper class communities) than others. In the U.S., Black and Brown youth have historically (and presently) been denied equal access to quality education and equitable schooling contexts. Critical race theory calls on researchers and members of the education community to more fully attend to the ways that race functions as a mitigating factor that determines the qualities and characteristics of schooling and how these are differentially afforded to members of society (Larkin & Hannon, 2020). As both students of and educators within the American public school system, we used critical race theory to better understand how we learned to teach in ways that resist whiteness and affirm our Black identities and pedagogies. It also speaks to how we engaged with our students to advocate for themselves in school systems that are not systemically affirming of their cultural ways of being.

We used the work of Hollins (1999) on racial identity development in teaching to enact what she describes as a Type III teacher who "view[s] culture as affect, behavior, and intellect" (p. 190). In this way, we, as Black educators, recognized how central "culture and ethnicity [are] in daily life" and how it impacts teachers' "selecting approaches to instruction, framing curriculum, and creating a social context for learning" (p. 190). According to Hollins (1999), Type III teachers "understand the centrality of culture in our existence as human beings" (p. 190). They understand that there is cultural knowledge and there are cultural understandings that contribute to students' learning, and those understandings should be an active part of the school curriculum. As such, these teachers will alter curricula to meet the needs of their students. They create student-centered classrooms that are collaborative and place a high value on cross-cultural understanding. Culture is central to Type III teachers. In this chapter, we argue that our racial identity development as Type III teachers often collided with the expectations of being public school teachers.

We refer to this phenomenon of racial and professional identity development as teaching Black. We were able to define teaching Black by responding to the statements: (a) teaching Black means knowing…; (b) teaching Black means feeling…; and (c) teaching Black means doing…by the end of our self-study. Implicit in these sentence stems is a recognition that being a Black teacher is inherently contradictory to the traditional values of teacher preparation (Petchauer & Mawhinney, 2017). In the U.S., these traditional values can mean subscribing to Euro-centric curricula, failing to include instructional resources and materials that reflect a diversity of socio-cultural identities and experiences, disciplinary practices that favor compliance over creativity, and teaching strategies that devalue the socio-cultural-racial identities of Black and Brown students while affirming those of White, mainstream, middle/upper class American backgrounds. For us, the reality of identifying as Black in America is both fundamental to and critical of the educational system given the harm it inflicts on Black students, some who then turn into Black teachers. Situated within pervasive whiteness and anti-Blackness, the inequitable academic opportunities for Black students have often mirrored the inequitable professional opportunities we experienced as Black teachers.

Throughout our sustained and deliberate engagement in this self-study (Loughran, 2004), we acknowledged how teaching Black meant being disruptive and subversive, as suggested by Ladson-Billings in her seminal book *The Dreamkeepers* (1994). Additionally, our meetings during the Covid-19 pandemic ultimately served as a means of sustaining connection and self-preservation. Together, we functioned as a support system to confront issues of anti-Blackness, abuse of power, and what it meant to be a Black educator. The racialized lens through which we examined our own teacher identity development is critical to the preparation, mentoring, and retention of Black educators.

5.2 Methods

This inquiry is a co/autoethnographic self-study that examined our experiences and narratives as five Black teachers who worked at the same urban school (Hannon, 2019; Taylor & Coia, 2009). We chose this methodology because it was important for us to understand if and how our individual experiences were reflective of a more congruent and telling collective experience as shared by other Black teachers in the same school context. Additionally, self-study (LaBoskey, 2004) enabled us to explore how our teaching practices were reflective of our racial identities and the tensions that existed between them. Critical to our self-study was understanding how our racialized teacher identities influenced the choices we made regarding our contributions to the classroom and school culture. Our self-initiated self-study aimed at understanding how our identities challenged or aligned with the normative expectations for teachers in the U.S. (Maloney, 2017). In this way, we desired to be better Black teachers. But to do this, we had to first define what it meant to be a Black teacher. We desired to improve the learning experiences of our students and understand the gendered and raced contributing factors in our meaning-making, mitigating circumstances, and commonalities in our professional decisions. Through our discussions, we unpacked if and how being Black influenced our decision-making and the possible tensions between our racial and professional identities. Thus, we set out to explore our experiences being Black teachers in an urban characteristic high school and how we believed we came to bring our whole selves to our school building and classrooms. This was a time when we were teaching in a way that was fully and unapologetically embracing of Black culture and who we are as Black teachers.

5.2.1 Participants

The lead author invited teachers to join this project based on the commonalities we shared. Our commonalities included working together at a vocational high school in the Northeastern United States with the same administrators and being academic content area teachers (as opposed to vocational teachers). All of us identify as middle-class Black Americans with at least one parent having a college degree. Malcom and LaChan joined the faculty in 2003, followed by Michael in 2006. Monique joined in 2009, and Lia joined in 2011.

5.2.2 Data Collection and the Research Process

Our data sources included the analytic memos and transcribed recordings from our nine meetings which were held primarily via Zoom over the course of 8 months. In order to help facilitate the discussions in our meetings, LaChan reviewed and developed guiding questions and prompts. Some of these prompts and questions were, "Describe how you came to the profession. What does it mean to you to teach Black? Talk about the evolution of your racialized identity." These were shared with our group members prior to our first meeting. While we did not provide each other copies of our individual written responses, we did utilize and draw from our responses to probe each other, share ideas or concepts, and collectively and collaboratively critique, question, and comment on what we were coming to understand.

It was important that we not just talk about what we experienced, but to also recall stories with examples of what we experienced.

During each meeting LaChan would take analytic memos, ask clarifying questions, and engage in member checking throughout the session. At the conclusion of each meeting, she summarized and synthesized the major points and themes from the discussion and asked for any further clarifications or corrections. Subsequent meetings would begin with a personal check-in, a restatement of the previous discussion's main points, and a continuation of the last salient topic we discussed. As a group, we were intentional about making sure that we discussed the feelings associated with our experiences. We did this by continuing to iteratively probe into the narratives we shared and the examples we provided regarding being Black teachers.

While during our initial meetings we focused on stories and examples of our teaching experiences, most of our sessions attended to unpacking how we understood what we experienced as tensions we felt in regard to being Black educators. This process allowed us not only to identified similarities and differences in our engagement at our school but also appreciate the perspectives we each possessed.

5.2.3 Data Analysis

After the conclusion of our final session, we reviewed our data sources and proceeded to identify salient themes from our engagement with each other. We collaborated to develop a code book based on our data. We utilized the online application Dedoose to code our transcripts. Drawing from these, we employed narrative analytic approaches (Clandinin & Connelly, 2004) and open coding (Saldaña, 2016) to discern what was being highlighted in individual data sources and collectively across all the data. We continued through this process and conferenced with one another to support the clarity and transparency of the analysis. Oftentimes, the experiences we recalled occurred concurrently in that we all had different perspectives of the same events, thus highlighting how important our discussions were in understanding ourselves, our students, and our environments. In this way, we were able to hear firsthand the recollections that we may have only had a cursory knowledge of. This aided in the promotion of the trustworthiness of this work (DeVault, 2018; Mena & Russell, 2017).

5.3 Findings

Our self-study supported us to understand and operationalize what teaching Black looks and feels like. In this section, we present our findings with the recognition that they are intersectional and overlapping. Bringing our whole selves into our school building and into our classrooms required a constant negotiation of personal investment, truth-telling, and transparency. We continuously had an internal conversation where we asked ourselves, "How Black can I be here today?" We were Black teachers teaching primarily Black and Brown students and surrounded by whiteness in the form of teachers, administrators, policies, disciplinary practices, curricula, expectations of professionalism, and mentorship. Despite microaggressions and cultural dissonance, we were able to build community with one another, speak truth into the curriculum, disrupt the status quo, and practice self-care. Ultimately, our self-study led us to identify salient aspects of our experiences which we discuss in alignment with Ladson-Billings's (1994) two main descriptors for teaching Black: disruptive and subversive.

5.3.1 Teaching Black as Disruptive

According to Merriam-Webster (n.d.-a), the business world definition for disrupt means, "to successfully challenge by using innovation to gain a foothold in a marginal or new segment of the market and then fundamentally change the nature of the market." This definition aligns with the aims of advocates for educational equity and applies equally to the education stratosphere and its impacts on historically marginalized students. During our self-study, it became very clear to us that our mere presence, voices, and ideas were often perceived as disruptive to school norms. Our desire to see ourselves in materials and curricula, our interest in advocating for disenfranchised students, and our aspiration for professional advancement were perceived as disruptive to the White-space power structure of schools. All of us were hired intentionally to disrupt the pervasive whiteness in our urban school, to help foster better relationships with students and families, and to improve the quality of instruction.

In the following, we provide examples of how we realized we were disruptive and the implications for disruptiveness. Malcom and Michael were the first and only Black male teachers in the physics and social studies departments, respectfully. Malcom remarked how our Black administrators wanted a teaching faculty that was more reflective of the student population. Michael remembered feeling protected by his Black administrators. He commented:

> I was [hired] because of what my perspective was going to add to the environment. Being Black was supposed to mean something, not just represent something, not because you got to check a box. I was told "You teach how you teach." And, I never changed when someone came into my room." (Zoom Meeting, July 31st)

LaChan, who was one of the first Black teachers in years to re-integrate the English department, recalled feeling a sense of privilege in her hiring. In a subsequent meeting, LaChan connected this with the notion of being disruptive. She shared:

> I didn't know that I was being disruptive. I thought I was just adding variety…just making myself comfortable. I was just putting [things into] a different perspective, bringing a different lens to the table. Because regardless of whether there are Black people or White people, schools are White spaces. Regardless of how many Black people that are in them or run them. They operate in the same way, with the same purpose, and the same functions. I

thought I was being helpful…innovative. And not that I wasn't, because I still believe that I am. It's just about how they see us. (Zoom Meeting, August 28th)

Malcom drew a distinction between how it felt to be disruptive and valued, and disruptive and devalued. He said, "When [Monique] said the word asset, that kind of triggered me, because I don't think they want us to know that we're assets. Even though they want us to be assets, they just don't want us to [know] it" (Zoom Meeting, July 31st).

During the time we worked at our school, our Black principal and vice principal, who viewed us as assets, retired and were replaced by White administrators. As teachers, we continued to push toward equity, counternarratives in curricula, and inclusive education, but we quickly learned that our new administrators did not view us in the same ways as our previous ones. The shift in leadership brought a shift in the expectations of us as teachers.

We were hired to be disruptive, but now being treated like a disruption reinforced the feeling that we did not belong in this space as Black teachers. These microaggressions reinforced the constant tension of how much of ourselves to share in our workspace and demonstrated itself in how and what we taught in our classrooms. Therefore, we had no choice by to make our teaching methods and lessons more subversive.

5.3.2   Teaching Black as Subversive

To subvert means to "undermine the power and authority of an institution" (Merriam-Webster, n.d.-b). As Black teachers, we were subversive by undermining the anti-Blackness in our curricula and including culturally and racially diverse instructional resources. We supplemented required texts with texts that amplified Black and Brown voices and provided counternarratives to dominant, White oriented narratives and perspectives. In our courses, we used primary and secondary sources that centered and highlighted the perspectives of Black and Brown people. We examined the real-life physical and sociocultural struggles of cause and effect when examining energy and force by exploring the phenomena of Black girl hair and the hegemonic White supremacist definitions of beauty. We did all of this to help our students understand that the narrative they had been given, the same narrative that we had been given as former students, was not a complete story and was told to them for a reason: to maintain a racist status quo and inequitable, socially unjust socio-cultural systems that people of color live through daily. Regardless of the novel, article, primary source, or experiment, we taught our students in ways that reflected the cultural understandings of being minoritized in America.

We learned in this self-study that because of our rapport with students and our valuing of who they were as individuals, we were able to productively keep students actively engaged in learning. Because of this and the trust that it enabled, our students largely did not have disciplinary issues in our classrooms, which contrasted with the experiences of teachers who failed to connect with them in meaningful ways. In keeping students engaged, we were challenging them to advocate for themselves, call out injustice, and make a positive impact in their school and community. We were teaching them to use their voices. Lia recalled one such experience teaching advanced placement (AP) Literature. She shared:

> I decided to incorporate literary lenses into my AP course…looking at marginalized people. And I had my students look at "Goldilocks and the Three Bears." They hit the ceiling, and then went to lunch. Somebody got in an argument because [they] told a White boy, "You're racist" because of the privilege of moving somebody else's book bag off the table where one of my Brown AP students put their book bag. And I was like, "Yeah I might have started that, because we just talked about White girls going into places and then claiming victim [like Goldilocks] and the Brown people who are likened to animals and not viewed as human." We did the whole spiel, and they were on "ten" when they left class. And then, there was almost a fight over White privilege about moving book bags in a space that had already been claimed. That was so distinct in my mind because I didn't anticipate that particular response, but I was very proud of it. I was glad that I instigated that. 100%. I owned it. (Zoom Meeting, August 28th)

Monique, a Spanish teacher, expressed a similar sentiment regarding the tension she experienced with the materials she was presented with. She shared:

> It's like you're constantly fighting this battle of, "I know that education is not set up for my students. The materials…they don't necessarily represent the people in front of me." So, I [need] the wherewithal to constantly research, make my own materials, make things and find things that reflect my students. (Zoom Meeting, August 28th)

Monique was not the only one with this subversive struggle. In our own ways, we all worked to bring "color", to diversify our curricular materials, lessons, assignments, and activities. Giving the students representations of themselves was a priority, and we knew this helped to engage them.

Michael also became a teacher with the aim to provide students with representations of themselves and the motivation to shake things up and present a more balanced accounting of history than he'd been exposed to as a student. Later in his career, he would become an assistant principal and shake up the social studies department at his new school by challenging teachers to include diverse perspectives in their teaching. The notion of shaking things up surfaced as important in our discussions yet not without its consequences. Lia shared the following:

> When we feel pushback [from colleagues and administrators], it's because we're smart. The disrupting [and subversion] comes in the fact that you have a cohort of very intelligent Brown teachers who push for excellence. And when we challenge, we're upsetting the power dynamic… our disruption and the rejection that we feel it's not necessarily because it's teaching while Black. It's because we're smart while Black. (Zoom Meeting, July 31st)

Despite all of the daily tensions we experienced as teachers, we recognized and valued each other's classroom as places of respite where we could decompress and recharge our minds and hearts. Working together to mutually make-meaning of our experiences enabled us to identify moments of pride and disappointment, appreciation and resentment, confidence and invalidation.

As is evident, teaching Black as subversive has its challenges. Yet, it also has its rewards, one being autonomy and electing when we wanted to subvert with our presence, ideas, and opinions. At moments, we appreciated being left alone in our classroom to teach our students as we saw best. But, when it was time to address an issue such as the application of inequitable dress code discipline or when students would complain about how White teachers would leverage microaggressions against them, we were encouraged by many of our colleagues, supervisors, and administrators to remain silent and invisible (e.g., Cooper, 2009). This only fueled our need to make sure that even if we could not challenge schoolwide practices, the students in our classrooms felt affirmed, validated, and appreciated. All too often, our tension between autonomy and invisibility was a shaky bridge to navigate. Our concerns were minimized and unsupported making our reliance on one another more critical because there was another person to validate one's point of view. As Black teachers, it was this sense of community that allowed us to care for and take care of our students and ourselves.

5.4   Discussion

In this section, we discuss what we learned from our self-study in relation to ourselves, preparing teachers for urban teaching and urban teacher education, and how our understandings are situated within the context of our theoretical frameworks. Considering our insights on teaching Black in alignment with Ladson-Billings's (1994) framing as disruptive and subversive, and the efficacy of self-study to elevate our awareness of our roles as Black teachers, a critical element of this work is that the practice of community building was an act of self-care. We take this up in the next subsection.

5.4.1   Community Building as Self-Care

For us, teaching was not just about the content we taught, but it was also about creating a community where everyone felt valued and celebrated for their contributions. In building community, we were bringing our Blackness to the workplace. Eventually, that would change. One by one, the Black teachers were leaving. Lia referred to it as an exodus. Roughly 12 Black teachers and support staff left over the course of a few years. Our community of Black teachers was dwindling, and no one had a commitment to replacing those who had left with other teachers of color. It became more difficult to advocate for change. Orienting all of the new White teachers to our Black and Brown students was challenging. Most importantly, the responsibilities of teaching our students in affirming and student-centered ways were not shared across disciplines by all the educators at the school. The pressures were sitting on the shoulders of a few Black teachers, pressures highlighted in other similar contexts (e.g., Will, 2020). With the progression of time, more expectations were imposed on us to assimilate to a shifting school culture that moved away from centering the experiences and identities of our students and back towards White, normative constructions of teaching and learning.

Teaching Black as self-care helped to balance the burdens with the blessings. It allowed us to tackle the responsibilities of teaching Black and Brown students with one another. Resisting Whiteness and affirming ourselves was a form of self-care in an institution that made it absolutely clear that you are only welcomed when you perform in the ways that were conventional, apolitical and colorblind (Martin & Kitchen, 2020). In some ways practicing self-care helped us mitigate the reality that we were becoming isolated from one another, but it also served to raise our awareness of the possibilities to transition to a new phase in our careers. Creating a sense of community for each other and for our students made us feel connected beyond the classroom. We were family, and we treated our students and each other as such. In a community, we felt safe to take pedagogical risks. We felt safe to be honest with one another. And, we felt safe being critical of one another (Shin & Im, 2020). What we did not fully appreciate was the impact of even the loss of one Black teacher in our school. After all, we had been intentionally hired to disrupt the status quo of pervasive whiteness in urban schools and classrooms and to affirmatively reflect diversity in our pedagogies. While we acknowledge that we wanted to fit in, we knew that was unlikely unless we built an internal community, a third space.

5.4.2 Schools as White Spaces

From a critical race theory perspective, U.S. systems of schooling were built upon, White supremacy and education itself is constructed as property. A challenge to this system arises through the questions we grappled with in this self-study such as who benefits from Black teachers' service to the system as it exists? What power structures are maintained when Black teachers assimilate? Who benefits from schooling system that shift away from normative practices as a result of teaching Black as disruption and subversion? We know from experience and from the literature (e.g., Carver-Thomas, 2018) that Black teachers are an asset to any school system. Yet, we are positioned as such that we have no right to make demands from a system in service to our students and the communities that we teach, especially those in urban contexts. As Black people and Black educators, the status quo maintains that we are to be deferential, appreciative, and compliant (Cooper, 2009). We are expected to know our place and not disrespect those in authority. In this way, being Black teachers in schools (which operate as White spaces) and teaching Black as disruption and subversion means taking risks, confronting microaggressions, and sometimes being isolated from your very own support systems. A critical race theory lens highlights how teaching Black is thus a material, socio-political and socio-cultural tool that can be yielded to dismantle schooling systems and structures that oppress both teachers and students of color.

Ultimately, we know that anti-Blackness is inextricably tied to Black suffering (Dumas, 2014). Whether intentional or not, when schools do not have safe spaces for Black teachers to share and support one another, Black teachers and students suffer. When there is no demonstrative effort and associated outcome to diversify the faculty and leadership, Black teachers and students suffer. When Black teachers' voices are stifled to maintain White middle-class norms of schooling, the entire school culture suffers. To be a Black teacher means to have courage. It means having a support system that helps Black teachers to push through a system that intentionally makes it difficult for them to fit in. It means that one must feel comfortable with not fitting in, confirming, or assimilating. It also means having a support system that provides safety and is validating of one another's experiences and identities. It means being willing and able to teach Black.

5.4.3   Teacher Quality and Urban Teacher Preparation

With fewer Black teachers in our school, more Black and Brown students were being taught in classrooms where their racial identities and cultural and community assets were not being honored. Subsequently, they were not experiencing the same levels of success as could have been the case with Black teachers in affirming classrooms. For example, Black teachers who used to teach honors classes were now teaching students whose skills had not been developed by their previous teachers and less-skilled White teachers were teaching honors classes. Even though all teachers at the school had equal access to instructional materials that reflected a diversity of culture and perspectives, what to do with those materials and how to integrate them into teaching practices emerged as an issue of teacher quality and teacher preparedness.

A great deal of teacher preparation is spent on the strategies of teaching and too little time is spent on teaching candidates how to support one another and work collaboratively to problem-solve and use both student data and teacher inquiry data to inform instruction. Such endeavors should also focus on providing teacher candidates, especially urban teacher candidates, with the knowledge, skills, and dispositions to honor and affirm the racial identities of their students (and, ultimately, develop as Type III teachers themselves. With so much emphasis placed on meeting the academic needs of P-12 students, it is still necessary to also teach candidates to handle the stressors and pressures of urban teaching. Part of this can be attended to by more fully engaging in teaching practices and a professional ethic as a Type III teacher that maintains the racial identities of students, especially Black and Brown students, as salient and valuable.

5.5   Recommendations and Conclusion

Over the course of this self-study, we experienced a range of feelings, understandings, and realizations. The tensions of teaching Black revealed several dispositional qualities that can be developed among teacher candidates in urban teacher preparation. These qualities reflect and are drawn from how we valued each other during our time working at our school and more recently throughout the self-study. These dispositional qualities are:

- A commitment to empathy for students and colleagues.
- A commitment to affirming Black and Brown students.
- A commitment to acknowledging whiteness and anti-Blackness.
- A commitment to fostering a supportive community for Black and Brown staff.

In addition, we believe that the following recommendations would support urban teacher preparation and the ongoing learning and professional development of in-service teachers (especially Black teachers and other teachers of color) who work in urban schools.

5.5.1   Leadership and Collaboration

Embedded within teacher preparation coursework should be opportunities for teacher candidates (TCs) to learning how to be resources and colleagues to one another. They can do this in their coursework by being taught how to authentically engage in peer reviews, peer observations, peer mentoring, and critical friends protocols. Additionally, sending TCs into clinical internships in cohorts with the expectations that they are committed to working with and supporting one another in structured ways, supports collaboration, TCs' learning and TCs' efficacy (Dinsmore & Wenger, 2006). For teaching in urban settings, this is even more critical as many urban schools are often staffed with novice teachers due to high attrition rates (Mawhinney & Rinke, 2019).

5.5.2   Racial Affinity Groups

Teacher educators and school leaders should reevaluate policies and practices that perpetuate silos and isolate preservice and in-service teachers from one another. In our experiences, when we were assigned to professional learning communities, the teachers of color were dispersed among the White teachers. In many cases, it would have been beneficial to enable us to work together or select our own groups. Many educator preparation programs have honor societies and education organizations that reflect a White majority. Having an educator group for TCs of color can help to serve the same purpose other education group whose mission is to support P-12 students of color.

5.5.3 Diverse Teacher Educators and Teachers

In teacher preparation programs teacher educators can be full and part-time faculty, cooperating teachers, mentor teachers, or clinical supervisors. Focusing on racially diversifying those who enact these roles is an excellent step in exposing TCs to instructors and guides who can provide multiple and insider perspectives on schooling as people of color. We know that P-12 students benefit from having teachers of color. The same applies to TCs. Therefore, an intentional commitment to hiring teachers and teacher educators is necessary.

5.5.4 Black and Brown School Leaders

Administrators of color may likely have the intentional goal of diversifying the teacher workforce as well as possess a social justice perspective and orientation to schooling. In our experiences, our Black administrators valued us because we were diverse and did not represent a monolith of Black culture. By encouraging and providing sustained opportunities for administrator/teacher and teacher/student mentorship, it provides a pathway for communication and relationship building. You cannot be what you cannot see. Giving teachers the opportunity to learn from one another and learn from Black and Brown school leaders builds relationship and can strengthen school communities. It also aids in perspective taking and sense-making. In our experiences, the opportunity to see each other teach and lead was transformative in our pedagogy and relationship with students.

5.6 Conclusion

To conclude this chapter, we individually define what teaching Black means to us. We believe it was most appropriate to allow our answers to speak to our findings and highlight the tensions that exist been being Black and being educators.

5.6.1 To Malcom, Teaching Black Means…

Teaching Black means knowing that I, as an individual also represent an entire group of people that are categorized based on the way they physically look. I'm looked at as an exception, and they don't cast that same generalization on the rest of that same group that they cast on when it's looked at on a negative scale. Teaching Black means doing whatever I can to make every student feel like I really care about them. And then it becomes easy to teach whatever your content is.

5.6.2 To Michael, Teaching Black Means…

Teaching Black means knowing specific things about Black culture, and the diversity within the Black culture. Teaching Black means navigating the standardized curriculum that's handed down and finding those areas that are biased, and teaching so that their voice, their identities, their experiences are not ignored, not minimized and are a part of education.

5.6.3 To Monique, Teaching Black Means…

Teaching Black means knowing that you're just as smart and just as capable, if not more. Teaching Black makes me feel resentment because everyone else gets to just exist as themselves, but there's always this voice in the back of my head, "You know you can't get away with that." Teaching Black means using empathy, knowing that you want to have more culturally aware students and be more culturally savvy. Teaching Black is being flexible and empathetic.

5.6.4 To Lia, Teaching Black Means…

Teaching Black means feeling that there's a sense of pride that goes with it. Teaching Black also means feeling lonely from the collective grieving that Brown people are doing in the U.S. right now. I do not want to have to go to work and pretend like I am okay and that life is normal when none of that is acknowledged. Teaching Black is a very precarious balancing act.

5.6.5   To LaChan, Teaching Black Means…

Teaching Black means knowing that you will always be against the grain and that can have an effect on how you see yourself, how you value yourself, and how you internalize those messages. Teaching Black means knowing that I'm always taking a risk to bring my whole Black self in any space I choose to occupy. Teaching Black means knowing that at some point, a limit will be imposed on me to be more silent, more compliant, and less of a troublemaker. Teaching Black means knowing that how people perceive me doesn't make it true.

5.6.6   From Then to Know: Where We Are Today

The experiences and engagement in this self-study led us to reflect upon the past, and to consider the present and all that has occurred in our lives since our time together at our school. Malcom transitioned to teach physics in a large urban district and owns a farm. Michael resigned as the only Black social studies teacher at the school thus far and became an assistant principal in a school with a large Black and Brown student population and majority White teachers. LaChan finished her doctoral program and accepted a director of teacher preparation position at an institution of higher education. Lia pursued a second master's degree as a clinical mental health counselor and is both a teacher and a licensed therapist. Monique remains a teacher of Spanish language, culture, and history at our school. She was recently awarded Teacher of the Year.

In summary, from this self-study we learned that we are keenly aware that teacher quality matters for teachers working in urban settings. We also learned that there is a hidden moving bar that we as Black teachers are supposed to be aiming for that our White counterparts seemingly do not have to attain. We learned that in order to provide students with an equitable and balanced education, we must be courageous enough to disrupt the current curricula even at the risk of being isolated. We learned that being a Black teacher means there is both an obligation and burden of shouldering the pressures of an entire schooling system that tells Black and Brown students that they are of lesser value than their White peers. And lastly, we learned that leaning on each other is one of the strongest forms of self-care that makes the commitment to being educators possible. Our experiences are bittersweet. So is teaching Black.

References

Carver-Thomas, D. (2018). *Diversifying the teaching profession: How to recruit and retain teachers of color*. Learning Policy Institute.

Chisanga, T., & Meyiwa, T. (2019). Reflexive Ubuntu, co-learning, and transforming higher education at a Rural University in South Africa. In J. Kitchen, M. Berry, S. M. Bullock, A. R. Crowe, M. Taylor, H. Guojonsdottir, & L. Thomas (Eds.), *International handbook of self-study of teaching and teacher education practices* (2nd ed., pp. 1491–1506). Springer.

Clandinin, D. J., & Connelly, M. (2004). Knowledge, narrative and self-study. In J. J. Loughran, M. L. Hamilton, V. K. LaBoskey, & T. Russel (Eds.), *International handbook of self-study of teaching and teacher education practices* (pp. 575–600). Springer.

Cooper, C. W. (2009). Parent involvement, African American mothers, and the politics of educational care. *Equity & Excellence in Education, 42*(4), 379–394. https://doi.org/10.1080/10665680903228389

DeVault, G. (2018). Establishing trustworthiness in qualitative research. *The Balance Small Business.* https://www.thebalancesmb.com/establishing-trustworthiness-in-qualitative-research-2297042

Dinsmore, J., & Wenger, K. (2006). Relationships in preservice teacher preparation: From cohorts to communities. *Teacher Education Quarterly, 33*(1), 57–74.

Dumas, M. J. (2014). 'Losing an arm': Schooling as a site of black suffering. *Race Ethnicity and Education, 17*(1), 1–29. https://doi.org/10.1080/13613324.2013.850412

Duncan, K. E. (2019). "They hate on me!" black teachers interrupting their white colleagues' racism. *Educational Studies, 55*(2), 197–213. https://doi.org/10.1080/00131946.2018.1500463

Hannon, L. V. (2019). Engaging my whole self in learning to teach for social justice. In J. Kitchen, M. Berry, S. M. Bullock, A. R. Crowe, M. Taylor, H. Guojonsdottir, & L. Thomas (Eds.), *International handbook of self-study of teaching and teacher education practices* (2nd ed., pp. 737–762). Springer.

Hannon, L. V. (2020). *You don't know my story: Engaging Black parents with culturally responsive school practices* (Publication No. 28089726). Doctoral dissertation, Montclair State University. ProQuest Dissertations and Theses Global.

Hollins, E. R. (1999). Relating ethnic and racial identity development to teaching. In E. H. Sheets (Ed.), *Racial and ethnic identity in school practices: Aspects of human development* (pp. 183–193). Routledge.

Kitchen, J., & Brown, N. (2022). Blind spots and eye-openers: Attending to the concerns of racialized teacher candidates in a social justice course. *Studying Teacher Education, 18*(1), 98–118. https://doi.org/10.1080/17425964.2022.2044586

LaBoskey, V. K. (2004). The methodology of self-study and its theoretical underpinnings. In J. J. Loughran, M. L. Hamilton, V. K. LaBoskey, & T. Russell (Eds.), *International handbook of self-study of teaching and teacher education practices* (pp. 817–869). Springer.

Ladson-Billings, G. (1994). *The dreamkeepers: Successful teachers of African American children.* Jossey-Bass.

Ladson-Billings, G., & Tate, W., IV. (1995). Toward a critical race theory of education. *Teachers College Record, 97*(1), 47–68.

Larkin, D. B., & Hannon, L. V. (2020). Preparing teachers for students in juvenile justice settings. *Contemporary Justice Review, 23*(4), 475–499. https://doi.org/10.1080/10282580.2019.1700374

Lopez, A. E., & Jean-Marie, G. (2021). Challenging anti-black racism in everyday teaching, learning, and leading: From theory to practice. *Journal of School Leadership, 31*(1–2), 50–65. https://doi.org/10.1177/1052684621993115

Loughran, J. J. (2004). Learning through self-study: The influence of purpose, participants and context. In J. J. Loughran, M. L. Hamilton, V. K. LaBoskey, & T. Russel (Eds.), *International handbook of self-study of teaching and teacher education practices* (pp. 151–192). Springer.

Maloney, T. (2017). Black teacher educator, white teacher interns: How I learned to bring my whole self to my work. In B. Picower & R. Kohli (Eds.), *Confronting racism in teacher education: Counternarratives of critical practice* (pp. 91–96). Routledge.

Martin, A. D. (2020). Tensions and caring in teacher education: A self-study on teaching in difficult moments. *Studying Teacher Education: A Journal of Self-study of Teacher Education Practices, 16*(3), 306–323. https://doi.org/10.1080/17425964.2020.1783527

Martin, A. D., & Kitchen, J. (2020). LGBTQ themes in the self-study of teacher educator practices: A queer review of the literature. In J. Kitchen, M. Berry, S. M. Bullock, A. R. Crowe, M. Taylor, H. Guojonsdottir, & L. Thomas (Eds.), *International handbook of self-study of teaching and teacher education practices* (2nd ed., pp. 589–610). Springer.

Mawhinney, L., & Rinke, C. R. (2019). *There has to be a better way.* Rutgers University Press.

Mena, J., & Russell, T. (2017). Collaboration, multiple methods, trustworthiness: Issues arising from the 2014 international conference on self-study of teacher education practices. *Studying Teacher Education, 13*(1), 105–122. https://doi.org/10.1080/17425964.2017.1287694

Merriam-Webster. (n.d.-a). *Disrupt.* https://www.merriam-webster.com/dictionary/disrupt

Merriam-Webster. (n.d.-b). *Subversive.* https://www.merriam-webster.com/dictionary/subvert

Milner, H. R. (2012). But what is urban education? *Urban Education, 47*(3), 556–561. https://doi.org/10.1177/2F0042085912447516

Petchauer, E., & Mawhinney, L. (Eds.). (2017). *Teacher education across minority-serving institutions: Programs, policies, and social justice.* Rutgers University Press.

Pithouse-Morgan, K., & Samaras, A. P. (2020). Methodological inventiveness in writing about self-study research. In J. Kitchen, M. Berry, S. M. Bullock, A. R. Crowe, M. Taylor, H. Guojonsdottir, & L. Thomas (Eds.), *International handbook of self-study of teaching and teacher education practices* (2nd ed., pp. 427–460). Springer.

Saldaña, J. (2016). *The coding manual for qualitative researchers.* Sage.

Sharma, M. (2022). Endemic racism in Trump's America: A racialized female faculty member's experience. *Studying Teacher Education, 18*(1), 5–22. https://doi.org/10.1080/1742596 4.2022.2057464

Shin, H. Y., & Im, C. (2020). Self-study in Korea: A case study on the improvement of classrooms with self-study. In J. Kitchen, M. Berry, S. M. Bullock, A. R. Crowe, M. Taylor, H. Guojonsdottir, & L. Thomas (Eds.), *International handbook of self-study of teaching and teacher education practices* (2nd ed., pp. 427–460).

Taylor, M., & Coia, L. (2009). Co/autoethnography: Investigating teachers in relation. In C. A. Lassonde & S. Galman (Eds.), *Self-study research methodologies for teacher educators* (pp. 169–186). Brill Sense. https://doi.org/10.1163/9789087906900_011

Taylor, M., & Coia, L. (2020). Co/autoethnography as a feminist methodology: A retrospective. In J. Kitchen, M. Berry, S. M. Bullock, A. R. Crowe, M. Taylor, H. Guojonsdottir, & L. Thomas (Eds.), *International handbook of self-study of teaching and teacher education practices* (2nd ed., pp. 565–588). Springer.

Will, Madeline. (2020, July). "No one else is going to step up": In a time of racial reckoning, teachers of color feel the pressure. *Education Week.* https://www.edweek.org/teaching-learning/no-one-else-is-going-to-step-up-in-a-time-of-racial-reckoning-teachers-of-color-feel-the-pressure/2020/07

Yosso, T. J. (2005). Whose culture has capital? A critical race theory discussion of community cultural wealth. *Race Ethnicity and Education, 8*(1), 69–91. https://doi.org/10.1080/1361332052000341006

Zamudio, M. M., Russell, C., Rios, F. A., & Bridgeman, J. L. (Eds.). (2010). *Critical race theory matters: Education and ideology.* Routledge.

LaChan V. Hannon, Ph.D., is a former high school teacher and the current Director of Teacher Preparation & Innovation in the Department of Urban Education at Rutgers-Newark. LaChan received her Ph.D. from Montclair State University in teacher education and teacher development with a focus on parent engagement and culturally responsive school practices. Her scholarly work investigates the intersectionality of race, disability, and parent involvement as they relate to the professional development for school leaders and educators. Her research and teaching interests are on culturally responsive school/parent partnerships, teacher self-study, and teaching for social justice. Her TEDx Talk titled *Young, Gifted & Black with Autism* was released in 2016. LaChan has published articles and chapters in academic texts including: *International Handbook of Self-Study* *of Teaching and Teacher Education Practices, Contemporary Justice Review,* and *Journal of Autism and Developmental Disorders.*

Lia M. Hannon, M.A, M.S.Ed., NCC, is a high school English/Language Arts teacher and a licensed clinical mental health professional. Lia received a Bachelor of Arts degree in English from Ursinus College and a Master of Science in Education degree with a focus in reading, writing, and literacy from the University of Pennsylvania. Lia began her career teaching elementary school in the School District of Philadelphia and found her home teaching secondary education in New Jersey. Throughout her career, Lia has contributed to her school community through curricular and professional development, student activities, and equity initiatives. In 2019, Lia completed a Master of Arts in Clinical Mental Health Counseling degree at Rider University. She currently works both as a nationally board-certified counselor specializing in the areas of grief and trauma and a full-time teacher. Recently, Lia was named her school's Teacher of the Year.

Monique S. Jenkins is a high school Spanish teacher and comes from a legacy of educators. Monique earned a Bachelor of Arts degree in Spanish Language and Literature with teacher certification from Rutgers University – Camden. As a New Jersey native and student in urban schools, Monique has made a career of working with students in urban schools for the last 15 years. Using language and literature to connect culture and student learning, Monique has reimagined curricula for both monolingual and bilingual students. In 2016, Monique was named her school's Teacher of the Year.

Michael R. Jones, M.Ed., is a former high school teacher and current assistant principal in the Black Horse Pike Regional School District. Michael received his Bachelor of Arts degree in history with a concentration in African American studies from Delaware State University. Michael began his career in education at McGraw-Hill before becoming a teacher of social studies in 2007. While teaching, he received a Master of Education degree in educational leadership from The College of New Jersey. During Michael's educational career he has participated in the New Jersey Amistad Commission Summer Institute and written ground-breaking curricula, functioned as an athletic coach, facilitated professional development, and worked on building and district-level equity consortiums.

Malcom A. Williams, M.Ed., is a high school physics teacher with over 18 years of classroom experience in urban schools. He has made a career as an urban educator committed to working with minoritized students in under-resourced schools. Malcom received a Bachelor of Science degree from Stockton University in applied physics with a minor in mathematics, and a Master of Education degree in educational leadership, management and policy from Seton Hall University. Malcom holds multiple teaching and administrative certifications, yet remains committed to full-time classroom teaching. He is a husband and father of three children with special interests in homesteading, environmentally friendly gardening practices, and woodworking.

Chapter 6
Who Gets to Ask "Does Race Belong in Every Course?": Staying in the Anguish as White Teacher Educators

Megan Madigan Peercy and Judy Sharkey

Abstract In our recent review of the literature regarding the use of self-reflexive methodologies among teacher educators (TEs) in English language teacher education, we noted a gap in attention to teacher educators' identities and the impact these have on their pedagogy. Given how deeply identity affects the pedagogy of TEs, it is crucial to carefully examine these connections. We particularly noticed a lack of White TEs recognizing race as foundational to their pedagogy, while TEs of color more frequently named their race/ethnicity as instrumental to their work. Given the significant role that race plays in issues of justice and equity and the ways in which we see and understand the world, we argue that White TEs' attention to issues of race and racism, and to challenging their own White complicity is needed to move the preparation of TESOL (Teachers of English for speakers of other languages) teachers, and others working in urban classroom settings, in humanizing and justice-oriented directions. We extend the findings of our review to explore our attempts to address issues of race in our pedagogy. Specifically, we use examples from the first author's teaching to illustrate how she found herself implicated in White complicity, and illustrate how the support of the second author as a critical friend was crucial to our joint learning. We offer recommendations for teacher educators committed to self-reflexivity and greater attention to equity in preparing teachers for urban classrooms.

Keywords Self-reflexive methodology · Language teacher education · Teacher educator identity · White complicity · White teacher educators · Anti-racist pedagogy

M. M. Peercy (✉)
University of Maryland, College Park, MD, USA
e-mail: mpeercy@umd.edu

J. Sharkey
University of New Hampshire, Durham, NH, USA

A. D. Martin (ed.), *Self-Studies in Urban Teacher Education*, Self-Study of Teaching and Teacher Education Practices 25,
https://doi.org/10.1007/978-981-19-5430-6_6

Students classified as English learners (ELs) comprise almost 15% of U.S. urban school populations, and more than three-quarters of ELs in U.S. schools identify as Hispanic/Latinx (NCES, 2020). Issues of race and language are often conflated and both are used as ways to "other" groups that are typically minoritized in the U.S. (e.g., Liggett, 2009; Shuck, 2006). The largest percentage of ELs are concentrated in urban areas (NCES, 2020), and ELs are more likely to face challenges often thought of as "urban issues," such as homelessness and low socioeconomic status (U.S. Department of Education, 2021). Often both racialized and linguicized (Flores & Rosa, 2015; Rosa, 2019), these students are most frequently taught by White teachers, who are themselves most frequently prepared by White teacher educators (AACTE, 2018; NCES, 2020). Both of these groups of educators generally have little experience with addressing issues of race in their teaching, and are often insulated from their own experiences of being minoritized, instead experiencing a relatively privileged status.

In our recent review of the literature regarding the use of self-reflexive methodologies among teacher educators (TEs) in English language teacher education (ELTE), including both the use of self-study methodology and studies that share methodological commitments with self-study, we noted a gap in attention to teacher educators' identities and the impact these have on their pedagogy (Peercy & Sharkey, 2020). Given how deeply identity affects the pedagogy of TEs (e.g., Brown, 2002, 2004; Hamilton & Pinnegar, 2014; Kim et al., 2018; McNeil, 2011; Skerrett, 2006; Smith et al., 2016), it is crucial to carefully examine these connections. We particularly noticed a lack of White TEs recognizing race as foundational to their pedagogy, while TEs of color more frequently named their race/ethnicity as instrumental to their work (Peercy & Sharkey, 2020). Given the significant role that race plays in issues of justice and equity and the ways in which we see and understand the world, we argue that White TEs' attention to issues of race and racism, and to challenging their own White complicity (Applebaum, 2010) is needed to move the preparation of TESOL (Teachers of English for speakers of other languages) teachers in humanizing and justice-oriented, directions (see also Peercy et al., 2019a). We acknowledge that as White, female, middle class, able-bodied researchers and practitioners we are deeply implicated in this "White complicity" ourselves (Sharkey et al., 2021a). We extend the findings of our review to explore our own attempts to address issues of race in our pedagogy, and use examples from Megan's teaching to illustrate how she found herself implicated in White complicity (Applebaum, 2010). This is particularly critical given that Megan prepares preservice and in-service teachers to work in local urban and suburban districts that educate a highly diverse student population, and she prepares doctoral students as novice TEs for those same settings (for instance, the racial composition of the district in which her teacher education program is located includes a student population that is 55% African American and 36% Latinx, 66% of the student body qualifies for free and reduced meals, and 21% of the student body is classified as ELs).

We note that the abiding presence of a critical friend is especially important in these efforts to recognize and interrupt White complicity "because whiteness constantly ambushes white subjects and implicates them in racism" (Yancy, 2012, p. 170), and we share some ways that our interactions as critical friends supported our inquiry and pedagogy.

6.1 Background

As Goodwin and Darity (2019) recently noted, we still know little about what TEs need to know and do to move from talking about social justice to enacting it in their practice. This is also true in ELTE: although there is increasing attention to race, ethnicity, and other issues of equity in the scholarship in TESOL (e.g., Kubota & Lin, 2009; Motha, 2020; Von Esch et al., 2020), we know little about TEs'—and especially White TEs'—own learning and development related to social justice issues in their practice, other than that they are generally ill-prepared to address them, and that they struggle to do so (e.g., Cross, 2003; Gordon, 2005; Gorski, 2016; Gorski et al., 2012; Gort & Glenn, 2010). The literature also illustrates that many TEs have not had the kind of experiences that prepare them to capitalize on the assets of students from a diverse set of backgrounds that differ widely from their own (e.g., Cochran-Smith et al., 2015; Goodwin & Darity, 2019; Gorski, 2016; Haddix, 2016). This gap in TE knowledge and experiences makes it especially challenging to prepare teachers for diverse urban settings, because they are often characterized by linguistic, cultural, racial/ethnic, and socioeconomic diversity.

As Cross (2003) articulates, significant disparity in the experiences of TEs, teachers, and the students whom the teachers are being prepared to teach comes in large part from racial differences, and thus "an enormous gap between who prepares teachers, who the teachers themselves are, and who they will likely teach…results in a significant detachment of White teacher educators and White teacher education students from children of color" (p. 204).

According to Gordon, this detachment is rooted in White TEs who do not engage in self-reflexivity about their race:

> the very issues that our [teacher education] students have failed to deal with or have not been exposed to are issues we have failed to deal with or have not been exposed to as White faculty....I am suggesting that there is a trickle down effect here. As White faculty members who have not acknowledged our own racial identities, we will be similarly unprepared to help teacher education candidates, those who are White and those of color, to recognize and affirm theirs. Nor can we be role models for teacher candidates who are struggling to understand and change the racial realities of the world in which they live. (pp. 137-138)

Gorski et al. (2012) frame this challenge as the need for TEs who are prepared to engage teachers in developing "equity- and justice-minded" approaches to teaching, including attentiveness to race and racial inequities alongside inequities related to sexuality and socioeconomic status. Similarly, Stillman and Beltramo (2019) and Carter Andrews and colleagues (Carter Andrews & Castillo, 2016; Carter Andrews et al., 2019) draw attention to the need for TEs who can engage in asset-oriented and humanizing pedagogy through greater awareness of how their own race, class, gender, sexuality, language ability, religion, and their intersections, all contribute to teaching, learning, interactions, and opportunities available to educators and students.

6.2 Theoretical Framework

Given the demands on all TEs to more deeply engage with their own identities to meaningfully prepare teachers for their work in classrooms, including the need to challenge and disrupt the "overwhelming presence of Whiteness" (Sleeter, 2001) in teacher education, we argue that more attention is needed regarding TEs' White complicity. We draw on Applebaum (2010) who defines White complicity in the following way:

> White people, through the practices of whiteness and by benefiting from white privilege, contribute to the maintenance of systemic racial injustice….the failure to acknowledge such complicity will thwart whites in their efforts to dismantle unjust racial systems and, more specifically, will contribute to the perpetuation of racial injustice….white people can reproduce and maintain racist practices even when, and *especially when*, they believe themselves to be morally good. (p. 2)

Drawing from this understanding of our complicity in maintaining systemic racial injustice, and framings of teacher education *as* a "practice of Whiteness" (e.g., Haddix, 2016; Matias, 2016; Sleeter, 2001; Souto-Manning, 2019; Souto-Manning & Emdin, 2020), we argue that it is critical to examine how White TEs can contribute to interrogating the impact of their race and their White privilege on their pedagogy, and what might be transformed about their pedagogy when they do so, especially in regard to their capacity to more critically attend to issues of equity in their preparation of teachers for urban schools. Several scholars have asserted that to move in the direction of anti-racism, Whites need to remain in spaces of "trouble," "anxiety," "discomfort," "vigilance," "apprehension," and "anguish" (e.g., Applebaum, 2015; Butler, 2005; Cutri & Whiting, 2015; Jenkins, 2010; Ohito, 2016; Warren, 2003; Yancy, 2008), because Whites cannot ever fully arrive at anti-racism. As Applebaum (2015) argues, "being an anti-racist white … is a project that always requires another step and does not end in a white person's having 'arrived' in the form of an idyllic anti-racist" (p. 11).

An important stance for "staying in the anguish" (Applebaum, 2015, p. 2) of these uncomfortable spaces regarding how Whiteness plays a part in maintaining injustice in and through one's pedagogy is a commitment to continued self-reflexivity, or "question[ing] of our own attitudes, thought processes, values, prejudices and habitual actions, to strive to understand our complex roles in relation to others," and to better understand how we might effect change (Bolton, 2010, p. 13). Indeed, several TEs have identified critical self-reflexivity as necessary to fostering equity-oriented approaches in teacher preparation (e.g., Carter Andrews & Castillo, 2016; Cochran-Smith et al., 2004; Gorski et al., 2012). Given the commitment of self-study methodology to "stay in the anguish" by self-reflexively examining and questioning how we are always in the process of becoming (Griffiths & Poursanidou, 2004; Taylor & Diamond, 2020), and have "a moral commitment to improving practice" (Bullough & Pinnegar, 2004, p. 317), we find self-study to be an especially appropriate way of engaging in work that is needed to problematize and challenge White complicity in teacher education.

6.3 Methods and Data Sources

As part of a larger effort to focus more deeply on practice-based pedagogies in my[1] research and teaching of preservice teachers, in-service teachers, and doctoral students, I (Megan) have spent the better part of a decade examining and developing practices that are central, or "core," to teaching multilingual students, in collaboration with early career teachers of multilingual students and a team of early career TEs (e.g., Fredricks & Peercy, 2020; Kidwell et al., 2021; Peercy et al., 2018, 2019b, 2020). During this time, however, I realized that by examining the practice-based scholarship, I was largely drawing on work by White U.S.-based, English-dominant scholars, and as a result was giving less attention to the issues of equity and justice that were an important part of my commitments (e.g., Peercy et al., 2019a). In this chapter, we examine my critical self-reflexive efforts to better understand my work as a TE, and to more intentionally center issues of equity and justice—through attention to race and racism, in particular—in my pedagogy. We highlight some of the challenges that emerged in this work, as well as the importance of Judy as a critical friend to help me examine and interrogate these efforts. Such inquiry is especially important for White TEs engaged in teacher preparation in urban contexts, given the frequent disparity in TEs' and teachers' experiences and backgrounds, and those of the PK-12 students in those settings.

As a place to begin examining my work as a TE and my attempts to center issues of equity and justice in my teaching, I engaged in weekly journaling about a doctoral course for novice teacher educators (NTEs) that I was teaching for the second time. This course explored the pedagogy of teacher education (PTE), and after co-teaching it the first time with a White male colleague, I wanted to reframe it from a justice- and equity-oriented lens, focusing especially on issues of race and racism in teacher education that have been emerging in ever more pressing and urgent ways in the TE scholarship (e.g., Daniels & Varghese, 2020; de los Ríos & Souto-Manning, 2015; Matias, 2016; Sleeter, 2017; Souto-Manning, 2019; Varghese et al., 2019). I asked Judy, a longstanding collaborator and critical friend, to join me in this work. It is important to note our positionality in this work: we are both White, middle class, able-bodied, female teacher educators with tenure, who benefit from numerous privileges that our identities make possible for us. Though we both have

---

[1] Given that the focus of this chapter is Megan's pedagogy, we use the first person to refer to Megan throughout the remainder of the chapter.

backgrounds that also confer different experiences than the demographics of many TEs (e.g., we are both from lower socioeconomic class upbringings, we are bilingual, and Judy is a cisgender lesbian), we are also able to strategically self-censor these aspects of our social identities. We are each researchers and TEs at two different research intensive universities on the east coast, and we have collaborated for several years on topics related to ELTE and self-reflexive approaches. We began our efforts on this project with a third ELTE colleague also involved as a critical friend, a woman of color who has engaged in significant work around issues of race and language teaching/learning. Although she initially agreed to participate, she asked to withdraw after our preliminary meetings in which it was clear that she had many lived experiences and significant pedagogical expertise related to race and racism, and she did not want to be in a position of educating me, given our otherwise "co-equal" positioning. This occurrence reflected an important tenet we have uncovered in critical friendship, that those engaging as critical friends are on equal footing (Sharkey et al., 2021b). We address the challenges and tensions of White educators striving to better understand race and racism while also not burdening colleagues of color, more fully in another publication in preparation.

I journaled at least weekly about my course, and we engaged in ongoing dialogue in the comment bubbles in the shared online document where the journal entries were located. We video-conferenced once a month to discuss my journal entries and what was going on in our pedagogy. Drawing from the notion of staying in the anguish of being a problem (Applebaum, 2015) as a White TE, the focus of both the journaling and our conversations focused on my pedagogical attempts, challenges, doubts, and questions as I explored my work to bring issues of equity—and race and racism more specifically—as more central to this course than I had in the past. The primary data sources for this work include 18 journal entries (with responses and reactions from Judy, and conversations between the two authors in comment bubbles), four recorded and transcribed debriefing conversations between the two authors (1–2 h each), 15 recorded and transcribed class meetings of my PTE course (class met weekly for 3 h), and seven recorded and transcribed interviews with students in the PTE course (interviews averaged an hour in length), that I conducted after the semester was complete and course grades were turned in. Other data sources include course materials from the PTE class (e.g., syllabi, texts, student assignments), and an ongoing online shared notes document where for several years both authors have regularly posted ideas and memos regarding our longitudinal work together on self-reflexivity in ELTE. The PTE doctoral course enrolled eight doctoral students: two international students from China who identified as female, and six students from the U.S., including four students who identified as White females, and two students who identified as White males.

Data were analyzed using the constant comparative method (Corbin & Strauss, 2015) and examined for emergent themes. While there were several themes that arose in the analysis, including my vulnerability and doubt about what I was doing pedagogically, here we use one vignette from my PTE class to illustrate my unpreparedness to address questions about issues of equity that arose in my classroom, and in my work as a teacher educator overall. We also discuss the importance of working with Judy as a critical friend to examine where we discovered White complicity in my practice, even while I was trying to address issues of race and racism and make topics of equity and justice central to my teaching.

6.4 "Does Race Belong in Every Course?": The White Savior Trope

We begin by illustrating an example of how I came to recognize my own lack of experience addressing issues of racial equity in my PTE course, and how over the course of the semester, I realized that this gap implicated my work in teaching teachers also. This particular instance arose in the third class meeting when Caroline, a first year doctoral student and NTE raised a question about how to challenge issues of inequity in the teacher education space without coming across as a White savior (e.g., Aronson, 2017) who would sweep in and save minoritized groups from their plight:

> Caroline: I have a question as it relates to teacher education....For me personally, I'm an advocate of bilingual education ... but I struggle with...I'm White, but I'm bilingual. I advocate for [bilingual] schools even though I'm not a minority, but I don't want to come across as preachy or stepping out of bounds, and I don't know how to manage that. It's a big concern that I have as I move forward.
>
> Megan: I would situate myself in a very similar space to what you're describing. I'm White, I'm bilingual, I've had some of those same situations. A lot of what you'll read and hear from colleagues and scholars of color is that White allies are important as well for advancing this. So I think [as far as] where to strike that balance, we have to ask our friends and colleagues of color, 'Does this feel appropriate? Does this seem appropriate for interacting with this group?' We only know our own experience, so that's what I've had to do, is reach out and ask other colleagues 'How does this seem?' It's hard, it's a tricky space to be in because you want to help promote and advocate, but you don't want to be...
>
> C: Like a White savior.
>
> M: Yes, exactly. Like the White teacher from MadTV from the first week of class (09-11-19 class transcript).[2]
>
> Later, I journaled about this interaction in class:
>
> Caroline (a White female) was expressing her interest in and discomfort with how to address issues of race without seeming like a White savior or someone who has the answers. I told her I was also grappling with that and trying to figure out how to do that.... I don't think my response was probably adequate or helpful. The truth is, I don't know how to do it well either. I feel like I'm just at the very starting point of figuring out how to do this. It's hard to know how much to share that with the doctoral students. (Berry talks about the tension of exposing one's vulnerability as a TE and of maintaining students' confidence in you as competent. I feel like that's the ground I'm on when addressing issues of equity and justice, particularly related to race.) (09-16-19 journal)

---

[2] One of the texts that I selected to frame the course was a MadTV parody of a teacher as White savior trope (https://www.youtube.com/watch?v=ZVF-nirSq5s) called *Nice White lady*.

At the time, I felt ill-prepared for this interaction, and realized that while getting excited about the transformation of this course to focus more deeply on situating teaching and teacher education in questions of equity and justice through a focus on race and racism, I had carefully planned the new readings and ideas that the course would examine. However, I naively had not given a lot of thought to the likelihood that doctoral students would have questions related to lived moments in their teacher education classrooms, with regard to how to do this. Reflecting then—and now—Caroline's question caught me off guard and I was not ready to answer it. Indeed, given my own experience with the withdrawal of our other colleague from this project, I am re-thinking my response about checking with friends of color—how do we engage our colleagues of color without placing the burden on them to help correct what is a White problem (Hytten & Warren, 2003; Matias, 2013; Richardson & Villenas, 2000; Varghese et al., 2019; WOC and Allies, 2017)?

A few weeks later I was struggling with how to address issues of power, agency, race, privilege, and equity in my teaching of the PTE course, and realizing how much I had taken on without a real understanding of how to do so. I expressed that I felt especially challenged to support NTEs in dealing with race in their pedagogy, noting how in contrast I felt more comfortable addressing language and gender:

> I don't think I'm really doing this successfully, and maybe that's because I don't feel like I know how to do it. I feel ill-equipped for it—pedagogically, experientially, emotionally…. (I realize that not having to address it is a privilege.)….I don't feel like a pedagogical model for this. Interestingly I don't feel so ill-equipped to discuss issues of language, gender—but maybe it's because I feel like I have lived experiences of being minoritized in those ways. (10-03-19 journal)

Knowing that as White teacher educators we participate in systems of oppression (Galman et al., 2010; Matias, 2016; Richert et al., 2008; Yancy, 2019), we need to engage in the challenging work of addressing race and racism in our courses, and "stay in the anguish" of feeling inadequate and unprepared while finding ways to address the gaps in our ability, knowledge, and lived experiences.

I decided to read more about discussing race while teaching the course (e.g., *So you want to talk about race*, *White fragility*, an interview with Ibram Kendi), and despite my hesitation about how competent I would appear to students, I began to share with the class what I was reading. I started regularly sharing that I was still learning and reading and trying to figure out how to engage around issues of inequity. During some class periods I took in examples of what I was reading and thinking about and read excerpts to them, noting when they asked questions that I was also wondering about or did not yet know how to address myself, such as in the exchange below with Samantha, a NTE in my course:

> Samantha: How do you get a group of people to that same place where it's not being derailed by 'Oh, you're making me uncomfortable [by talking about racism]'? So people aren't defensive and you can get everybody to the place where 'Okay, let's actually look at how we can use counter-narratives to realize that there are problems and that we're living in this, and we are living in the dominant culture, and we are perpetuating the dominant culture'?

Megan: Well, I just got this [holding up a book] from the library. It's brand new, 2019. I'm wondering if it will be helpful in this regard, it's called *Race Dialogues: A Facilitator's Guide to Tackling the Elephant in the Classroom*. So it's going to be on my to-read pile. (10-16-19 class transcript)

Even re-reading this now, I cringe. That I had no response to this other than what I was reading is painful to me as an educator. I never felt like what I was doing was adequate, or informed enough, but to my surprise students noted that it had an important impact on their own efforts as emerging teacher educators. As one NTE in my class articulated at the end of the semester:

We started off with Whiteness in teacher education [in this course in] week one, and I got excited….Often we pay lip service and say like, 'Yes, equity, and race should be in all of our conversations' and instead it's given to like one course….And we know, research tells us, that's not how it should be done. And so you were treating, modeling that it should be done throughout. I really appreciated that you are continuing to bring in the books that you were reading….You are showing us that you that you are still learning and growing…. And so I think I tried to also do that in my own teacher education courses, to show my students that I will make mistakes. And I'm still learning and growing. And here's where I'm at. And you as a teacher will also make mistakes. And so I also tried to approach teacher education and my research in it from a place of vulnerability, but also openness and willingness to grow. (Belinda, 12-17-19 interview)

Hearing that my transparency about my learning experience was a helpful model to students was somewhat reassuring, but I still felt unease and a sense of failure as an educator who did not have this all worked out in ways that I could use to clearly and confidently answer questions from the NTEs in my class.

Reflecting each week on the data from this class, I started to realize that it was challenging for me to engage with NTEs' questions about how to leverage the ideas we were discussing because despite all my years of experience in ELTE teaching about cultural and linguistic diversity, *I had limited experience with discussing issues of race and racism with teachers myself.* This brought to mind Loughran and Berry's (2005) argument that "teacher educators face the same difficulty [as novice teachers do] in their learning of teaching about teaching…in many situations, teacher educators also need to develop their understanding through phronesis [knowing through experience]" (p. 199). It was startling to me to realize how little experience I had discussing race in my courses for teachers or in my day-to-day life.

After many years as a teacher educator in ELTE, I was comfortable talking about linguistic, cultural, and socioeconomic disparities, and about equitable access to content for multilingual students, but somehow my facility with those topics had allowed me to not discuss race and racism in the context of language teaching and learning. I was surprised when I thought about the many times I had taught ESOL methods courses, and realized that I had not talked about race with the teachers in my classes. In fact, the very same semester that I was teaching the PTE course, I was teaching an ESOL methods course, and I had not considered that what I was doing in PTE would or should have intersections and impact on what I was doing in my methods course. Later in the semester I journaled about this:

Something I haven't thought much about are ways to develop teachers' pedagogical ability to issues of equity, justice, race, in my teacher education courses themselves. This semester I have focused more on how to bring more awareness and attention to those issues in my doctoral course….Perhaps ironically, I haven't been spending as much time and energy trying to do that with the teachers myself….[In my ESOL Methods course] I am attending to … issues that relate to equitable access to content, rigorous instruction, and high expectations for ELLs. What I'm realizing is that I didn't explore, directly, with these teachers, topics related to race and justice, and I think it's hard to decide where and how to do that- and does that belong in this course? Does that belong in every course?…This raises an enduring question that I have about doing the work of preparing teachers in ways that bring together a fine-grained attention to practice AND a focus on equity—and that both are necessary. How do we do both? Do they need to both happen in all courses?… Is there a way of embedding attention to equity and justice in ways that are not just token mentions or single readings or a single class period about equity, in methods coursework? (11-21-19 journal)

It was interesting to me how much race had been a part of my thinking and planning for the PTE course, and yet I did not give it much thought in my ESOL Methods course, where careful attention to issues of race and racism and the ways in which they are intertwined with language learning and use, could help support teachers in engaging in more equitable practice in urban schools. It was only through careful examination of my experiences in the PTE class—journaling, discussing with Judy, and grappling with moments in the PTE class when I did not have clear answers to NTE questions, that I even started to identify this gap. That it is even possible for me to ask such a question about whether race belongs in every course speaks volumes about my privileged position and my complicity; my colleagues of color cannot avoid questions about race and skin color, no matter what the course topic is (e.g., McNeil, 2011; Peercy et al., 2019a). Judy's comments and ideas as my critical friend were central to helping me raise my awareness and grow in my understanding. For TEs who are committed to addressing race and racism in their classrooms, and especially for White TEs who have much work to do, the assistance of a critical friend is crucial.

6.5   I Think Race Does Need to Be in every Course

Embedded in my journal entry about my lack of attention to issues of race in my teacher education courses, I also noted: "I wonder whether Judy's comments about how my journaling is raising questions for her in her teacher education courses has brought [the ESOL Methods course] to the front of my mind more?" (11–21-19 comment bubble). And a couple of weeks later, in response to my journaled questions "Does [race] belong in [the Methods] course? Does [race] belong in every course?", Judy responded, and provided examples from her pedagogy of how she addressed issues of race when she taught methods courses:

I think it does need to be in every course. It's more challenging for White people to see race in everything when we are in the majority, but race is always present….I've been working on analyzing the readings in my courses to see who we are reading in terms of race, gender, geography, etc. I started thinking about including the pictures of the authors so that this work is more visible for students—and myself. The whole 'how White is this syllabus?' question. (12-2-19 comment bubble)

Here Judy pushed my thinking, giving suggestions for how to include more attention to race when teaching methods courses. She also illustrated a specific assignment and how she had been changing it over time to connect more directly and intentionally raise interconnections between identity and pedagogy:

I started off my course this semester (Teaching Multilingual Learners) with some autobiographical/self-reflexive work. The guiding question for the course—since I started teaching it in 2002 has been 'How do language and culture affect teaching and learning?' But I've been trying to shift more attention to the teacher learners answering 'How does *my* culture, *my* language, affect how I teach and affect students' learning?' We do some easy stuff like 'Where I'm from' poems, but this year I had them do some implicit bias tests—they do at home and in private and share what they are willing to share—and they read Christine Sleeter's blog. They also have to do a final reflective essay on the guiding question. (12-2-19 comment bubble)

Judy's suggestions provided much for me to consider and reflect on. Our collaboration did not push only my thinking about incorporating issues of race and racism in my pedagogy. Our interactions also had impact on Judy's pedagogical decision-making. She shared:

It's very interesting, my role as a critical friend reading your journals. I think because I'm in that role it's having some effect on what I'm doing with my [Introduction to Educational Studies] class....I'm talking about race a lot more. I'm thinking about when and how and if I bring up different issues of race in my conversations with them. I don't know if I'm just trying to like *normalize* these comments....so I'm wondering if we just keep doing this more, maybe it creates a different kind of space. (11-11-19 meeting)

Judy went on to describe our collaboration as having an influence on her pedagogy:

Judy: How do I characterize the effect that [reading and responding to] your journal is having on my thinking, on what I'm doing? Maybe it's like a watermark, like if you don't have a coaster on your table... (11-11-19 meeting)

I added to Judy's watermark image, describing the reciprocal impact our collaboration was having:

It's been like, this dialogic process....The data we've been focusing on happens to come from my teaching, but I would say that the watermark is, I don't know, it's like a mirrored watermark. Like you got a watermark on a piece of paper and then you fold it in half, and then it made its mark on both sides. (11-11-19 meeting)

In a later meeting, Judy shared more about how her pedagogy had been affected through our collaborative interactions during the semester, and how she was more intentionally trying to weave race into her teaching in informal and regular ways throughout the semester:

I can be sitting down and talking to [my students], so then it's not like I'm in the front of the room lecturing. Then I can make these kind of personal connections [with them about race]....So it's stuff that I'm intentional about inserting into the conversation....I think we were able to have that conversation [in my class this semester] in a way that, to me, felt more authentic, where in the past, sometimes those conversations have been very didactic. (12-16-19 meeting)

In an experience common to critical friendship work (e.g., Baskerville & Goldblatt, 2009; Schuck & Russell, 2005), our shared conversations ended up being a learning experience for us both, moving us toward greater consideration of how to embed discussions of race and racism in our teaching. In a recursive way, reading my journals encouraged Judy to think more about race in her courses, and her descriptions about what she was doing in response made me think more about my methods instruction.

6.6 Discussion and Implications

The power and persistence of race and racism and their impact on our teaching and on students' learning experiences (e.g., Gershenson et al., 2021), the growing disparity in the demographics of the educator workforce and the students in U.S. PK-12 classrooms (NCES, 2020), alongside the impact of humanizing, responsive pedagogies that support students of varying backgrounds and experiences (e.g., Ladson-Billings, 1994; Paris & Alim, 2017), all mean that we must carefully and thoughtfully attend to creating both a more diverse educator workforce *and* preparing White educators to proactively address inequities and center the assets students bring to the classroom. In urban classrooms, these assets are likely to be different than the ones that monolingual White TEs and teachers are accustomed to recognizing, and therefore require especially careful attention. Given the challenges that TEs, and especially White TEs, face in recentering their pedagogy around equity and justice, particularly related to issues of race and racism (e.g., Galman et al., 2010; Picower & Kohli, 2017), it is important to highlight that White TEs frequently lack lived experiences of discussing race and racism in their teaching (and other parts of their lives), and without specific attention and commitment, we too often ignore and are unaware of this, perhaps intentionally so (e.g., Applebaum, 2010; Mills, 1997). My struggle to more deeply address race and racism has made it clear to me that this will be an ongoing and challenging investment. As Yancy (2019) asserts, we must understand "white, antiracist praxis as a process, *not an arrival*" (p. 19). Grappling with our understanding of race and racism, and getting to questions about whether "race belong[s] in every course" brings us closer to race-visible teacher education, which recognizes the centrality of race in any discussion about justice, and doesn't allow us to "overgeneralize dimensions of difference and to skirt issues of race" (Hambacher & Ginn, 2021, p. 329).

Furthermore, my attention to issues of race cannot involve only covering important new scholarship on the topic. Instead, I must also consider what this looks like enacted in my pedagogy and in my life—as a parent, as a neighbor, as a church member, as a voter, as a friend, and how to extend that to my work preparing mostly

White NTEs who are themselves preparing mostly White teachers for multilingual and multiracial classrooms. How might we all "stay in the anguish" together, in productive ways? Trying to change my pedagogy and challenge my White complicity is ongoing, non-linear, messy, and requires staying in uncomfortable places. The presence of similarly dedicated critical friends can be one way of pushing ourselves to examine the ways in which we can be doing this work. Drawing again from Applebaum (2015), we need to cultivate new relationships with the feelings of apprehension and vulnerability that this creates, and understand that these are places to dwell and not try to transcend. According to Applebaum (2015), "Understanding that one is a problem in this sense can lead to ways of being newly accountable and can encourage an acknowledgment that there is always so much more to learn" (p. 16). Indeed, I have much to learn, and White TEs have much to learn, from staying in the anguish of these uncomfortable spaces. We recommend that other TEs also consider the ways that their race and other identities play a significant role in their pedagogy and the ways that they prepare teachers for urban settings. As we found, journaling, examining one's pedagogical materials and interactions, and working with critical friends are all valuable means of doing so.

6.7 Conclusion

We hope that by sharing areas where Megan's pedagogy needs greater attention to her own racial positioning and awareness to expand the possibility of addressing issues of equity in her work with NTEs and teachers preparing for work in urban contexts, we may encourage other White TEs to do this much-needed work as well. Until we can understand ourselves as part of the problem, it is difficult to move toward equity and justice in authentic ways. Self-study methodology offers an important structure for self-reflexive inquiry into our practice, as we learn to "do whiteness differently" (Warren, 2003, p. 465).

References

AACTE. (2018). *Colleges of education: A national portrait.* Retrieved from https://aacte.org/2019/02/report-identifies-student-diversity-in-u-s-colleges-of-education-by-race-and-ethnicity/.

Applebaum, B. (2010). *Being white, being good: White complicity, white moral responsibility, and social justice pedagogy.* Lexington Books.

Applebaum, B. (2015). Flipping the script...and still a problem: Staying in the anxiety of being a problem. In G. Yancy (Ed.), *White self-criticality beyond anti-racism: How does it feel to be a white problem?* (pp. 1–20). Lexington Books.

Aronson, B. A. (2017). The white savior industrial complex: A cultural studies analysis of a teacher educator, savior film, and future teachers. *Journal of Critical Thought and Praxis, 6*(3), 36–54. https://doi.org/10.31274/jctp-180810-83

Baskerville, D., & Goldblatt, H. (2009). Learning to be a critical friend: From professional indifference through challenge to unguarded conversations. *Cambridge Journal of Education, 39*(2), 205–221. https://doi.org/10.1080/03057640902902260

Bolton, G. (2010). *Reflective practice: Writing and professional development.* SAGE Publications.

Brown, E. R. (2002). The (in)visibility of race in narrative constructions of the self. In J. Loughran & T. Russell (Eds.), *Improving teacher education practices through self-study* (pp. 145–160). Routledge Falmer. https://doi.org/10.4324/9780203018637-19

Brown, E. R. (2004). The significance of race and social class for self-study and the professional knowledge base of teacher education. In J. J. Loughran, M. L. Hamilton, V. K. LaBoskey, & T. L. Russell (Eds.), *International handbook of self-study of teaching and teacher education practices* (pp. 517–574). Springer. https://doi.org/10.1007/978-1-4020-6545-3_14

Bullough, R. V., & Pinnegar, S. E. (2004). Thinking about the thinking about self-study: An analysis of eight chapters. In J. J. Loughran, M. L. Hamilton, V. K. LaBoskey, & T. L. Russell (Eds.), *International handbook of self-study of teaching and teacher education practices* (pp. 313–342). Springer. https://doi.org/10.1007/978-1-4020-6545-3_9

Butler, J. (2005). Giving an account of oneself. *Fordham University Press.* https://doi.org/10.5422/fso/9780823225033.001.0001

Carter Andrews, D. J., & Castillo, B. M. (2016). Humanizing pedagogy for examinations of race and culture in teacher education. In F. Tuitt, C. Haynes, & S. Stewart (Eds.), *Race, equity and higher education: The continued search for critical and inclusive pedagogies around the globe* (pp. 112–128). Stylus.

Carter Andrews, D. J., Brown, T., Castillo, B. M., Jackson, D., & Vellanki, V. (2019). Beyond damage-centered teacher education: Humanizing pedagogy for teacher educators and preservice teachers. *Teachers College Record, 121*(6), 1–28.

Cochran-Smith, M., Davis, D., & Fries, K. (2004). Multicultural teacher education: Research, practice, and policy. In J. Banks & C. Banks (Eds.), *Handbook of research on multicultural education* (2nd ed., pp. 931–975). Jossey-Bass.

Cochran-Smith, M., Villegas, A. M., Abrams, L., Chavez-Moreno, L., Mills, T., & Stern, R. (2015). Critiquing teacher preparation research: An overview of the field, part II. *Journal of Teacher Education, 66*(2), 109–121. https://doi.org/10.1177/0022487114558268

Corbin, J., & Strauss, A. (2015). *Basics of qualitative research: Techniques and procedures for developing grounded theory* (4th ed.). Sage. https://doi.org/10.4135/9781452230153

Cross, B. E. (2003). Learning or unlearning racism: Transferring teacher education curriculum to classroom practices. *Theory Into Practice, 42*(3), 203–209. https://doi.org/10.1207/s15430421tip4203_6

Cutri, R. M., & Whiting, E. F. (2015). The emotional work of discomfort and vulnerability in multicultural teacher education. *Teachers and Teaching, 21*(8), 1010–1025. https://doi.org/10.1080/13540602.2015.1005869

Daniels, J., & Varghese, M. (2020). Troubling practice: Exploring the relationship between whiteness and practice-based teacher education in considering a raciolinguicized teacher subjectivity. *Educational Researcher, 49*(1), 56–63. https://doi.org/10.3102/0013189x19879450

de los Ríos, C., & Souto-Manning, M. (2015). Teacher educators as cultural workers: Problematizing teacher education pedagogies. *Studying Teacher Education, 11*(3), 272–293. https://doi.org/10.1080/17425964.2015.1065806

Flores, N., & Rosa, J. (2015). Undoing appropriateness: Raciolinguistic ideologies and language diversity in education. *Harvard Educational Review, 85*(2), 149–171. https://doi.org/10.17763/0017-8055.85.2.149

Fredricks, D., & Peercy, M. M. (2020). Youth perspectives on humanizing core practices. In L. Cardozo-Gaibisso & M. V. Dominguez (Eds.), *Handbook of research on advancing language equity practices within immigrant communities* (pp. 107–128). IGI Global. https://doi.org/10.4018/978-1-7998-3448-9.ch006

Galman, S., Pica-Smith, C., & Rosenberger, C. (2010). Aggressive and tender navigations: Teacher educators confront whiteness in their practice. *Journal of Teacher Education, 61*(3), 225–236. https://doi.org/10.1177/0022487109359776

Gershenson, S., Hansen, M., & Lindsay, C. A. (2021). *Teacher diversity and student success: Why racial representation matters in the classroom.* Harvard Education Press.

Goodwin, A. L., & Darity, K. (2019). Social justice teacher educators: What kind of knowing is needed? *Journal of Education for Teaching, 45*(1), 63–81. https://doi.org/10.1080/0260747 6.2019.1550606

Gordon, J. (2005). Inadvertent complicity: Colorblindness in teacher education. *Educational Studies, 38*(2), 135–153. https://doi.org/10.1207/s15326993es3802_5

Gorski, P. C. (2016). Making better multicultural and social justice teacher educators: A qualitative analysis of the professional learning and support needs of multicultural teacher education faculty. *Multicultural Education Review, 8*(3), 139–159. https://doi.org/10.108 0/2005615x.2016.1164378

Gorski, P. C., Zenkov, K., Osei-Kofi, N., & Sapp, J. (2012). Introduction. In P. Gorski, K. Zenkov, N. Osei-Kofi, & J. Sapp (Eds.), *Cultivating social justice teachers* (pp. 1–10). Stylus.

Gort, M., & Glenn, W. J. (2010). Navigating tensions in the process of change: An English educator's dilemma management in the revision and implementation of a diversity-infused methods course. *Research in the Teaching of English, 45*(1), 59–86.

Griffiths, M., & Poursanidou, K. (2004). Collaboration and self-study in relation to teaching social justice issues to beginning teachers. In L. M. Fitzgerald, M. L. Heston, & D. L. Tidwell (Eds.), *Journeys of hope: Risking self-study in a diverse world. Proceedings of the fifth international conference of the self-study of teacher education practices* (pp. 129–132). Queen's University.

Haddix, M. M. (2016). *Cultivating racial and linguistic diversity in literacy teacher education.* Routledge. https://doi.org/10.4324/9781315850665

Hambacher, E., & Ginn, K. (2021). Race-visible teacher education: A review of the literature from 2002 to 2018. *Journal of Teacher Education, 72*(3), 329–341. https://doi.org/10.1177/0022487120948045

Hamilton, M. L., & Pinnegar, S. (2014). Self-study of teacher education practices as a pedagogy for teacher educator professional development. In *International teacher education: Promising pedagogies (Part A).* Emerald Group Publishing Limited. https://doi.org/10.1108/s1479-368720140000022010

Hytten, K., & Warren, J. (2003). Engaging whiteness: How racial power gets reified in education. *International Journal of Qualitative Studies in Education, 16*(1), 65–89. https://doi.org/10.108 0/0951839032000033509a

Jenkins, F. (2010). Judith Butler: Disturbance, provocation and the ethics of non-violence. *Humanities Research, 16*(2), 93–115. https://doi.org/10.22459/hr.xvi.02.2010.05

Kidwell, T., Peercy, M. M., Tigert, J., & Fredricks, D. (2021). Novice teachers' use of pedagogical language knowledge to humanize language and literacy development. *TESOL Journal.* https://doi.org/10.1002/tesj.590

Kim, J., Wee, S. J., & Kim, K. J. (2018). Walking the roads as immigrant mothers and teacher educators: A collaborative self-study of three Korean immigrant early childhood educators. *Studying Teacher Education, 14*(1), 22–38. https://doi.org/10.1080/17425964.2017.1411255

Kubota, R., & Lin, A. M. (Eds.). (2009). *Race, culture, and identities in second language education: Exploring critically engaged practice.* Routledge. https://doi.org/10.4324/9780203876657-5

Ladson-Billings, G. (1994). *The dreamkeepers: Successful teachers of African American children.* Jossey-Bass. https://doi.org/10.3726/978-1-4539-1735-0/39

Liggett, T. (2009). Intersections of language and race for English language learners. *Northwest Journal of Teacher Education, 7*(1), 27–37. https://doi.org/10.15760/nwjte.2009.7.1.4

Loughran, J., & Berry, A. (2005). Modelling by teacher educators. *Teaching and Teacher Education, 21*(2), 193–203. https://doi.org/10.1016/j.tate.2004.12.005

Matias, C. E. (2013). On the "flip" side: A teacher educator of color unveiling the dangerous minds of white teacher candidates. *Teacher Education Quarterly, 40*(2), 53–73. https://doi.org/10.1007/978-94-6300-450-3_2

Matias, C. E. (2016). "Why do you make me hate myself?": Re-teaching whiteness, abuse, and love in urban teacher education. *Teaching Education, 27*(2), 194–211. https://doi.org/10.1080/10476210.2015.1068749

McNeil, B. (2011). Charting a way forward: Intersections of race and space in establishing identity as an African-Canadian teacher educator. *Studying Teacher Education, 7*(2), 133–143. https://doi.org/10.1080/17425964.2011.591137

Mills, C. W. (1997). *The racial contract.* University Press. https://doi.org/10.5406/illinois/9780252040863.003.0006

Motha, S. (2020). Is an antiracist and decolonizing applied linguistics possible? *Annual Review of Applied Linguistics, 40*, 128–133. https://doi.org/10.1017/s0267190520000100

NCES. (2020). https://nces.ed.gov/programs/coe/indicator_clr.asp

Ohito, E. O. (2016). Making the emperor's new clothes visible in anti-racist teacher education: Enacting a pedagogy of discomfort with white preservice teachers. *Equity & Excellence in Education, 49*(4), 454–467. https://doi.org/10.1080/10665684.2016.1226104

Paris, D., & Alim, H. S. (Eds.). (2017). *Culturally sustaining pedagogies: Teaching and learning for justice in a changing world.* Teachers College Press.

Peercy, M. M., & Sharkey, J. (2020). Self-study in English language teaching: Emerging considerations about the intersection of teacher educators' identities and pedagogies. In J. Kitchen, A. Berry, S. M. Bullock, A. Crowe, H. Guðjónsdóttir, & M. Taylor (Eds.), *International handbook of self-study of teaching and teacher education* (2nd ed.). Springer. https://doi.org/10.1007/978-981-13-1710-1_28-1

Peercy, M. M., DeStefano, M., Sethna, K., & Bitter, M. (2018). Scaffolding scaffolding: A collaborative effort to understand and enact appropriate scaffolding for EL learning in science. In J. Sharkey (Ed.), *Engaging research: Transformative practice for elementary settings* (pp. 133–148). TESOL Press.

Peercy, M. M., Sharkey, J., Baecher, L., Motha, S., & Varghese, M. (2019a). Exploring TESOL teacher educators as learners and reflective scholars: A shared narrative inquiry. *TESOL Journal, 10*(4). https://doi.org/10.1002/tesj.482

Peercy, M. M., Tigert, J., Feagin, K., Kidwell, T., Fredricks, D., Lawyer, M., Bitter, M., Canales, N., & Mallory, A. (2019b). "I need to take care of myself": The case for self-care as a core practice for teaching. In C. R. Rinke & L. Mawhinney (Eds.), *Opportunities and challenges in teacher recruitment and retention: Teacher voices across the pipeline* (pp. 303–325). Information Age Publishing.

Peercy, M. M., Kidwell, T., Lawyer, M., Tigert, J., Fredricks, D., Feagin, K., & Stump, M. (2020). Experts at being novices: What new teachers can add to practice-based teacher education efforts. *Action in Teacher Education, 42*(3), 212–233. https://doi.org/10.1080/01626620.2019.1675201

Picower, B., & Kohli, R. (Eds.). (2017). *Confronting racism in teacher education: Counternarratives of critical practice.* Taylor & Francis. https://doi.org/10.4324/9781315623566

Richardson, T., & Villenas, S. (2000). "Other" encounters: Dances with whiteness in multicultural education. *Educational Theory, 50*(2), 255–273. https://doi.org/10.1111/j.1741-5446.2000.00255.x

Richert, A. E., Donahue, D. M., & LaBoskey, V. K. (2008). Preparing white teachers to teach in a racist nation. In W. Ayers, T. Quinn, & D. Stovall (Eds.), *Handbook of social justice in education* (pp. 640–653). Routledge. https://doi.org/10.4324/9780203887745-62

Rosa, J. (2019). *Looking like a language, sounding like a race: Raciolinguistic ideologies and the learning of Latinidad.* Oxford University Press. https://doi.org/10.1093/oso/9780190634728.001.0001

Schuck, S., & Russell, T. (2005). Self-study, critical friendship, and the complexities of teacher education. *Studying Teacher Education, 1*(2), 107–121. https://doi.org/10.1080/17425960500288291

Sharkey, J., Peercy, M. M., Daniels, J., Hebard, H., & Liggett, T. (2021a, March). *Naming and disrupting White complicity in TESOL teacher education.* Paper presented at the annual meeting of the teachers of English for speakers of other languages international convention. Virtual meeting.

Sharkey, J., Peercy, M. M., Solano-Campos, A., & Schall-Leckrone, L. (2021b). Being a reflexive practitioner and scholar in TESOL: Methodological considerations. In E. R. Yuan & I. Lee (Eds.), *Becoming and being a TESOL teacher educator: Research and practice.* Routledge.

Shuck, G. (2006). Racializing the nonnative English speaker. *Journal of Language, Identity, and Education, 5*(4), 259–276. https://doi.org/10.1207/s15327701jlie0504_1

Skerrett, A. (2006). Looking inward: The impact of race, ethnicity, gender, and social class background on teaching sociocultural theory in education. *Studying Teacher Education, 2*(2), 183–200. https://doi.org/10.1080/17425960600983213

Sleeter, C. E. (2001). Preparing teachers for culturally diverse schools: Research and the overwhelming presence of whiteness. *Journal of Teacher Education, 52*(2), 94–106. https://doi.org/10.1177/0022487101052002002

Sleeter, C. E. (2017). Critical race theory and the whiteness of teacher education. *Urban Education, 52*(2), 155–169. https://doi.org/10.1177/0042085916668957

Smith, P., Warrican, S. J., & Kumi-Yeboah, A. (2016). Linguistic and cultural appropriations of an immigrant multilingual literacy teacher educator. *Studying Teacher Education, 12*(1), 88–112. https://doi.org/10.1080/17425964.2016.1143811

Souto-Manning, M. (2019). Toward praxically-just transformations: Interrupting racism in teacher education. *Journal of Education for Teaching, 45*(1), 97–113. https://doi.org/10.1080/02607476.2019.1550608

Souto-Manning, M., & Emdin, C. (2020). On the harm inflicted by urban teacher education programs: Learning from the historical trauma experienced by teachers of color. *Urban Education*, 1–33. https://doi.org/10.1177/0042085920926249

Stillman, J., & Beltramo, J. L. (2019). Exploring Freirean culture circles and Boalian theatre as pedagogies for preparing asset-oriented teacher educators. *Teachers College Record, 121*(6), 1–38.

Taylor, M., & Diamond, M. (2020). The role of self-study in teaching and teacher education for social justice. In J. Kitchen, A. Berry, S. M. Bullock, A. Crowe, H. Guðjónsdóttir, & M. Taylor (Eds.), *International handbook of self-study of teaching and teacher education practices* (2nd ed., pp. 509–543). Springer. https://doi.org/10.1007/978-981-13-6880-6_16

U. S. Department of Education. (2021). Retrieved from https://www2.ed.gov/datastory/el-characteristics/index.html

Varghese, M., Daniels, J., & Park, C. (2019). Structuring disruption: Race-based caucuses in teacher education programs. *Teachers College Record, 121*(6), 1–34.

Von Esch, K. S., Motha, S., & Kubota, R. (2020). Race and language teaching. *Language Teaching, 53*(4), 391–421. https://doi.org/10.1017/s0261444820000269

Warren, J. (2003). *Performing purity: Whiteness, pedagogy, and the reconstitution of power.* Peter Lang.

Women of Color (WOC) and Allies. (2017). *White people, stop asking us to educate you about racism.* Retrieved from https://medium.com/@realtalkwocandallies/white-people-stop-asking-us-to-educate-you-about-racism-69273d39d828.

Yancy, G. (2008). *Black bodies, white gazes: The continuing significance of race in America.* Rowman & Littlefield.

Yancy, G. (2012). *Look a white! Philosophical essays on whiteness.* Temple University Press.

Yancy, G. (2019). Guidelines for whites teaching about whiteness. In S. D. Brookfield (Ed.), *Teaching race: How to help students unmask and challenge racism* (pp. 19–41). Wiley. https://doi.org/10.1002/9781119548492.ch2

Megan Madigan Peercy, Ph.D., is Professor and Associate Dean in the College of Education at the University of Maryland. Her research focuses on pedagogies of teacher education; the development of teacher educators; and the preparation and development of teachers throughout their careers, as they work with linguistically and culturally diverse learners. Her research has been funded by the Spencer Foundation and the Institute of Education Sciences. Examples of her recent work appear in *Teaching and Teacher Education, Action in Teacher Education, Language Teaching Research, TESOL Quarterly*, and *TESOL Journal*.

Judy Sharkey, Ph.D., is the John & H. Irene Peters Professor & Chair of the Education Department at the University of New Hampshire. Within critical second language and literacy education, her research focuses on decolonizing approaches to teacher/teacher educator learning and development in plurilingual, transmigrant and diaspora communities in the U.S., Colombia, and Pakistan. Recent research has appeared in *Language Teaching Research, TESOL Journal*, and *Journal of Teacher Education.* She is the co-editor (with Megan Madigan Peercy) of *Self-Study of Language and Literacy Teacher Education Practices: Culturally and Linguistically Diverse Contexts.*

Part III
The Academic Content Areas and Urban Teacher Education

Chapter 7
A Self-Study in PreK-4 Science Teacher Preparation: Supporting Teacher Candidates' Professional Development and Critical Consciousness Using Science as the Context

Shondricka Burrell

Abstract In this chapter the author uses self-study methodology to examine her experience as a science teacher educator implementing and supporting the development of experiential learning, place-based science practices, and critical consciousness among teacher candidates. The chapter explores the process of preparing pre-service teachers enrolled in an elementary science methods class to develop lessons that leverage science as connected with the lived experiences of school-aged children. The practice of embedding both science content and scientific investigative practices in the collective experiences of local communities makes science learning relevant. In addition, for the purposes of this self-study, it serves as a mechanism to promote critical consciousness. Teacher candidates could thus possess a deeper knowledge and understanding of historically segregated urban communities. More so, this could serve to bring awareness of environmental injustices that can be understood through the lens of life, chemical, Earth, and physical sciences, the subjects the teacher candidates will eventually teach in their own classrooms. Using culturally responsive pedagogy as a theoretical framework, the self-study provides insights into how to support the development of teacher candidates' abilities to support diverse learners in the science classroom.

Keywords Science teacher preparation · Science education · Experiential learning · Equity pedagogy · Critical consciousness · Self-study

S. Burrell (✉)
Morgan State University, Baltimore, MD, USA
e-mail: shondricka.burrell@morgan.edu

© The Author(s), under exclusive license to Springer Nature Singapore Pte
Ltd. 2022
A. D. Martin (ed.), *Self-Studies in Urban Teacher Education*, Self-Study of
Teaching and Teacher Education Practices 25,
https://doi.org/10.1007/978-981-19-5430-6_7

Urban communities (communities located in cities) can serve as an extension of the science classroom. They can serve as both a laboratory and a resource for the teaching and learning of both science content and numerous scientific practices, such as identifying problems, asking questions, modeling, investigation, analyzing and interpreting data, and mathematical reasoning (National Research Council [NRC], 2012). More so, for teacher candidates, urban communities can be leveraged as a resource to promote critical consciousness (Ladson-Billings, 2006). The process of identifying and grappling with science content as manifest in the conditions of local communities is instructive and promotes social awareness. For pre-service teachers who will teach science, doing so can enable them to identify patterns of environmental injustice and disparities in the contexts that they will teach in and may serve to help them provide a quality science education.

Unfortunately, a persistent pattern exists where school-aged children in the United States who live in poor and racially segregated urban neighborhoods are disproportionately exposed to environmental toxicants through air, soil, and water, and may attend schools adversely impacted by these environmental hazards (Balazs et al., 2011; Balazs & Ray, 2014; Pastor et al., 2006). Furthermore, students living in these historically redlined communities are projected to be the most vulnerable to the adverse impacts of climate change (Hoffman et al., 2020; Shonkoff et al., 2011). Besides the documented disproportionate exposure to environmental toxicants and correlation to adverse health outcomes, there is a correlation between physical proximity to pollution and academic outcomes for children attending schools in these impacted communities (Pastor et al., 2004).

The science content areas of biology, chemistry, geology, and physics can be applied to understand such environmental injustice. Yet there is an educational opportunity gap in connecting science content with the lived experiences of students in under-resourced urban schools (Basu & Barton, 2007). I believe we can begin to close this gap by supporting critical awareness among teacher candidates and preparing them to enact equity grounded instructional approaches such as experiential learning and place-based science.

Supporting this critical awareness among teacher candidates is compounded by a demographic disconnect as many are not residents of the communities they work in nor are they of the same racial background as their students. For example, the U.S. Department of Education National Center for Education Statistics [NCES] (2020a) reported that of the students enrolled in United States (U.S.) elementary and secondary schools during the 2017–2018 academic year, 47.6% identified as White, 15.2% Black, 26.8% Hispanic, 5.2% Asian, 0.4% Pacific Islander, 1.0% American Indian/Alaska Native, and 3.9% as two or more races. NCES (2020b) also found that public school teachers in 2017–2018 were 79.3% White, 6.7% Black, 9.3% Hispanic, 2.1 Asian, 0.2% Native Hawaiian/Pacific Islander, 0.5% American Indian/Alaska Native, 1.8% two or more races and that teachers were 76% female and 24% male. This means that the teaching workforce is predominantly White and female.

The social and racial incongruence between teachers and students surfaces in modes of classroom instruction. Dominant trends in teaching reflect a pedagogical disconnect within the urban context and in the classroom, as teachers replicate traditional, positivist pedagogies, specifically when teaching science (Mensah & Jackson, 2018). This approach centers the learning of science as an understanding of loosely connected concepts that are potentially and tangentially related to the realities of students attending schools in urban communities. Consequently, explicit connections between science and the proximal world are absent in the education of many students in urban schools. Given such a context, I conducted a self-study examining how I support teacher candidates' understanding of the relevance and value of making connections between their students' lives, communities, and science instruction. In doing so, I gained insights that informed my practice (Bullock, 2020) into how I implemented and supported knowledge of experiential learning, place-based pedagogy, and the development of critical consciousness among teacher candidates.

In this chapter, I take an inquiry stance to examine my teaching experiences supporting pre-service teacher exploration of and learning about science content in urban communities and in the lived experience of students. Specifically, I discuss my enactment of teaching practices with undergraduate students enrolled in a methods class for preschool through fourth grade (PreK-4) science with the intention of understanding the efficacy of my approach, and to learn about myself and the tensions that arose in this undertaking. This self-study will inform the improvement of my teaching practices with the aim to support the development of critical awareness among science teacher candidates and also inform the work of science teacher educators.

7.1   Theoretical Framework

My self-study was informed by culturally relevant pedagogy as constructed by Gloria Ladson-Billings (1995b). According to Ladson-Billings (1995a), culturally relevant pedagogy results in student academic success (academic skill development leading to competence), supports the maintenance of cultural competence/integrity (i.e., minoritized students' backgrounds are not rejected but leveraged as an asset in classroom learning), and aids the development of critical awareness (i.e., sociopolitical consciousness). Culturally relevant pedagogy is intended to disrupt the pattern in classrooms where students are managed rather than meaningfully engaged in learning, with such management resulting in their "academic failure, dropout, suspension, and expulsion" (Ladson-Billings, 2014, p. 77). Two components of culturally relevant pedagogy were particularly salient in this self-study—skill development that supports student competence and critical consciousness.

Furthermore, three pedagogical constructs also informed the pedagogical activity I explored and the meaning-making of this inquiry. These three constructs were experiential learning, place-based pedagogy, and critical consciousness. I chose these three constructs to incorporate in my instruction and professional development of elementary science teacher candidates. These constructs support meaningful learning opportunities, serve as a catalyst to employ science for problem solving and promote social justice, and have the potential to disrupt patterns of inequity and injustice (Taylor & Diamond, 2020) in PreK-4 education. Collectively, these can support a learner's perception of the relevance of science to everyday life, specifically that it is not something that other people study or do somewhere else, but rather that science is done by students contextualized in their lived experiences, and is relevant to their immediate community. I discuss these three constructs in relation to science education.

7.1.1 Experiential Learning

Experiential learning is learning by *doing*. For science instruction, this means that it is active, cognitively engaging science experiences where students learn science concepts in conjunction with the direct use or application of their understandings. My approach to experiential learning is influenced by both Dewey (1916) and Bandura (1986). According to Dewey (1916), learning happens organically when students have "something to do, not something to learn; and the doing is of such a nature as to demand thinking, or the intentional noting of connections" (p. 119). This approach of learning by doing is foundational to the development of self-efficacy in that students develop a sense of competence through mastery experiences (Bandura, 1986). Students reinforce their learning by performing specific scientific skills such as measuring, modeling, experimenting, or evaluating. During experiential learning experiences students take up science content and scientific practices through both physical and cognitive engagement.

7.1.2 Place-Based Pedagogy

In place-based pedagogy, science concepts are contextualized in what is familiar and in relation to a learner's local community. Place-based pedagogy is an equity-based approach to science teaching and learning in which the educator makes meaningful connections amongst student interests, experiences, the local community, and science concepts (NRC, 2012). For example, students can observe photosynthesis in the leaves of green plants collected along their walk to school, from a tree located near their home, or from the school's garden. Similarly, students could also learn about water quality by testing the pH level of water sampled from their home kitchen, from a local stream, or from rainfall. This approach can support student interest and academic development in relation to science (Clark et al., 2015; Kraft et al., 2011). In addition, place-based pedagogy demonstrates the relevance of science to the lived experiences of the student. It frames the community as the context for understanding science concepts and scientific practices.

7.1.3   Critical Consciousness

Critical consciousness is the intentional observation of power dynamics and patterns in communities, human interactions, and social structures that probes and asks questions to understand the contributing factors and relationship to equity/inequities. According to Ladson-Billings (2006), critically conscious educators are intentional about understanding the local community as the context for their teaching and for student learning. Critically consciousness educators critique prevalent narratives about student learning that frame assessment outcomes as an achievement gap and as a valid, accurate reflection of student academic progress (Ladson-Billings, 2011). Such educators are cognizant of the relationship between school funding and the inequitable distribution of resources and opportunities for students to learn (Ladson-Billings, 2006, 2011). Critically conscious teachers of science can provide access to high-quality science content to help students understand science as relevant to their lived experiences (Basu & Barton, 2007) and to prepare them to critically examine patterns of equity and inequity in society at large (Moje, 2007).

7.2   Methodology

Recently researchers have used self-study to examine their efforts to bring change to their institutions (Brown & Schneider, 2020; Chisanga & Meyiwa, 2020); positionality as researchers and practitioners (Pinnegar et al., 2020); and intersectional identities while teaching social justice (Hannon, 2020). In addition, the methodology has been used to examine the impact of self-study on the experience and quality of the practice of teacher education (Ritter & Hayler, 2020); approaches to prepare educators to teach for social justice (Sowa & Schmidt, 2020); and how various individuals within teacher preparation and higher education could leverage self-study to generate education research, or in conjunction with other methodologies, to expand the framing of their work (Ritter & Quiñones, 2020). I chose self-study as a research method because I sought to increase the understanding of my practice in preparing pre-service teachers and increasing my understanding of myself in relation to teaching and learning within my work as a teacher educator (Bullock, 2020; Loughran, 2004). I engaged in this self-study as a means of acquiring a new and reframed (LaBoskey, 2004a) understanding specific to my practice in preparing pre-service teachers. As part of this study, I addressed the following research questions:

1. How effective is my practice with respect to supporting the understanding of experiential and place-based pedagogies, and with respect to supporting the development of critical consciousness in PreK-4 teacher candidates?
2. How can I improve upon my practice in these areas?
3. How do I understand myself and my role as a science teacher educator?

Thus, I hoped to utilize the insights from this inquiry to inform my own professional development, and to potentially "trigger further deliberations, explorations, and change by other educators in their contexts" (LaBoskey, 2004b, p. 1170).

To explore the research questions, I collected and analyzed multiple data sources, including design notes that outlined the intent and content for the learning experiences implemented during my teaching of a science methods course, lecture slides from the class sessions, and the feedback provided from two critical friends. My critical friends also reviewed three video recorded lessons that I taught along with notes I compiled about my teaching. My hope is that the learning I gained from this self-study will improve my future teaching and support the development of critical consciousness among science teacher candidates as well as their understandings of experiential and place-based pedagogies.

7.2.1   My Positionality with Respect to Science Teaching and Learning

I self-identify as an African American female, descendant of survivors of slavery on both sides of my family. Professionally, I identify as a geoscience education researcher and teacher educator. I come to the work of science education with a background in disciplinary science—geology—and a career trajectory that includes roles as a science teacher at an alternative high school designed for students who did not experience academic success in traditional school settings, adjunct geoscience faculty who taught general education geoscience courses, and a contract employee in education and outreach at a federal aerospace agency who mentored community college students as they performed both research and mission support duties as interns. In each space, both in-school and out-of-school, I aimed to create opportunities for students to learn science and engage in scientific practice.

In more recent years, as part of my doctoral work, I have contributed to the development and testing of instructional scaffolds to help students develop critical thinking and evidence-based reasoning skills (Lombardi et al., 2018a, b). I also developed a water quality-themed curriculum using Flint, Michigan as a case study (Burrell, 2019a). In this work I framed science as useful for problem-solving, specifically, regarding cases of environmental injustice (Burrell, 2020). I tested the efficacy of the curriculum designed to engage secondary students in learning science content, scientific practices, and problem solving related to environmental justice with 300 students in four different high schools across the U.S. My aim was to determine whether embedding science content in a current issue of environmental injustice would support student learning of science concepts, investigative practices, and lead to other desired outcomes such as knowledge gains, interest in science, and attitudinal shifts in the perception of science as relevant and applicable. I found that students retained conceptual understanding, science interest, and a positive attitudinal shift in their perceptions of science (Burrell, 2019b). Contextualizing science content and scientific practices, in a pressing socio-scientific issue, exemplifies my approach to science teaching and learning. In my teaching, I am intentional in designing science learning experiences that are experiential, place-based, and contextualized in my students' communities. My positionality in the courses that I teach, and specifically, the course that is the context for this self-study, is that science is relevant to all students' lives and can be taught and learned from a perspective of utility in addressing pressing societal problems.

7.2.2   Research Context

At the time of this study, I was a tenure track assistant professor of secondary science methods at a Predominantly White Institution (PWI). The university is in a state where there is a shortage of classroom teachers and educational leaders due to decreased enrollment in teacher preparation programs and educator turnover (Levis, 2018). More locally, the university is in a county where 95.5% of public elementary school teachers are White and 32% of students are of color (Fontana & Lapp, 2018). The context for this self-study is an undergraduate course in elementary school science methods. The class is for pre-service teachers in their third year of the degree program. This iteration of the course was unique in that it was delivered in a hybrid online and in-person format. This meant that there would be three groups of students—one group learning remotely, and two groups of students rotating on alternate weeks for in-person instruction. Class sessions were conducted in this combined on-line and in-person modality for a compressed 14-week semester. Remote instruction was mediated by a videoconference platform with recording capability. Three recorded sessions totaling 7.5 h of instruction were the focal point for this self-study.

7.2.3   Self-Study Methods

Self-study as a formal approach to research seeks to increase understanding of "oneself; teaching; learning; and the development of knowledge about these" (Loughran, 2004, p. 9). It represents part of a larger "trend away from modernism and its assumptions about legitimate knowledge and knowledge production toward broadening what counts as research" (Bullough & Pinnegar, 2001, p. 13). Although self-study is not a prescriptive approach to research, it does require critical reflexivity to reframe thinking, and confirm or challenge developing understandings, though multiple methods intended "to gain different, and thus more comprehensive, perspectives on the educational processes under investigation" (LaBoskey, 2004a, pp. 859–860).

Contrary to what the name might imply, self-study is not synonymous with personal reflection. Indeed, as part of the multiple methods used to collect and analyze data, it is commonplace to invite others to play a role in self-study. Two critical friends supported me in this inquiry. One critical friend was a tenured colleague at the institution where the research was conducted and the second was a former colleague who is now a tenured faculty member at a four-year Hispanic Serving Institution (HSI). Both critical friends are teacher educators at their respective institutions, and were members of the Self-Study Faculty Learning Group (Ritter et al., 2018). I joined this faculty group in my second semester at my institution as a means of connecting with colleagues as part of the research community and to become familiar with self-study as a methodology. I asked these colleagues to serve as critical friends for this current study as they are each familiar with the methodology and because I have observed their honesty when discussing their work and professional experiences with the group. I believed the skills of critical evaluation and clear communication of observation would be important for this study. Thus, they bring their experience and expertise to this self-study project.

7.2.4 Data Sources

Data sources for this project include a number of different course artifacts. First, I employed design notes which were generated for each class session and aligned with the intention outlined in the course catalog description and the course syllabus. These notes consisted of an agenda for the class session and the student learning objectives. I also included presentation slides from each session. The slides included the title of the class session, the session agenda, notes, discussion questions, an outline of experimental procedure for any in-class investigation, prompts to deconstruct the learning experience from the perspective of a student and from the perspective of a teacher, and next steps for the class. Following each class session, the slides were made available to students via our learning management platform.

Another primary data source were the recordings from three class sessions that were analyzed for this project. I selected three class sessions to focus on as in each, I attended to one of the three pedagogical constructs (experiential learning, place-based pedagogy, and critical consciousness). In each session I sought to implement the session agenda, the intended learning outcomes, address the state academic standards in alignment with my planned learning experience, and facilitate whole-group and small group discussions. I sought to provide my students with the opportunity to deconstruct science learning experiences from the perspective of an elementary grade student and from the perspective of a classroom teacher. As each session concluded, I highlighted next steps in the class and any relevant information for the upcoming class session. Each of the class sessions was aligned with one of the pedagogical constructs—experiential learning, place-based pedagogy, and critical consciousness. The recordings for the class sessions were reviewed by the critical friends. Each shared their reflections on how my instructional approach aligned with experiential learning, place-based pedagogy, and critical consciousness.

7.2.5   Data Analysis

Through iterative content coding (Creswell, 2013) I identified convergent and divergent ideas from my data sources and from the insights shared by my critical friends. My coding process included: organizing the written content of the data into categories, labeling emergent themes from these categories, identifying convergent and divergent themes, and interpreting the possible significance of these themes as related to my teaching practice. I also continued my dialogue with each critical friend. We individually met for a 60 min follow up session. During each meeting, we discussed my insights and meaning making. These conversations provided an opportunity for them to ask clarifying questions and provide additional feedback. I used the insights generated from these conversations and my data analysis to identify elements of my instructional practice that aligned with the pedagogical constructs I focused on. I discuss what I have learned in the following section.

7.3   Findings

I now discuss what I learned according to the pedagogical construct that I focused on in each class session—experiential learning, place-based pedagogy, and critical consciousness. I begin by providing a summary of the class session. In the summary I include my intended learning outcomes and content of the learning experience. Then, based on my data analysis, I share my insights and how these inform supporting Pre-K preservice teachers to engage with meaningful science instruction.

7.3.1   Experiential Learning

The class session where I focused on experiential learning was the first meeting of the semester. I designed the learning experience around introducing and engaging the teacher candidates with scientific practices as these skills are foundational to the teaching and learning of science content. During the session students were not provided with lists of scientific practices, but rather learned them by *doing*; in other words, they asked questions, designed an experiment, and critically evaluated the available data prior to learning the terms for each action.

My intention was to: frame science as a means of solving problems in society and a means for contributing to social justice; review the scientific practices as outlined by the National Research Council (2012) as a benchmark for both quality science education and equity; provide a foundation for the class to become a community of learners; and introduce the course using the syllabus as the guiding document. To do this, I developed an ice breaker during which students introduced themselves, shared their favorite subject, and shared something that represented them as a teacher. During the learning experience students assumed the role of Earth scientists investigating the water quality issue in Flint, Michigan (lead content has been at a dangerously high level in this city). Assuming the roles of Earth scientists, my students looked at a chronology of events, considered the questions they would like to pose in an investigation, and designed an investigation to answer those questions. Using both whole-group and smaller collaborative learning groups, students employed scientific practices and discussed the issue of environmental injustice. The class ended with students deconstructing the learning experience from the perspective of an elementary grade student and then from the perspective of a teacher.

I learned that enacting experiential learning aligns well with my overall approach to teaching, which is to create a space for the learner to construct knowledge. It also allowed me to support the teacher-candidates' development both as science learners and as future science educators. In other words, using questioning techniques in the learning of science concepts and participation in scientific practices helped them learn the content while observing an instructional approach they could adapt in their future classrooms.

7.3.2 Place-Based Pedagogy

For the class where I focused on place-based pedagogy, I designed the session for students to learn a process that occurs in their immediate surroundings—photosynthesis—and to become familiar with science, curricular resources, and community partnerships that they could leverage to teach science in their future classrooms. Awareness of local resources are particularly important for new teachers tasked with developing learning experiences their first few years in the profession. For teachers with positions in schools in urban communities, this approach facilitates making meaningful connections between science content and the students' surroundings.

The lesson was based on an investigation and learning activity adapted from the Exploratorium Science Snack, *Photosynthetic floatation: Light leaves light* (n.d.), a biology lesson for grades 3–5. My intention was to focus on supporting student understanding of the role of green plants in producing oxygen through photosynthesis; to connect oxygen production to air quality and global climate change; and to incorporate leveraging community resources in the teaching of PreK-4 science content. During the lesson students discussed photosynthesis from a biological and chemical perspective, and used the scientific practices of asking questions, investigating, and constructing explanations (NRC, 2012). Students also connected the science content to environmental justice in Pittsburgh, specifically related to the presence of trees in urban spaces versus suburban, and the associated air quality based on the presence of trees. There were two guest speakers from local community organizations in this session—Urban Hilltop Farm and One Tree per Child/Tree Pittsburgh. Their presentations served to extend the in-class science experiment to our local environment.

After these presentations, I recognized that students did not raise or ask any questions. I had previously provided students with information about these community-based organizations and asked them to generate questions for the speakers. I realized I must consider more ways for students to submit prepared questions prior to the session. For example, after reviewing the websites for the organizations, students might be curious about their work and possibilities for potential community-educator partnerships. Questions this might raise could then be shared during the class session or be asked to the speakers.

Notably, it was during this session that I felt vulnerable and experienced internal conflict. I introduced the session with a photo that I took of Emancipation Oak, a historic tree at the entrance of Hampton University's campus where my relative, Reuben V. Burrell worked as an instructor and photographer. I used the image to trigger interest in the topic of trees, their environmental benefit with respect to clean air, and how their greater concentration in suburban versus urban communities correlates to differential air quality in each of these settings.

This site of Emancipation Oak was an outdoor classroom for freed people during the 1860s when educating African Americans was illegal, and it is a place where the intersection of history and science is meaningful. Further, it serves as a space where history remains part of our collective consciousness. Inserting this content was seamless on a surface level, but personally meaningful. However, I did grapple with questions about the amount of science content to include in the lesson. As a former high school science teacher and geoscience faculty where disciplinary science was the focus, I was transitioning to preparing PreK-4 educators for whom teaching science will not be a specialized focus or primary responsibility. In this relatively new role preparing elementary grade teachers, I felt an internal tension navigating the balance of teaching science content and teaching science pedagogy and avoiding what might be perceived as an over-emphasis on science content. I found myself navigating this relatively new space and calibrating my teaching not against my prior teaching experiences, but rather for the teacher-candidates' reality which was less familiar. With respect to place-based pedagogy, as a teacher educator, it is an easy decision to contextualize science with real life experiences, even when it connected to injustice; I believe this can serve as a contribution to disrupt patterns of inequity, but I accept that it will not always be simple to navigate such learning scenarios.

7.3.3   Critical Consciousness

In the class session where I focused on critical consciousness, I designed the learning experience to foster my students' awareness of various forms of inequity and injustice in school settings and for them to more deeply engage with such topics by exercising agency in formulating approaches that could address them. I categorized this class session as aligned with critical consciousness because of the focus on marginalization and minoritization.

My intention was to discuss socially just teaching versus teaching for social justice and to identify strategies that could create a safe learning space for students from historically marginalized demographic groups. I presented statistics about discipline, suspension, and expulsion rates for Black girls and boys compared to White girls and boys (Crenshaw et al. 2015). Throughout the session, students made connections between the assigned readings, instructional strategies reviewed in the course thus far, and their own experiences. In collaborative learning groups, students applied their knowledge to four case scenarios that I developed; they responded to probing questions that required them to identify strategies for creating an emotionally and cognitively safer learning environment for students from minoritized identities.

For example, in one scenario, students discussed how to use visual formative assessment and reflections in science journals as equity strategies to make their students' thinking visible. In another scenario, the teacher-candidates assumed the role of second grade teachers in a school undergoing efforts to racially de-segregate. In this scenario, new teachers at the school observe that the new incoming students (who are predominantly African-American/Black and from Latinx communities) are curious, eager to learn, and seek to actively participate in class. Yet, veteran teachers at the school use deficit-based language to describe the new students as loud and having behavioral issues, and thus refer them frequently to the principal's office. The teacher-candidates in my class were tasked to consider what might contribute to the discrepancy in perspective between the new and veteran teachers and to identify strategies that they themselves could implement in their future classrooms to ensure a more equitable and safer learning space for all students. Overall, the teacher-candidates interpreted data on inequity in school discipline, discussed the difference between socially just science teaching, and teaching for social justice, and applied strategies learned throughout the course to different school-based scenarios.

When I designed and planned for the session on critical consciousness I found myself second-guessing my approach. It did not include the kinds of questioning techniques that I would typically utilize, such as questions about the best activity to support student learning of the content, or the sequence of activities needed to build understanding. And it was not a question of the importance of this instructional approach (i.e., critical consciousness) as part of the professional preparation of the teacher candidates.

I questioned how this kind of learning experience would be received by my students, and the implications of taking up critical consciousness in the classroom relative to my status as a tenure track junior faculty member. I questioned whether it would be perceived (by my students) as too much, too heavy, and that I would be considered as teaching with an agenda or not presenting science content objectively. Admittedly, in this session, my focus was not on the efficacy of the instructional approach or my teaching, but rather how the teacher candidates would perceive and evaluate what I was teaching and seeking for them to engage with. I was very much aware of the disparity in student evaluations of teacher effectiveness for White faculty versus faculty of color, and particularly female faculty of color in the

U.S. (Boring et al., 2016; Williams, 2018). I felt professionally vulnerable, not because of my skills or identity as a science teacher educator, but because of my identify as an African American female professor. I invested time, and cognitive and emotional energy as I contemplated, internally deliberated, and reflected upon this. I believe that I ultimately enacted a pedagogy aligned with critical consciousness, but it was against the background narrative of concern about my professional position in relation to my positionality. Perhaps, if this concern was not a factor, I may have developed prompts that more deeply engaged students to critique patterns of injustice. I encouraged my teacher-candidates to lean into our discussions and the potential discomfort that could arise. I realize that as I teach and promote critical awareness, I am leaning into vulnerability (Wilkerson, 2020). In the future, I believe I can highlight to my students that the purpose of examining the contentious issues of inequity, exclusion, and injustice is not to convince or indoctrinate towards a particular view, but rather that it is a learning opportunity about the persistent experience of injustice in our society (Martin, 2020).

7.4 Discussion

During this process of self-inquiry, I chose to examine my practice related to implementing instruction that supports teacher candidates' professional development with respect to instructional strategies aligned with experiential learning and place-based pedagogy while simultaneously promoting their critical consciousness of patterns of marginalization among students in urban schools. Using multiple sources of qualitative data, I examined both the intent of the class session and the efficacy of my practices in working towards the intended learning outcomes. I believe the three pedagogical constructs investigated in this self-study can promote equity and inclusion in the classroom and serve to amplify the necessity of employing science content in relation to efforts for social justice. In alignment with Bullock's (2020) conceptualization of self-study methodology in science education as form of professional development, I believe that this self-study will help to inform my teaching and enhance the quality of my course with respect to preparing elementary science teacher candidates to enact meaningful pedagogical practices in their future classrooms.

This self-study is an examination of my implementation of experiential and place-based pedagogies, and support of teacher candidate development of critical consciousness. My choice of these three approaches was intentional in supporting the professional development of pre-service elementary science teacher candidates on the teaching of science content and scientific practices particularly in schools located in cities/urban communities. These instructional approaches align with culturally relevant pedagogy, in three areas: academic skill development, cultural integrity, and critical awareness (Ladson-Billings, 1995a). Specifically, experiential learning emphasizes learning by doing, or direct engagement with science content. This contributes to skill development through mastery experiences (Bandura, 1986) or what culturally relevant pedagogy would frame as competence that leads to academic success (Ladson-Billings, 1995a). My practice also aligns with culturally relevant pedagogy through the opportunity for teacher candidates to assume the role of Earth scientists and design an investigation of lead-contaminated water in Flint, MI. The teacher candidates learned the scientific practices outlined by the NRC (2012) such as asking questions, making observations, designing and implementing investigations, critical evaluation of data, and evidence-based reasoning through their application. Place-based pedagogy is inherently an asset-based approach to teaching and learning as the immediate surroundings become the context for developing scientific understanding. In other words, the community becomes an educational resource for science education. In the study, teacher candidates were able to connect the learning of photosynthesis and the collocation of trees with air quality. The development of critical awareness or socio-political consciousness was supported by the examination of statistics of school discipline and considering the underlying factors contributing to disproportionate discipline rates for students of color. In these ways, experiential learning, place-based pedagogy, and critical consciousness align with and illustrate culturally relevant pedagogy, and support competence in the learning of science content and investigative practices, use of the local community as a resource for applying science learning, and the critical examination of societal patterns. The confluence of experiential learning, place-based pedagogy, and culturally relevant pedagogy is a mechanism for science teaching and learning; to understand the socio-scientific issues in local communities, such as air and water quality; and to potentially disrupt the persistent patterns of environmental injustice.

A few areas for further research have emerged from this study. First, to access a more robust understanding of the efficacy of my practice, I would like to extend this study by collecting and analyzing artifacts generated by teacher candidates as part of the course. For example, the teacher candidates create a science journal where they document their thoughts on various in-class experiments and discussions, and respond to reflective prompts. These reflections along with other course projects could serve as a rich dataset for qualitative analysis to potentially provide evidence of the efficacy of my instructional method in meeting the intended learning outcomes. In other words, artifacts can be used to triangulate my findings about my enactment of experiential and place-based pedagogies, and methods to support development of critical consciousness (Creswell, 2013) and potentially identify new understandings. In addition, there are new lines of inquiry that have opened up based on this work specifically around my perceived role as a science teacher educator. I believe a collaborative self-study of faculty preparing early childhood science teachers exploring the tensions of teaching science content and pedagogy, enacting culturally relevant pedagogy, and examining the science teacher-educator's role as it relates to positionality when addressing issues of educational equity and justice would be productive. The current work and the identified areas for further research have implications for practice in the field of science teacher education. These implications are significant and include identifying: effective practices for positioning self in relation to the professional development of teacher candidates, approaches for preparing teacher candidates to enact equity-oriented practices, and effectively contributing to the quality of science learning experiences for school-aged children in urban community schools.

7.5 Conclusion

This work was an opportunity for me to engage in inquiry into my practice as a science teacher educator. In the process I connected with the potential of experiential learning as a mechanism for competence building, place-based pedagogy as a mechanism to position the local community as a resource for teaching science content and the applying investigative practices, and critical consciousness as a mechanism to support teacher candidate understanding of educational contexts. In the process, I gained key insights about my practice and the field that will inform my future work. Given the tension that surfaced for me as secondary science educator teaching elementary science methods, I intend to continue the study of my teaching practices in preparing elementary school science teachers. I would also like to investigate artifacts produced by teacher candidates to gain insight into how my instructional practices translate into their professional development. This work is also important with respect to preparing teacher candidates to work in urban schools. It supports a re-envisioning of the local community as an educational resource. Just as science is not confined to the classroom, place-based science learning is not restricted to distant places but can effectively take place in the student's immediate surroundings. Professional development of science teacher candidates can include an asset-based perspective of the local community as an educational resource.

References

Balazs, C., & Ray, I. (2014). The drinking water disparities framework: On the origins and persistence of inequities in exposure. *American Journal of Public Health, 104*(4), 603–611. https://doi.org/10.2105/2FAJPH.2013.301664

Balazs, C., Morello-Frosch, R., Hubbard, A., & Ray, I. (2011). Social disparities in nitrate- contaminated drinking water in California's San Joaquin Valley. *Environmental Health Perspectives, 119*(9), 1272–1278. https://doi.org/10.1289/ehp.1002878

Bandura, A. (1986). *Social foundations of thought and action: A social cognitive theory* (Prentice-Hall series in social learning theory). Prentice-Hall.

Basu, S. J., & Barton, A. C. (2007). Developing a sustained interest in science among urban minority youth. *Journal of Research in Science Teaching, 44*(3), 466–489. https://doi.org/10.1002/tea.20143

Boring, A., Ottoboni, K., & Starck, P. B. (2016). Student evaluations of teaching (mostly) do not measure teaching effectiveness. *Science Open Research*, 1–11. https://www.scienceopen.com/hosted-document?doi=10.14293/S2199-1006.1.SOR-EDU.AETBZC.v.

Brown, N., & Schneider, S. (2020). Exploring intersectionality as a means to precipitating change: A collaborative self-study of institutional transformation. In J. Kitchen, M. Berry, S. M. Bullock,

A. R. Crowe, M. Taylor, H. Guðjónsdóttir, & L. Thomas (Eds.), *International handbook of self-study of teaching and teacher education practices* (2nd ed., pp. 1507–1520). Springer.

Bullock, S. M. (2020). Self-study of science teaching and science teacher education practices: Considering and contesting knowledge and authority. In J. Kitchen, M. Berry, S. M. Bullock, A. R. Crowe, M. Taylor, H. Guojonsdottir, & L. Thomas (Eds.), *International handbook of self-study of teaching and teacher education practices* (2nd ed., pp. 933–954). Springer.

Bullough, R. V., & Pinnegar, S. (2001). Guidelines for quality in autobiographical forms of self-study research. *Educational Researcher, 30*, 13–21. https://doi.org/10.3102/2F0013189X030003013

Burrell, S. (2019a). Testing the efficacy of a place-based geoscience curriculum that embeds science content in a current environmental issue of water quality. *Geological Society of America Abstracts with Program, 51*(5). https://doi.org/10.1130/abs/2019AM-341009

Burrell, S. (2019b). *Towards a geoscience pedagogy: A socio-cognitive model* [Unpublished doctoral dissertation] Temple University.

Burrell, S. (2020). Geoscience to advance justice: A pedagogical perspective. *Society of America Abstracts with Program, 52*(6). https://doi.org/10.1130/abs/2020AM-360098

Chisanga, T., & Meyiwa, T. (2020). Reflexive Ubuntu, co-learning, and transforming higher education at a rural University in South Africa. In J. Kitchen, M. Berry, S. M. Bullock, A. R. Crowe, M. Taylor, H. Guðjónsdóttir, & L. Thomas (Eds.), *International handbook of self-study of teaching and teacher education practices* (2nd ed., pp. 1491–1506). Springer.

Clark, L., Majumdar, S., Bhattacharjee, J., & Hanks, A. C. (2015). Creating an atmosphere for STEM literacy in the rural south through student-collected weather data. *Journal of Geoscience Education, 63*(2), 105–115. https://doi.org/10.5408/13-066.1

Crenshaw, K., Ocen, P., & Nanda, J. (2015). *Black girls matter: Pushed out, overpoliced, and underprotected.* Center for Intersectionality and Social Policy Studies, Columbia University.

Creswell, J. W. (2013). *Qualitative inquiry & research design: Choosing among five approaches* (3rd ed.). SAGE.

Dewey, J. (1916). *Democracy in education.* Project Gutenberg.

Exploratorium. (n.d.). *Photosynthetic floatation—Light leaves light.* Science Snacks. https://www.exploratorium.edu/snacks/photosynthetic-floatation.

Fontana, J., & Lapp, D. (2018). A PACER Policy Brief: New data on teacher diversity in Pennsylvania. *Research for Action.* https://8rri53pm0cs22jk3vvqna1ub-wpengine.netdna-ssl.com/wp-content/uploads/2018/09/RFA-New-Data-on-Teacher-Diversity-PACER-FINAL.pdf

Hannon, L. (2020). Engaging my whole self in learning to teach for social justice. In J. Kitchen, M. Berry, S. M. Bullock, A. R. Crowe, M. Taylor, H. Guðjónsdóttir, & L. Thomas (Eds.), *International handbook of self-study of teaching and teacher education practices* (2nd ed., pp. 737–762). Springer.

Hoffman, J. S., Shandas, V., & Pendleton, N. (2020). The effects of historical housing policies on resident exposure to intra-urban heat: A study of 108 US urban areas. *Climate, 8*(1), 1–15. https://doi.org/10.3390/cli8010012

Kraft, K. J., Srogi, L., Husman, J., Semken, S., & Fuhrman, M. (2011). Engaging students to learn through the affective domain: A new framework for teaching in the geosciences. *Journal of Geoscience Education, 59*(2), 71. https://doi.org/10.5408/1.3543934a

LaBoskey, V. K. (2004a). The methodology of self-study and its theoretical underpinnings. In J. Loughran, M. L. Hamilton, V. K. LaBoskey, & T. Russell (Eds.), *International handbook of self-study of teaching and teacher education practices* (pp. 817–869). Springer.

LaBoskey, V. K. (2004b). Afterword. Moving the methodology of self-study research and practice forward: Challenges and opportunities. In J. J. Loughran, M. L. Hamilton, V. K. LaBoskey, & T. Russell (Eds.), *International handbook of self-study of teaching and teacher education practices* (pp. 1169–1184). Springer.

Ladson-Billings, G. (1995a). But that's just good teaching! The case for culturally relevant pedagogy. *Theory Into Practice, 34*(3), 159–165.

Ladson-Billings, G. (1995b). Toward a theory of culturally relevant pedagogy. *American Educational Research Journal, 32*(3), 465–491. https://doi.org/10.3102/00028312032003465

Ladson-Billings, G. (2006). From the achievement gap to the education debt: Understanding achievement in US schools. *Educational Researcher, 35*(7), 3–12. https://doi.org/10.3102/2F0013189X035007003

Ladson-Billings, G. (2011). Yes, but how do we do it? Practicing culturally relevant pedagogy. In J. G. Landsman & C. W. Lewis (Eds.), *White teachers/diverse classrooms: Creating inclusive schools, building on students' diversity, and providing true educational equity* (p. 365). Stylus Publishing LLC.

Ladson-Billings, G. (2014). Culturally relevant pedagogy 2.0: a.k.a. the remix. *Harvard Educational Review, 84*(1), 74–84.

Levis, E. (2018, July 12). *Governor Wolf announces $2 million to retain more teachers, school leaders*. https://www.media.pa.gov/Pages/Education-Details.aspx?newsid=474

Lombardi, D., Bailey, J. M., Bickel, E. S., & Burrell, S. (2018a). Scaffolding scientific thinking: Students' evaluations and judgments during earth science knowledge construction. *Contemporary Educational Psychology*. https://doi.org/10.1016/j.cedpsych.2018.06.008

Lombardi, D., Bickel, E. S., Bailey, J. M., & Burrell, S. (2018b). High school students' evaluations, plausibility (re) appraisals, and knowledge about topics in earth science. *Science Education, 102*(1), 153–177. https://doi.org/10.1002/sce.21315

Loughran, J. J. (2004). A history and context of self-study of teaching and teacher education practices. In J. J. Loughran, M. L. Hamilton, V. K. LaBoskey, & T. Russell (Eds.), *International handbook of self-study of teaching and teacher education practices* (pp. 7–39). Springer.

Martin, A. D. (2020). Tensions and caring in teacher education: A self-study on teaching in difficult moments. *Studying Teacher Education, 16*(3), 306–323. https://doi.org/10.1080/1742596 4.2020.1783527

Mensah, F. M., & Jackson, I. (2018). Whiteness as property in science teacher education. *Teachers College Record, 120*(1), 1–38.

Moje, E. B. (2007). Developing socially just subject-matter instruction: A review of the literature on disciplinary literacy. *Review of Research in Education, 31*, 1–44. https://doi.org/10.3102/2F0091732X07300046001

National Center for Education Statistics. (2020a). *Digest of education statistics Table 203.50, Enrollment and percentage distribution of enrollment in public elementary and secondary schools, by race/ethnicity and region: Selected years, fall 1995 through fall 2029*. U.S. Department of Education. https://nces.ed.gov/programs/digest/d20/tables/dt20_203.50.asp.

National Center for Education Statistics. (2020b). *Race and ethnicity of public school teachers and their students*. (NCES 2020–103). U.S. Department of Education. https://nces.ed.gov/pubs2020/2020103/index.asp.

National Research Council. (2012). *A framework for K-12 science education: Practices, crosscutting concepts, and core ideas*. National Academies Press.

Pastor, M., Jr., Sadd, J. L., & Morello-Frosch, R. (2004). Reading, writing, and toxics: Children's health, academic performance, and environmental justice in Los Angeles. *Environment and Planning C: Government and Policy, 22*(2), 271–290. https://doi.org/10.1068/2Fc009r

Pastor, M., Jr., Morello-Frosch, R., & Sadd, J. L. (2006). Breathless: Schools, air toxics, and environmental justice in California. *Policy Studies Journal, 34*(3), 337–362. https://doi.org/10.1111/j.1541-0072.2006.00176.x

Pinnegar, S., Hutchinson, D. A., & Hamilton, M. L. (2020). Role of positioning, identity, and stance in becoming S-STTEP researchers. In J. Kitchen, M. Berry, S. M. Bullock, A. R. Crowe, M. Taylor, H. Guðjónsdóttir, & L. Thomas (Eds.), *International handbook of self-study of teaching and teacher education practices* (2nd ed., pp. 97–133). Springer.

Ritter, J. K., & Hayler, M. (2020). Challenges in engaging in self-study within teacher education contexts. In J. Kitchen, M. Berry, S. M. Bullock, A. R. Crowe, M. Taylor, H. Guðjónsdóttir, & L. Thomas (Eds.), *International handbook of self-study of teaching and teacher education practices* (2nd ed., pp. 1225–1251). Springer.

Ritter, J. K., & Quiñones, S. (2020). Entry points for self-study. In J. Kitchen, M. Berry, S. M. Bullock, A. R. Crowe, M. Taylor, H. Guðjónsdóttir, & L. Thomas (Eds.), *International handbook of self-study of teaching and teacher education practices* (2nd ed., pp. 1–37). Springer.

Ritter, J. K., Lunenberg, M., Pithouse-Morgan, K., Samaras, A. P., & Vanassche, E. (Eds.). (2018). *Teaching, learning, and enacting of self-study methodology: Unraveling a complex interplay.* Springer.

Shonkoff, S. B., Morello-Frosch, R., Pastor, M., & Sadd, J. (2011). The climate gap: Environmental health and equity implications of climate change and mitigation policies in California—A review of the literature. *Climatic Change, 109*(1), 485–503. https://doi.org/10.1007/s10584-011-0310-7

Sowa, P. A., & Schmidt, C. (2020). Preparing teachers to teach for social justice: Mirrors and windows. In J. Kitchen, M. Berry, S. M. Bullock, A. R. Crowe, M. Taylor, H. Guðjónsdóttir, & L. Thomas (Eds.), *International handbook of self-study of teaching and teacher education practices* (2nd ed., pp. 545–564). Springer.

Taylor, M., & Diamond, M. (2020). The role of self-study in teaching and teacher education for social justice. In J. Kitchen, M. Berry, S. M. Bullock, A. R. Crowe, M. Taylor, H. Guðjónsdóttir, & L. Thomas (Eds.), *International handbook of self-study of teaching and teacher education practices* (2nd ed., pp. 509–543). Springer.

Wilkerson, I. (2020). *Caste (Oprah's Book Club): The origins of our discontents.* Random House.

Williams, J. A. (2018). Being othered and finding my voice: Using self-study to better understand my experiences as an early childhood teacher educator. In J. K. Ritter, M. Lunenberg, K. Pithouse-Morgan, A. P. Samaras, & E. Vanassche (Eds.), *Teaching, learning, and enacting of self-study methodology: Unraveling a complex interplay* (pp. 77–83). Springer. https://doi.org/10.1007/978-981-10-8105-7_10

Shondricka Burrell, Ph.D., is an Assistant Professor of secondary science education in the Department of Advanced Studies, Leadership, and Policy, School of Education and Urban Studies, at Morgan State University. Dr. Burrell is a socio-cognitive researcher who applies both quantitative and qualitative analytical methods to the study of science teaching and learning. With advanced degrees in the geosciences and curriculum and instruction, Dr. Burrell's research interests include: transformative learning experiences, science interest development, self-efficacy, Earth science, geoscience education, science for problem solving, science for social justice, educational equity, and environmental justice.

Chapter 8
A Closer Look at Equitable Outcomes: A Self-Study in Urban Mathematics Teacher Education

Natalie Odom Pough and Craig Willey

Abstract Inequitable opportunities to learn mathematics has plagued the U.S. for decades. Given the challenges facing urban children and families (e.g., systemic racism; deficit orientations; limited resources for schools), it is particularly important for prospective urban teachers (PTs) to not only be proficient with mathematics content and develop skillful pedagogy, but also be able to understand historical and social phenomena that have created inequitable opportunities to learn and thrive with mathematics. This collaborative self-study is fundamentally rooted in the belief that an examination of our histories and experiences can serve to provide insights into the productive practices that might help us define effective mathematics teaching and break free from the stalemate of uncritical, mediocre mathematics teaching that has persisted despite major, concerted efforts from leading organizations and local agencies. Drawing on narrative data from our elementary mathematics methods courses, we show an interrogation into the origins of our beliefs and pedagogical moves that can help surface mathematics teacher education practices that hold the potential to disrupt the perpetuation of stubborn inequities in mathematics teaching and learning. Furthermore, we analyze classroom discourse and PT work samples from our methods courses as a means of further reflection and to correlate the impact of—or lack of—our curriculum and instructional approach. Our findings spotlight the ways we have had to be resilient in the face of entrenched mathematics and racial ideologies, and we discuss the relationship between these reflections and our views on the mathematics learning experiences urban children deserve.

Keywords Self-study · Mathematics · Education · Equity · Race

N. O. Pough (✉)
The Ron Clark Academy, Atlanta, GA, USA
e-mail: pough@ronclarkacademy.com

C. Willey
Indiana University, Bloomington, IN, USA

A. D. Martin (ed.), *Self-Studies in Urban Teacher Education*, Self-Study of Teaching and Teacher Education Practices 25,
https://doi.org/10.1007/978-981-19-5430-6_8

We, the authors and investigators of this self-study, are mathematics teacher educators (MTEs) whose work is focused on preparing urban teachers. Our objectives are manifold. We are tasked to guide our prospective teachers (PTs) through their education program with the knowledge and skills needed to teach effectively. Concurrently, we are committed to helping them hear, resist, and challenge deficit-oriented narratives about urban schools and communities, and about the individuals who attend the schools and reside in these communities; without active and intentional confrontation of deficit notions, we can expect urban youth to continue to be mischaracterized and misunderstood as systemic racism thrives and evolves (Foote et al., 2013; Milner, 2008). We work collaboratively with PTs to establish productive narratives, where children's cultural, linguistic, personal, and community assets are valued and positioned as resources for learning (Turner et al., 2016, 2019). In the case of elementary teachers, we do this through our teaching practices, and how we assess their growth and success; then we broadcast that. With respect to mathematics, we dispel myths that narrowly define what it means to do math and who can do math competently. We build confidence in doing math among PTs where insecurities once dominated. And, we aggressively articulate belief systems about the brilliance of children of color and the corresponding math teaching practices that act on these beliefs.

Given this backdrop and these goals, there are countless questions that surface as we make curricular and pedagogical decisions (Kitchen, 2020; Oda, 1998). For example, how do we frame course content and learning experiences to make clear to PTs that issues of equity and justice are central to developing math teaching practices designed to augment success for children of color? If we are serious about equity and justice in mathematics education, then a candid examination of the efficacy of our practices is the least we can do. As a result, we will know where we are having an impact and where we are experiencing limited success (Clandinin & Connelly, 2004). Given that this self-study is aimed squarely at enhancing the mathematics learning experiences of children of color and has the potential to offer opportunities for growth and improvement, this model could serve as a tool for others to critically interrogate their teaching practices and dispositions as well.

This collaborative self-study (Chang et al., 2016), inherently involves an examination of self, as well as our relationships with PTs, urban communities, and teaching mathematics. We recognize that we are a part of multiple, complex systems: schooling, mathematics teaching and learning, and justice, economic, and political systems that do not provide equal respect and dignity for people of color (Battey & Leyva, 2016; Griffiths & Poursanidou, 2005). It might seem futile to focus our gaze on an individual, or pair of individuals, as a means to dismantle inequitable systems that all too often perpetuate injustices. Systems (including schooling and pedagogical systems) are the products of the actions and legacies of individuals (Billett, 2006). Therefore, to combat and change inequitable systems, we need to center and interrogate the effectiveness and impact of our work (i.e., our actions as MTEs) in preparing urban teachers to resist deficit notions about students of color and to adopt affirmative perspectives. We believe that an interrogation of our own dispositions and professional practices can increase the likelihood that our PTs (our community's next generation of teachers) see and hear students of color from an equity, asset-based orientation and, in relation to mathematics, honor their mathematical contributions to the classroom. Such an interrogation can more fully inform our own teacher education practices and contribute to how our PTs teachers resist racist policies and practices, and advocate for tolerance and justice—in mathematics and beyond. For us, engagement in this self-study is central to our work, as without this interrogation of our practices, we might feel confident in what we present and teach our PTs (in the form of curriculum and pedagogy), yet perhaps it might be with little regard to previous notions they might possess about urban settings and students of color. Scant attention to this perpetuates the status quo of inequitable schooling practices.

In this chapter, we situate this collaborative self-study in the larger context of city schools and urban teacher education, describe the parameters and self-study methods deployed, and report key themes that emerged from our data analysis. We follow with a discussion of these themes in relation to urban teacher education. We conclude by raising important implications for the field of teacher education and for self-study research.

8.1 Theoretical Framework

Two theoretical constructs are particularly salient to this self-study: *whiteness* and *consciousness*. Whiteness does not refer to an individual's phenotype, but rather to the attitudes and behaviors that serve to maintain systemic racism and white dominance (Hayes & Hartlep, 2013). Decades ago, Frankenberg (1993) stated, "As a collection of everyday strategies, whiteness is characterized by the unwillingness to name the contours of racism, the avoidance of identifying with a racial experience or group, the minimization of racist legacy, and other similar evasions" (p. 32). While this might resonate with some of the more overt forms of racism demonstrated today, whiteness also involves the more insidious forms of racism that may prove difficult to name and address. In higher education contexts, these might include centering one's (White) self and the associated emotions in tenuous situations (Matias, 2016), an unwillingness to hold oneself accountable and instead assigning blame on others (particularly people of color), undermining the authority of people of color, avoiding direct or contentious interactions with people of color, and/or circumventing people of color in search for a (White) authority figure (DiAngelo, 2018). Regardless of race or ethnicity, we are all imbued in whiteness by nature of its prevalence in *all* the social institutions where we work and live; there are no exceptions. To what degree we enact whiteness is likely a result of our cultural experiences and socialization into (anti)racism.

We use the notion of consciousness to represent the level of awareness and mindfulness of others' lived experiences, perspective and realities. Furthermore, consciousness indicates a willingness to locate oneself within racist structures and institutions (Ullucci & Battey, 2011). Gutiérrez (2013) argues urban mathematics teachers need political knowledge to:

> (a) negotiate their practice with colleagues, students, parents, administrators, colleges, and members of for-profit organizations who may not agree with their definitions of "mathematics," "education," or "learning"; (b) work with fewer material and human resources than teachers in more wealthy school districts; (c) support their students to compete on an unfair playing field that constantly changes; and (d) buffer themselves from images of students as unmotivated, not having the proper amount of "grit," lacking role models in their community, and having cultural and linguistic obstacles to overcome, as well as images of urban teachers as slackers, saviors, or people who simply could not obtain work elsewhere. (pp. 7–8)

In this study, the concepts of whiteness and consciousness are applied directly to the teaching and learning of mathematics (e.g., Battey & Leyva, 2016). The myth of political neutrality in mathematics continues to stigmatize mathematics teaching and learning (Martin, 2015). Educators who believe and teach the ideology that mathematics is *just* numbers have yet to fully analyze and critically appraise the ways that statistics and other measurements that feign political neutrality have been used to "prove" learning deficiencies among students of color and the academic achievement gap between them and their White mainstream peers. Without incorporating culturally relevant pedagogical practices into mathematics teaching (and mathematics teacher education), teachers will continue to deliver a one-size-for-all curriculum that fails to connect with a large percentage of students, namely urban students of color. The students who are successful under the traditional methodology of teaching mathematics risk being indoctrinated into believing that only certain people are good at math, further perpetuating the negative reputation attached to mathematics teaching and learning. Furthermore, acknowledging and combatting whiteness contributes to dismantling the myth that mathematics/mathematics education is politically and culturally neutral, which is an effort that can help facilitate equitable school experiences for P-12 learners.

8.2 Methods

Self-study methodology afforded us the opportunity to scrutinize our teaching practices and experiences in light of our broader goals (Kitchen, 2020; Pinnegar et al., 2020). In the following section, we share our teacher education context, our methodological approach to self-study, and our data sources and analysis.

8.2.1 Context

The setting for this inquiry is the four-year undergraduate elementary education program located in the midwestern United States in a large, urban area. The program is focused on preparing teachers for city schools. It is conceptually anchored and informed by a shared commitment to helping PTs develop anti-racist, culturally relevant pedagogies. When PTs are admitted into the program, they are assigned to a cohort, and the cohort is assigned to a partnership school. Normally, nearly all courses are taught in a designated K-6 classroom at the partnership school. The program employs a clinically-centered model of teacher education (e.g., Dennis et al., 2017), and field experiences are integrated with each course. For example, the mathematics method course meets on Wednesdays from 9:00 AM–12:00 PM for 16 weeks. During eight to ten of those class sessions, PTs can expect to plan and implement lessons with actual elementary students. Debriefing these field experiences and making explicit connections to course content/readings is a common practice for our PTs.

This study drew from two university courses we taught during the 2020–2021 school year amid the COVID-19 pandemic. Therefore, all courses had synchronous online virtual class meetings. There were thirteen 90-min class meetings. The first two courses, which occurred in the fall 2020 semester, examined methods for teaching mathematics in the early elementary grades (kindergarten through second grade). This introduction to the teaching profession challenged PTs' beliefs and assumptions about teaching and learning while providing exposure to critical sociocultural learning theory and its use in the process of inquiry. The second course focused on third through sixth grades and was in the spring 2021 semester. This course emphasized the developmental nature of the arithmetic process, how this leads to algebraic reasoning, and how both of these connect to the cultural and mathematical experiences of elementary school children. In planning for these courses, we referenced the Association of Mathematics Teacher Educators (AMTE) *Standards for Preparing Teachers of Mathematics* (2017). The standards allowed us to develop tasks, activities, and a variety of means to assess our students' understanding of the material covered in each course.

Throughout the preparation for our classes, we focused on improving the effectiveness of PTs' mathematical instructional practices and decision making. This began with developing their understanding of key concepts (e.g., students' mathematical thinking, community funds of knowledge) to encourage a positive orientation to learning and teaching mathematics. We also sought to include opportunities to critically reflect upon and develop PTs' consciousness of their own former experiences as students in P-12 mathematics classes. Additionally, as teacher educators, we planned for, developed, and supported learning experiences for our PTs that emphasized the need for equitable teaching practices and methods to support the success of all students.

Reflecting on our experiences, we recognized that PTs who commence their work with an orientation towards equitable mathematics education (as evidenced in their lessons and instructional practices), compared to those that do not, experience greater satisfaction in their field experiences. It is during this stage of development that PTs begin to draw connections between the pedagogical practices they were exposed to as P-12 students and their current work. We have observed that our PTs are also reckoning with their former P-12 mathematics learning experiences that had a heavy emphasis on memorization of facts and procedures rather than the development of a deep understanding of number sense and how to problem solve. It is during the teacher preparation period that PTs learn that reasoning skills are just as important as memorization. As PTs learn how to employ research-based practices and methods, they are also working through years of stress and anxiety as they transition towards becoming mathematics educators (Young & Dyess, 2021). We aim to implement encouraging learning environments so that our PTs are able to study math pedagogies through a different, more critical lens while recognizing the root causes of their anxieties towards mathematics.

8.2.2 Self-Study Methodology

The use of self-study research methodology focuses on self-understanding and the enhancement of professional practice based on the analysis of one's professional experiences (LaBoskey, 2004). We concur with Samara's (2011) definition of self-study of practice methodology as, "a personal, systematic inquiry situated within one's own teaching context that requires critical and collaborative reflection in order to generate knowledge, as well as inform the broader educational field" (p. 10). In particular, we focused on the tenuous moments engaging PTs (A. Martin, 2020), vis-à-vis our expressed pedagogical goals, in order to more fully take up efficacious teaching methods with our prospective mathematics teachers.

8.2.2.1 Self-Study Team

Dr. Natalie Odom Pough is a mathematics teacher educator. She is a Black female who holds the position of Visiting Clinical Assistant Professor. Her primary role is to teach mathematics methods courses to undergraduate students majoring in elementary education. Pough taught middle school mathematics and social studies for 8 years. She served as a former school administrator and former lecturer prior to her current position. Pough is passionate about instilling the joy and excitement she feels about mathematics teaching and learning into every PT she serves.

Dr. Craig Willey is a mathematics teacher educator. He is a White male with more than 10 years of experience in urban teacher preparation, primarily teaching mathematics methods for prospective elementary teachers. Prior to his current roles as Associate Professor and department chair, Willey was a bilingual middle school mathematics teacher in Denver Public Schools and a research fellow with the Center for Mathematics Education of Latinas/os (CEMELA) in Chicago. He believes

(White) teachers and teacher educators have a responsibility to examine their beliefs and practices in an effort to confront systemic racism.

8.2.3   Data Sources and Analysis

We drew on both historical and contemporary data in this self-study. For example, we analyzed journal entries from Pough's time as a teacher, including entries from her first year of teaching. We also both wrote extensive autobiographies describing the events and narratives that shaped our decisions and perspectives as teachers and mathematics teacher educators in urban contexts. In an effort to further contextualize our work as mathematics teachers educators, we wrote narratives centered on the aims and goals for our mathematics methods courses, as well as explanations for why equity in mathematics education is so hard to achieve. Finally, to hone in on the experiences of PTs and better understand the shifts (or lack of) towards re-conceptualizing mathematics for urban youth, we documented our in-class and out-of-class assignments and activities in our methods courses, assessing the intent and the degree to which these assignments and activities made explicit connections to children's multiple mathematics knowledge bases (e.g., community, familial, cultural, linguistic) (Turner et al., 2019).

We examined and coded the data individually. We then conferred weekly to share our respective codes, discuss, and reach consensus on our understandings of the most salient codes. These discussions and consensus building involved highlighting specific examples/experiences and grounding these experiences within the concepts of whiteness and consciousness. We were also guided by Anfara et al.'s (2002) process to ensure that the data sources directly evidenced and addressed our research aims through iterative coding.

The close, professional proximity between us provided plentiful opportunities for candor and vulnerability when discussing our PTs' learning goals, successes, and failures. The themes presented below reveal how we frame course content and learning experiences to make clear to PTs that issues of equity and justice are central to developing math teaching practices designed to augment success for children of color; they also highlight the tensions that surfaced as a result of a teacher education program focused on equity and justice.

8.3   Findings

Our findings center on our experiences confronting PTs' existing perspectives and ideologies in order for them to provide more equitable mathematics learning experience for children, particularly urban youth of color. We share our experiences and sentiments through the lens of resilience (Lam, 2015), where we persist despite the complexity of the issues at hand and the deeply embedded belief systems of PTs. As alluded to earlier, PTs' beliefs and conventional wisdom are the products of decades of socialization towards what counts as good mathematics teaching. Further, they are often the recipients of deficit-laden narratives about urban youth and communities. Our findings reveal how we as MTEs persist to recast mathematics ideologies, as well as confront and combat oppressive racial ideologies. We have embedded our analysis in the reporting of the findings, which are presented in the form of composite descriptions of recurring events and discussions from our courses.

8.3.1   Resilience in the Face of PTs' Mathematics Ideologies

One of our goals is to support PTs to interrogate taken-for-granted approaches to mathematics teaching and learning that are often deemed effective. In this way, they can develop consciousness about equitable mathematics teaching and the role of whiteness in status quo approaches to mathematics instruction. For example, we have had multiple, lengthy discussions centered on the use of timed tests, as the merits of timed tests appear frequently in PTs' journal entries. It spotlights PTs' affinity for competition and repetitive practice in the mathematics classroom with little regard to the research that details how timed tests build anxiety towards mathematics. The negative consequences of such approaches are harmful to all students, but especially students of color, who often do not possess the cultural and financial capital to perform well academically in such a context. PTs themselves have detailed their own negative experiences with mathematics instruction in their former schooling years. For many, this highlighted a personal disdain for the content area. We believe that there is a prime opportunity in teacher education to make connections between conventional mathematics teaching practices and negative sentiments towards mathematics. Nonetheless, it has proven difficult to help PTs expand their consciousness about what could be productive, effective, and equitable mathematics pedagogy.

Still, there were glimmers of hope in what new mathematics instructional practices PTs took up. For example, a common theme throughout out-of-class assignment data was the use of games in mathematics classrooms. The feelings highlighted in PTs' assignment reflections, however, had more to do with how they felt while playing the games in class. PTs provided positive recollections of these games when they considered themselves successful, a shift in their own consciousness on how they could approach mathematics instruction as future teachers. However, if they felt embarrassed and/or anxious during a game, as a winner or otherwise, there was a negative connection towards mathematics.

There was also a connection between PTs' beliefs about mathematics and how they critically reflected on their beliefs. We worked to build upon these connections throughout our methods courses. The tasks we presented during these courses encouraged students to recognize the advantages of games and the need to pair them with equitable instructional practices. We believe this experience can increase the chances of PTs designing lessons that fully benefit students during instruction and review sessions. Our goal was for PTs to be able to internalize the value of games for learners who have been marginalized by traditional mathematics instructional structures and maximize the effectiveness of these instructional strategies.

Furthermore, when asked to discuss their personal history with mathematics, our PTs often wrote about specific activities they were exposed to. Seldom was there a discussion over a specific mathematical concept or routine the PTs were particularly fond of or successful with. Stand-alone celebrations or games, such as Pi Day, Around the World, and cooking activities, were common responses describing their most positive experiences. The only mention of mathematical concepts throughout class discussions and assignment reflections surfaced when discussing third grade. There was a consensus amongst PTs surrounding the stress of third grade mathematics which typically involved fractions, multiplication facts, and timed tests. We recognized that these instances (presented as scattered memories) suggest our PTs were coming in with minimal understandings or minimally consciousness of culturally relevant pedagogical practices that could be adopted to make such content meaningful to all students. Such practices could be used to co-construct an ambitious mathematics pedagogy (e.g., Lampert et al., 2013) that aims to include and engage diverse learners than have historically been under-served. Ironically, however, the above-mentioned negative sentiments, combined with some entrenched, default practices (e.g., timed test, repetitive practice over rich problem-solving activities) have shown to be inhibiting in the development of new pedagogical approaches.

We acknowledge that this is an ongoing project to contribute—through pre-service teacher education—to shifts in mathematics pedagogy. We believe our self-study has helped us build not only resilience, but also motivated us to re-think and re-shape the experiences we provide PTs. PTs need more than to be told how to do something and why it is important; they need to feel worthwhile themselves as math students and future teachers of mathematics, possess an understanding of and consciousness about the role of whiteness in the education of diverse children, and believe that they can make a difference in the education of urban youth.

As MTEs, we discovered the need to investigate the common activities discussed by our PTs and explore what makes them popular. The use of these activities, such as Pi Day and Around the World, were common practices across the numerous school districts represented in our classes. As we discussed these with each other, we began to investigate widely used channels of mathematics teaching professional development. Subsequently, we had discussions with classroom teachers and determined that many of the practices used in their classroom are activities that they themselves engaged in when they were students. As we analyzed our methods courses and sought to more fully promote our students' consciousness, we integrated activities, projects, and assignments that were challenging but also engaging, and even entertaining. We learned that offering a detailed purpose and rationale to the assignment enabled our students to see why the activity was engaging to them and to learn ways to integrate the assignment into their own pedagogical index. Throughout this process, we also recognize the impact of social media and websites such as teacherspayteachers.com, on our students' approach towards understanding and teaching mathematics. Although many of these digital resources lack the critical lens (e.g., fails to take up whiteness and consciousness) that we stress in our classes, we cannot ignore the significant reach that these educators have. As MTEs, we must be aware of this shaping influence on our PTs.

8.3.2   Resilience in the Face of PTs' Racial Ideologies

As professors of undergraduate and graduate PTs working towards initial licensure as elementary education teachers, it is commonplace that they bring their unchecked biases into the learning environment, whether our own classrooms or in their clinical practice. When watching a YouTube video of a fifth grade class of White and Asian students in Canada, one PT stated, "I can't even do that! They're really smart." As discussed in Pough's journal entry about that class session, the student highlighted how the teacher scaffolded the discussion about numbers and prepared the students for the activity. Yet, while watching a video from the textbook, *Making Sense of Mathematics for Teaching Grades 3–5* (Dixon and Nolan, 2016), of a classroom of Black and Latinx students successfully navigating a rigorous word problem in a model similar to the one in the YouTube video, the same student exclaimed, "These have to be paid actors!" and further noted this comment in her own field journal. As we discussed this situation, we realized that all biases do not surface as readily as this one, but we recognized that they exist as part of the racial narratives that dominate throughout the U.S. and permeate mathematics classrooms (Shah, 2017). Pough highlighted these two comments and brought them to the student's attention within the evaluation feedback to her journal grade. We recognized such an instance as an opportunity to elevate students' consciousness about race, whiteness, and the learning experiences of diverse students and teachers' responsibilities to support and affirm all children.

Whiteness and biases often interfere with PTs' ability to imagine and enact high academic expectations for urban youth—and youth of color in particular—in the mathematics classroom. When we hear PTs questioning what kind of mathematics pedagogy is possible in urban classrooms, this signals a set of lower expectations for children of color, and we interpret these lower expectations as both whiteness and a way to mask educators' struggles with mathematics content. What emerges as whiteness is the struggle to reconcile the race-based, differentiated images of math teaching and learning: robust cognitive capacity and problem-solving skills for White children, and memorization and skill-based learning for children of color. With respect to their own insecure math content knowledge, PTs appear to be stuck in a cyclical dilemma: they fear their weaknesses in mathematics being exposed and subsequently find themselves relying heavily on textbooks and workbooks that hold extraordinarily little rigor and rely heavily on rote memorization. We recognized this in PTs' reflections after they worked with students one-on-one during field experiences. The expressed need to have resources, exemplars, or textbooks to develop their activities and lessons became a source of concern for us. Feelings about mathematics and mathematical ideologies compound racial/ethnic biases, and vice versa, and this combination contributes to racialized mathematics teaching and learning experiences (Battey & Leyva, 2016; Gholson & Martin, 2019).

Additionally, we realized that many of our PTs focused on incorporating classroom management protocols into their lesson rather than on the mathematical concepts we presented in our courses. It was evident that some PTs were more concerned with the behavior of students as opposed to the assessment of what their students should have learned. For example, in one lesson plan, a PT wrote about how the students should behave in class during her lesson and very little about the instruction or how she would engage her students. In the feedback provided to the PT, it was suggested that she modify the activity to more fully support student participation and engagement rather than focusing on behavior or punishment for off-task behavior. We believe that such a focus and attention to student behavior rather than learning highlights that this PT was grappling with dominant racial narratives and the need for us as MTEs to focus our energy towards conceptualizing an ambitious mathematics pedagogy for urban youth.

Our self-study has helped us appreciate the importance of discussions about race and racial ideology in mathematics education. The omission of such discussions can lead to an underdeveloped understanding of the relationships among student-teacher relationships, socio-economical and sociopolitical dimensions of schooling, and community activism. It leaves mathematics excluded when other content areas might be subjected to examinations as to how they are implicated in racist systems and structures.

However, when mathematics educators take the time to place mathematics within the day-to-day discussions that impact society, a stronger emphasis is placed on the importance of mathematics. Some may believe these are discussions for the secondary mathematics classroom and beyond, but a PT's understanding of equitable mathematics teaching is directly connected to how well they can understand and incorporate culturally relevant pedagogy (Ladson-Billings, 1995; Magee et al., 2020) into their instructional practices. We acknowledge that there are layers to PTs' ability to name and enact culturally relevant math teaching practices (Magee & Willey, 2021). Sustained and interconnected discussions are needed to help make explicit connections among our beliefs about mathematics, our experiences with mathematics, racial narratives, whiteness, and our pedagogical tendencies. The lack of discussions on race leave PTs uncomfortable when discussing the implications of racism in education. Teacher education programs are ideal places for PTs to explore race, social change and social justice, and engage with and take up knowledge of unfamiliar ideas and concepts to build profound understandings of mathematics.

As we analyzed our experiences in this inquiry, we came to terms that our desire for change often conflicted with the lessons and ideas that have been ingrained into our PTs since their youth. There are PTs who engage with students with "genuine intentions of making each of them better regardless of how many adjustments or accommodations need to be made" (Barksdale, 2021, p. x). These are the individuals who will possess consciousness about whiteness, see the components of culturally relevant pedagogy, and actively work to improve their teaching practices and expand their pedagogy. There are also individuals who have or will succumb to the "pressures of bureaucratic expectation and overzealous perceptions" (Barksdale, 2021, p. x) and allow their instruction to be dictated by standards and other procedures rather than guided by their students' needs. Lastly, there are educators who, "cannot be influenced or changed about how they choose to teach, interact with, and interpret the success of students" (Barksdale, 2021, p. xi). These are the individuals who choose to not connect with the needs and backgrounds of every child. In discussions during class, these are the students who usually use their own success as a benchmark for the success of others from similar backgrounds. They are not willing to connect with or understand whiteness or culturally relevant pedagogy and thus further the cycle of ill-prepared mathematics educators.

This self-study exposed us to the purpose behind our work. We must develop the tools we need to further improve on our pedagogical approach and continue to study how mathematics teachers are working to facilitate desired change. We collaborated to design courses and tasks that challenged our students and pushed them outside of their comfort zones. We, as mathematics teacher educators, have learned how to work through uncomfortableness in our classroom environments when we push our students in directions they are not familiar with. We have found comfort in leaning on one another for guidance and support. During our collaborative sessions, we have discovered ways to create a safe and productive learning environments. We have also designed techniques to restore and repair our learning environment when PTs disconnect with us or one another. As we continue to grow, we will modify our approaches so that students are leaving our programs with a solid approach towards their first year of teaching that includes the ability to constantly strengthen their critical lens.

8.4 Discussion

We acknowledge the complexity of teaching mathematics in urban spaces. This complexity translates into a similar complexity when identifying the needs of our PTs and designing mathematics methods courses. We have mentioned the need to provide mathematics learning experiences for PTs (e.g., problem solving or teaching problem solving to peers) so they can develop confidence in mathematical reasoning. We have also needed to scrutinize underlying beliefs about mathematics (e.g., some people are math people) and urban youth (e.g., their families don't care about education). When examining the most crucial, high impact domains of mathematics teaching and learning (e.g., content knowledge or facilitating discursive classrooms), we have found ourselves gravitating towards shifting PTs' attitudes towards mathematics as a critical starting point. This is a priority area for us in an effort to broaden perspectives on the teaching and learning of mathematics for urban youth.

With an understanding that our PTs are products of "the same school system and societal treatment of math" (Zager, 2017, p. 3) which we are asking them to critically analyze and change, it is imperative that we take the time to study the variations of mathematics teaching PTs have been exposed to. Similarly, it is essential for MTEs to take a step back and study how they are working to facilitate the desired changes. The use of visual representations, for example, via video lessons or in-class demonstration lessons of instructional strategies being taught, strengthens the chances of PTs feeling comfortable with employing these strategies in the future.

Teaching PTs about the intention, rationale, and focus of a lesson in alignment with fully including all students but especially urban children of color can serve to cultivate joy in the teaching and learning of mathematics.

8.5 Implications and Conclusions

Careful examinations of program/course goals, PTs' backgrounds and experiences, and MTEs' curriculum and instruction are crucial if we are to continue to develop an elementary mathematics education program that supports anti-racist, culturally relevant teachers. This self-study has made us more resolute to engage our elementary mathematics education team of professors and instructors in ongoing dialogue and professional development about mathematics and racial ideologies as priority areas for the design of mathematics learning experiences for PTs. This and subsequent models of interrogation serve as the basis for further growth, which is essential as our mathematics education instructional staff expands and changes (Baker & Bitto, 2021; Marin, 2014). Furthermore, the analysis of course assignments vis a vis PTs' learning products will offer direction and focus for our future work and collaborations.

This self-study also supports our continued efforts to fortify our partnerships between school districts, community leaders, and businesses throughout the city. Understanding how our work is directly connected to the strength and health of the community, we will continue our research efforts to provide our current and future PTs with the space to grow, flourish, and connect with mathematics at high levels and equitable teaching practices for urban students. This self-study offers an exploration of urban math teacher preparation. We analyzed our practices and the outcomes of our assignments in order to understand how our instruction was received by PTs, and how this related to the development of their mathematics teaching practices. We highlighted the ways in which PTs' beliefs and ideas are reflected in our courses, and what this suggests for teaching urban youth. It was our intent to explore the critical consciousness of our students, and we were able to create a snapshot of how our students were constructing an understanding of equitable mathematics instructional practices. Additionally, we were able to recognize and challenge mathematics ideologies that can exclude math learners by naming and confronting dominant conceptualizations of what it means to be "good at math", and share images of inclusive mathematics learning environments.

The findings reveal that our practices, strategies, and approaches are aimed at providing transformative educational experiences for our PTs. While we attempt to model the instructional practices that we would expect from our PTs, future research is needed (Bell et al., 2021). We would like to expand our work to include further analysis of the success of our PTs as they began their careers, and trace the ways in which their work, dispositions towards mathematics, and the success of their students might be influenced by our practices. Of course, there is always the need to be candid when assessing the ways in which equitable practices are not developing among novice teachers. Here lies an opportunity for future self-study research: it affords mathematics teacher educators the opportunity to do better (i.e., improve their practices), which allows PTs to deepen the knowledge and skills that are designed to transform (mathematics) learning experiences for urban youth. Working with self-study to explore the relationship between MTEs' and PTs' practices and the development of their respective professional mathematics identities is a promising mechanism that supports MTEs' insight of teacher development from multiple angles (Baker & Bitto, 2021). Ultimately, we argue that MTEs should take up self-study research of their pedagogical practices which, in turn, can support PTs in their preparation to becoming equitable and just urban mathematics teachers.

References

Anfara, V. A., Jr., Brown, K. M., & Mangione, T. L. (2002). Qualitative analysis on stage: Making the research process more public. *Educational Researcher, 31*(7), 28–38. https://doi.org/10.310 2/2F0013189X031007028

Association of Mathematics Teacher Educators. (2017). *Standards for preparing teachers of mathematics*. amte.net/standards.

Baker, C. K., & Bitto, L. E. (2021). Interrogating the tensions of becoming antiracist mathematics teacher educators via critical friendship and rehearsals. *Studying Teacher Education*, 1–18. https://doi.org/10.1080/17425964.2021.1997737

Barksdale, T. J. (2021). *First things first: Putting students before standards* (pp. x–xi). Hadassah's Crown Publishing.

Battey, D., & Leyva, L. A. (2016). A framework for understanding whiteness in mathematics education. *Journal of Urban Mathematics Education, 9*(2), 49–80. https://doi.org/10.21423/jume-v9i2a294

Bell, T., Lolkus, M., Newton, J., & Willey, C. (2021). Exploring power and oppression: An examination of mathematics teacher educators' professional growth. *Mathematics Teacher Educator, 9*(3), 184–201. https://doi.org/10.5951/MTE.2020.0036

Billett, S. (2006). Relational interdependence between social and individual agency in work and working life. *Mind, Culture, and Activity, 13*(1), 53–69. https://doi.org/10.1207/s15327884mca1301_5

Chang, A., Rak Neugebauer, S., Ellis, A., Ensminger, D., Marie Ryan, A., & Kennedy, A. (2016). Teacher educator identity in a culture of iterative teacher education program design: A collaborative self-study. *Studying Teacher Education, 12*(2), 152–169. https://doi.org/10.108 0/17425964.2016.1192030

Clandinin, D. J., & Connelly, M. (2004). Knowledge, narrative and self-study. In J. J. Loughran, M. L. Hamilton, V. K. LaBoskey, & T. Russell (Eds.), *International handbook of self-study of teaching and teacher education practices* (pp. 575–600). Springer.

Dennis, D. V., Burns, R. W., Tricarico, K., van Ingen, S., Jacobs, J., & Davis, J. (2017). Problematizing clinical education. In R. Flessner & D. R. Lecklider (Eds.), *The power of clinical preparation in teacher education* (pp. 1–20). Rowman & Littlefield Publishers.

DiAngelo, R. (2018). *White fragility: Why it's so hard for white people to talk about racism.* Beacon Press.

Dixon, J. K., & Nolan, E. C. (2016). *Making sense of mathematics for teaching: Grades 3–5.* Solution Tree Press.

Foote, M. Q., McDuffie, A. R., Turner, E. E., Aguirre, J. M., Bartell, T. G., & Drake, C. (2013). Orientations of prospective teachers toward students' family and community. *Teaching and Teacher Education, 35*, 126–136. https://doi.org/10.1016/j.tate.2013.06.003

Frankenberg, R. (1993). *White women, race matters: The social construction of Whiteness.* University of Minnesota Press.

Gholson, M. L., & Martin, D. B. (2019). Blackgirl face: Racialized and gendered performativity in mathematical contexts. *ZDM, 51*(3), 391–404. https://doi.org/10.1007/s11858-019-01051-x

Griffiths, M., & Poursanidou, D. (2005). A self-study of factors affecting success in two collaborations on the teaching of social justice. *Studying Teacher Education, 1*(2), 141–158. https://doi.org/10.1080/17425960500288317

Gutiérrez, R. (2013). Why (urban) mathematics teachers need political knowledge. *Journal of Urban Mathematics Education, 6*(2), 7–19. https://doi.org/10.21423/jume-v6i2a223

Hayes, C., & Hartlep, N. D. (Eds.). (2013). *Unhooking from whiteness: The key to dismantling racism in the United States.* Springer Science & Business Media.

Kitchen, J. (2020). Self-study in teacher education and beyond. In J. Kitchen, M. Berry, S. M. Bullock, A. R. Crowe, M. Taylor, H. Guojonsdottir, & L. Thomas (Eds.), *International handbook of self-study of teaching and teacher education practices* (2nd ed., pp. 1023–1044). Springer.

LaBoskey, V. K. (2004). The methodology of self-study and its theoretical underpinnings. In J. J. Loughran, M. L. Hamilton, V. K. LaBoskey, & T. Russell (Eds.), *International handbook of self-study of teaching and teacher education practices* (pp. 817–869). Springer.

Ladson-Billings, G. (1995). But that's just good teaching! The case for culturally relevant pedagogy. *Theory Into Practice, 34*(3), 159–165. https://doi.org/10.1080/00405849509543675

Lam, K. D. (2015). Teaching for liberation: Critical reflections in teacher education. *Multicultural Perspectives, 17*(3), 157–162.

Lampert, M., Franke, M. L., Kazemi, E., Ghousseini, H., Turrou, A. C., Beasley, H., et al. (2013). Keeping it complex: Using rehearsals to support novice teacher learning of ambitious teaching. *Journal of Teacher Education, 64*(3), 226–243. https://doi.org/10.1177/2F0022487112473837

Magee, P. A. & Willey, C. (2021). Iceberg of culturally relevant science and mathematics pedagogy: A pedagogical and analytical tool for teacher education. Unpublished Manuscript

Magee, P. A., Willey, C., Ceran, E., Price, J., & Cervantes, J. B. (2020). The affordances and challenges of enacting culturally relevant STEM pedagogy. In C. C. Johnson, M. J. Mohr-Schroeder, T. J. Moore, & L. D. English (Eds.), *Handbook of research on STEM education* (pp. 300–310). Routledge.

Marin, K. A. (2014). Becoming a teacher educator: A self-study of the use of inquiry in a mathematics methods course. *Studying Teacher Education, 10*(1), 20–35. https://doi.org/10.1080/17425964.2013.873976

Martin, D. B. (2015). The collective black and principles to actions. *Journal of Urban Mathematics Education, 8*(1).

Martin, A. D. (2020). Tensions and caring in teacher education: A self-study on teaching in difficult moments. *Studying Teacher Education, 16*(3), 306–323. https://doi.org/10.1080/17425964.2020.1783527

Matias, C. E. (2016). *Feeling white: Whiteness, emotionality, and education.* Brill.

Milner, H. R., IV. (2008). Disrupting deficit notions of difference: Counter-narratives of teachers and community in urban education. *Teaching and Teacher Education, 24*(6), 1573–1598. https://doi.org/10.1016/j.tate.2008.02.011

Oda, L. K. (1998). Harmony, conflict and respect: An Asian-American educator's self-study. In *Reconceptualizing teaching practice: Self-study in teacher education* (pp. 113–123). Falmer Press.

Pinnegar, S., Hutchinson, D. A., & Hamilton, M. L. (2020). Role of positioning, identity, and stance in becoming S-STTEP researchers. In J. Kitchen, M. Berry, S. M. Bullock, A. R. Crowe, M. Taylor, H. Guojonsdottir, & L. Thomas (Eds.), *International handbook of self-study of teaching and teacher education practices* (2nd ed., pp. 299–338). Springer.

Samaras, A. P. (2011). *Self-study teacher research: Improving your practice through collaborative inquiry*. Sage.

Shah, N. (2017). Race, ideology, and academic ability: A relational analysis of racial narratives in mathematics. *Teachers College Record, 119*(7), 1–42.

Turner, E. E., Foote, M. Q., Stoehr, K. J., McDuffie, A. R., Aguirre, J. M., Bartell, T. G., & Drake, C. (2016). Learning to leverage children's multiple mathematical knowledge bases in mathematics instruction. *Journal of Urban Mathematics Education, 9*(1), 48–78. https://doi.org/10.21423/jume-v9i1a279

Turner, E., Bartell, T. G., Drake, C., Foote, M., McDuffie, A. R., & Aguirre, J. (2019). Prospective teachers learning to connect to multiple mathematical knowledge bases across multiple contexts. In K. Beswick & O. Chapman (Eds.), *International handbook of mathematics teacher education* (pp. 289–320). Brill Sense.

Ullucci, K., & Battey, D. (2011). Exposing color blindness/grounding color consciousness: Challenges for teacher education. *Urban Education, 46*(6), 1195–1225. https://doi.org/10.117 7/2F0042085911413150

Young, E. S., & Dyess, S. R. (2021). Supporting prospective teachers in problem solving: Incorporating mindset messaging to overcome math anxiety. *Mathematics Teacher Educator, 10*(1), 9–28. https://doi.org/10.5951/MTE.2020-0047

Zager, T. (2017). *Becoming the math teacher you wish you'd had: Ideas and strategies from vibrant classrooms*. Hawker Brownlow Education.

Natalie Odom Pough, Ed.D., is the sixth and seventh-grade mathematics teacher at the Ron Clark Academy in Atlanta, Georgia and an adjunct professor. With over 15 years of experience in public schools and higher education, Dr. Pough has served as a middle school math and social studies teacher, assistant principal, college lecturer, and visiting clinical assistant professor. Dr. Pough's research focuses on equitable mathematics instructional practices, preservice and in-service teacher preparation, and new teacher attrition. Dr. Pough was named an ASCD Emerging Leader in 2018. In 2019, she was appointed to the Teaching Tolerance Advisory Board.

Craig Willey, Ph.D., is an Associate Professor of Mathematics Education and Teacher Education at Indiana University-Purdue University Indianapolis, as well as the department chair of Urban Teacher Education. His research focuses on (1) teachers' design and implementation of mathematics discourse communities with urban students, primarily Latinas/os; (2) the ways teachers mine and leverage children's community and cultural knowledge to make sense of math; (3) the development and incorporation of curricular features that provide bilingual learners better access to mathematical ideas and opportunities to engage meaningfully; and (4) the limitations and affordances of a school-university partnership model of urban teacher development. Dr. Willey is the PI on the NSF-funded project, *Teacher Collaborative for Culturally Relevant Mathematics and Science Curriculum (CR-MASC)* and Associate Editor for the *Journal of Educational Supervision*.

Part IV
Rethinking the Boundaries of Online, Rural, and Urban Teacher Education

Chapter 9
Reimagining My Self-in-Practice: Relational Teacher Education in a Remote Setting

Brie Morettini

Abstract In this chapter the author aims to better understand her self-in-practice as a relational teacher educator who takes up social justice, in part, through modeling humanizing pedagogies. Specifically, she examined her pedagogical practices to see how these might reimagine her identity as a relational teacher educator when teaching remotely. To do this, she conducted a self-study and analyzed the data set through the dimensions of relational teacher education with a nod to extant self-studies. The findings are within the dimensions of relational teacher education. In this way, the self-study to explores her practice in times of radical change. By analyzing the data through the dimensions of relational teacher education, the saw how teaching remotely actually enhanced the scope of her role and the intentionality of her efforts to relate to students. In particular, there were instances when she took on the role of caregiver for students, transcending the role of teacher educator, and providing support for preservice teachers even beyond the purview of the course. In sum, this inquiry prompted a reimagining of previously-held manifestations of relational teacher education. Findings from this study extend the conversations about humanizing, person-centered pedagogies in remote teaching and learning environments.

Keywords Relational teacher education · Self-in-practice · Humanizing pedagogies · Remote teaching

In the last several years, the term "social justice" has appeared frequently in the lexicon of educational research and has come to represent a larger pantheon of ideas related to advocating for the rights of marginalized people and working against systemic oppression. I take up social justice in teacher education by designing and

B. Morettini (✉)
Rowan University, Glassboro, NJ, USA
e-mail: morettini@rowan.edu

A. D. Martin (ed.), *Self-Studies in Urban Teacher Education*, Self-Study of
Teaching and Teacher Education Practices 25,
https://doi.org/10.1007/978-981-19-5430-6_9

teaching courses that acknowledge, examine, and scrutinize the powers and privileges that extend from differences in groups' and individual's racial, cultural, linguistic, gendered, socio-economic, and neurodiverse identities in our social institutions and settings. In this way, a major goal of my work as a social justice-oriented teacher educator is to prepare prospective teachers to create more equitable classroom practices through my own modeling of humanizing, person-centered pedagogies.

Such pedagogies include learning experiences that critically address equity issues both through classroom instruction and also through prospective teachers' emerging professional identities (Martin, 2018a). The relational nature of my pedagogy has always been *a way in* to building more equitable and socially just learning experiences for prospective teachers. How I relate to prospective teachers, how I scaffold classroom conversations through critical questions, how I model active listening and thoughtful responses *in the classroom* are some examples of how I use relational teacher education to foster equitable learning environments. In this way, I take up the notion of a relational teacher educator (Kitchen, 2002, 2005a, 2005b). Relational teacher education is the heart of my commitment to social justice; and, as an S-STTEP (self-study of teaching and teacher education practices) researcher, I turned to self-study to navigate changing and trying times.

In the fall of 2020, given the COVID-19 pandemic and with a pivot to remote teaching from traditional in-person teaching, I felt suddenly unmoored—how would I transfer my relational pedagogy to an online platform? How would I design equitable learning experiences without physically being with students[1]? I realized I needed to operationalize this as a self-study in order to learn and grow as a relational teacher educator.

The following questions guided my study:

- How does teaching remotely shape my identity as a relational teacher educator?
- What can I learn about my own relational practice by teaching remotely?
- How does teaching remotely influence the ways I convey respect and empathy for my students?

9.1 Conceptual Framework

I drew on relational teacher education (Kitchen, 2002, 2005a, 2005b) to theoretically frame the study. As a teacher-researcher with a commitment to criticality in my own practice, I acknowledge the power and privilege I carry with me into my work as a

---

[1] I use the terms prospective teachers, preservice teachers, and students interchangeable so as to avoid repetition.

teacher educator. Reflection on my practice allows me to critique the power and privileges I have as a teacher educator and the ways I leverage my role to model more equitable and humanizing learning environments for prospective teachers.

Specifically, I employed the dimensions of relational teacher education (Kitchen, 2002, 2005a, 2005b) to make sense of my changing identity as a relational teacher educator in a remote setting. To do this I analyzed my data sources through the dimensions of relational teacher education. Like others (e.g. Trout, 2018), I situated the findings within these dimensions to explore relational teacher education in a remote setting. In this way, self-study was ideally suited to explore my teaching practice during this exceptional time of radical change (Berry & Kitchen, 2020).

9.1.1 Relational Teacher Education

Relational teacher education captures how I have built my identity and understand myself as a teacher educator committed to social justice. Kitchen (2002) developed the framework of relational teacher education to encompass an approach to working with preservice teachers grounded in conveying respect and building relationships. He developed this based on the perspective that we live and know in relation to others (2005a, 2005b). Relational teacher education comprises seven dimensions as defined in Table 9.1.

Relational teacher education resonates with me because it aptly describes my approach to working with prospective teachers, and yet a great deal of my relationship building with students has been achieved informally during the moments before or after class sessions, in the hallways, or through running into students

Table 9.1 Dimensions of relational teacher education

Dimension	Definition
Understanding one's own personal practical knowledge	Drawing on past experiences to inform one's practice
Improving one's practice in teacher education	Enriching one's knowledge and skills through ongoing reflection and inquiry
Understanding the landscape of teacher education	Framing individual's challenges as extensions of larger institutional and societal challenges
Respecting and empathizing with preservice teachers	Recognizing that preservice teachers face difficulties when confronted with the realities and complexities of teaching
Conveying respect and empathy	Demonstrating consistent respect and empathy to preservice teachers
Helping preservice teachers face problems	Supporting preservice teachers as they reconcile tensions in personal and professional issues
Receptivity to growing in relationship	Being open to co-learning with preservice teachers

Adapted from Kitchen (2002, 2005a, 2005b)

on campus. My self-study is, therefore, situated at the tension (Berry, 2008) between creating authentic connections with prospective teachers and engaging with them remotely.

9.2 Methodology

This study centers my relational practices and the (re)formation of my professional identity in a new context, and hence self-study methodology is employed. I used two well-established frames for self-study research in this inquiry: intimate scholarship (Hamilton & Pinnegar, 2015) and personal history self-study (Samaras et al., 2004). Together, these approaches helped me to explore the influence of past experiences on my relational practices and allowed me to envision new possibilities in my practice. Specifically, intimate scholarship represents a subjective onto-epistemological commitment to meaning-making through relational understanding (Hamilton & Pinnegar, 2015). Intimate scholarship acknowledges the inherently relational nature of teaching and asserts that educators' practices are shaped in relationship to the needs of those with whom we share a context (Hamilton et al., 2016).

Intimate scholarship was theoretically salient because the inquiry was conducted from my perspective and prompted me to acknowledge and share my vulnerabilities (Hamilton & Pinnegar, 2015). My inquiry also focused on the particular—the nuances of my identity as a remote relational teacher educator with a particular group of prospective teachers. In alignment with intimate scholarship, I made myself vulnerable by opening up about my feelings and experiences teaching remotely. Thus, the study unfolded on shifting ground as I considered my self-in-practice (Fletcher, 2020) throughout a semester of teaching remotely and during the ensuing research process (Hamilton & Pinnegar, 2015).

In addition to intimate scholarship, I took up personal history self-study (Samaras et al., 2004). Like intimate scholarship, personal history self-study is perspective-driven, and it can uncover tacit and hidden influences on teachers by looking for "connections between what educators think and feel and how they teach" (Samaras et al., 2004, p. 908). Personal history self-study is defined as "the history or life experiences related to personal and professional meaning making for teachers and researchers" (Samaras et al., 2004, p. 910) and is used to explore identity formation by uncovering the hidden personal narratives and stories we live by (Clandinin & Connelly, 1999) that influence how teachers relate to and work with students (Samaras et al., 2004). Self-study scholars acknowledge that personal history is useful for "self-knowing and forming – and reforming – a professional identity" (Samaras et al., 2004, p. 913) as it requires us to scrutinize our identity and "risk needing to reform and recreate the self" (Samaras et al., 2004, p. 915).

In my own stance as a self-study scholar, I embrace the process of always *becoming* based on changing perceptions that account for my social, cultural, and material contexts (Hordvik et al., 2021; Martin, 2018b). And, intimate knowledge of my own personal history opens me up to new understandings of self-in-context (Greene, 1978, 1995). While self-study scholars embrace many methods for conducting personal history self-study, I call upon two specific forms: journaling and my education-related life history (Samaras et al., 2004). Taken together, intimate scholarship and personal history self-study are appropriate approaches for this inquiry because they opened me up to creating new understandings of self as I embarked on enacting relational teacher education in a remote setting. In the spirit of personal history self-study, I now offer up my personal history narrative as a teacher educator.

9.2.1 My Personal History as a Teacher Educator

I entered teacher education as a happy accident (Mayer et al., 2011). I was quite content as a kindergarten teacher. I taught in what can be called an urban characteristic (Milner, 2012) school with a significant immigrant population; my students were treated unfairly by the system, and over time I began to have bigger questions about the U.S. education system. I knew some of my students would be completely disenfranchised by the school system before they reached eighth grade; by that time, they would lack the academic record to attend one of the magnet schools that many students wanted to attend. I recall speaking with teacher colleagues about how to best draw on students' home languages and my colleagues' responses that I needed to stop allowing that and to make sure my students spoke only English.

I strove to provide resources to my students and their families only to be met with colleagues' suggestions that I just needed to put some of my students in basic skills instruction (i.e. segregated remedial classrooms) or retain them for another year of kindergarten. It was in my graduate program that I was exposed to critical race theory (Crenshaw et al., 1995). Critical race theory gave me the vocabulary to articulate the systemic racism I witnessed through my lived experience as an urban kindergarten teacher. Critical race theory, therefore, anchored me and sustained me; it gave me hope that others thought like I did, and my resistance could be part of larger social justice efforts to change how schools operate and how we educate young children. Now, as a teacher educator, I draw on my lived experience and social justice commitments to inform my practice. One of my goals, for example, is for prospective teachers in my classes to realize the systemic and institutionalized forces that empower some and disempower others.

My experiences have shaped my understanding of the relationship between teaching and learning. I acknowledge "the reciprocal learning between teachers and students" (Freire, 1998, p. 67). I believe there is no teaching without learning, and as a result, I strive to learn from my students, to critically reflect on my own practice, and to disrupt deficit-based perspectives of urban students and communities. My identity as a teacher educator, therefore, attends to the relational nature of teachers' work and advances a social justice commitment.

9.2.2 Context of the Study

The focal course for this self-study is *Working with Families and Communities*. This course is offered in both programs with which I am affiliated—urban education and inclusive education—and is intended to deepen prospective teachers' understandings of the roles that families and communities play in the education and development of children. The course situates communities and families from an asset-based perspective in which children are understood in the contexts of their families, communities, schools, and the wider society. Prospective teachers in this course develop skills in working effectively with diverse families in order to provide positive educational outcomes for children in urban and inclusive settings.

The assignments in the class assist students in identifying community cultural wealth (Yosso, 2005) and recognizing the importance of students' funds of knowledge (Gonzalez et al., 2005; Moll et al., 1992). Studying and working with diverse communities different from their own requires prospective teachers to engage in an ideological examination of their assumptions and biases. Since I am a teacher educator in the U.S. where the vast majority of teachers are White females (U.S. Department of Education, 2020), this course can be a heavy lift for students. With that in mind, I use three overarching questions (specified in my course syllabus) as a way to promote prospective teachers' emergent critical consciousness of systemic oppression:

1. What sorts of families and communities do schools empower?
2. What makes you think so?
3. How could schools empower all families and communities?

To unpack these questions, I craft assignments, discussions, and exercises that help students realize the myriad systemic injustices in our society and how they play out in schools, particularly urban and urban characteristic schools (Milner, 2012).

To support students' thinking and speaking openly about systemic oppression, I facilitate conversations to foster trusting relationships *with and among* my students so they do not shut down and shy away from these challenging topics. In the fall 2020 semester I felt unsure of how my course would unfold in a remote setting given its sensitive nature. How, if at all, would (or could) I enact relational practices without sharing a physical classroom? And, could this change in the teaching context help me develop new understandings of self-in-practice? These wonderings sparked the self-study detailed in this chapter.

9.2.3 Data Sources

For this chapter, I drew on the following data sources from *Working with Families and Communities*:

1. 14 Lesson Plans for classes
2. 14 Weekly Reflective Notes

3. 14 Course Meeting Transcripts
4. Course Syllabus
5. Email Communication with Students
6. Anonymous Student Course Evaluation Document

Institutional Review Board approval was obtained for the use of these data sources. Some of the data sources were developed before I taught the course (course syllabus and draft lesson plans), some of the data were developed while I taught the course (weekly reflective notes, course meeting transcripts, email communication with students), and some of the data were developed after the course ended (anonymous student course evaluation). The sequenced data collection was purposeful; I wanted the corpus of data to capture the progression of my thoughts over time, and I wanted to be intentional about the construction of the data corpus so as to establish trustworthiness (Feldman, 2003).

9.2.4 Data Analysis

The entire corpus of data was compiled after the course ended and after final grades were submitted. I compressed all of the data sources into one electronic file; then, I engaged in an immersive engagement through multiple readings (Ravitch & Carl, 2016). Next, I conducted a document analysis (Bowen, 2009) of the data set. Building off extant self-studies (e.g. Forgasz & Clemens, 2014) the data were first analyzed holistically and iteratively to engage in the "deeply reflexive process [which] is key to sparking insight and meaning" (Srivastava & Hopwood, 2009, p. 77). As I began coding my data, I collapsed the relational teacher education dimensions of *respecting and empathizing with preservice teachers* and *conveying respect and empathy* into one code, *feeling and conveying respect and empathy for preservice teachers,* given that these dimensions were overlapping in my analysis. Then, I used the five remaining dimensions as a priori codes to look for instances wherein teaching remotely influenced my self-in-practice (Fletcher, 2020). I specifically looked for critical moments in which my role and identity as a relational teacher educator were stretched or altered as a result of remote teaching. After a round of initial coding, I reexamined my data sources to support triangulation and more fully develop the codes into emergent findings.

To enhance the trustworthiness of the study I attended to collaboration and openness (Barnes, 1998) in two ways; first, I held bi-weekly consultations with a thought partner, a colleague teaching another remote section of this course. In our consultations, we discussed challenges and successes of translating this course to an online platform. We also discussed changes and adaptations we were making to specific assignments and in our own pedagogies along the way. Next, I shared the findings of this study with another teacher education colleague as an additional mechanism for establishing trustworthiness. Trustworthiness was further bolstered by my attending to three suggestions in self-study literature (Feldman, 2003): an explicit description and identification of data collection methods; an explanation of how I constructed the corpus of data; and, evidence of the value of the pedagogical changes this study prompted, which comprise the findings below.

9.3 The Dimensions of Relational Teacher Education in a Remote Setting

Having engaged with intimate scholarship and personal history self-study methods, I analyzed the data through the dimensions of relational teacher education. I have organized the findings within those dimensions to offer a nuanced understanding of myself and my pedagogical practices in a remote context.

9.3.1 Understanding One's Personal Practical Knowledge

I drew on my personal practical knowledge from prior semesters to adapt the course for online instruction using a balanced approach for readings and assignments. I knew from years of personal experience as a teacher educator that as the semester progresses and more assignments become due, students start to skim assigned readings, which makes meaningful discourse harder to achieve. To account for this, I decided to balance readings with podcasts in the second half of the semester and suggested for students to "listen to these podcasts while going for a walk or sitting outside if possible" (Class Meeting Transcript, 10/20/2020). Also, I thought podcasts would be more manageable for prospective teachers who might be over-saturated with screen time. Below is an excerpt from my reflective notes that details this moment:

> I told students about my pedagogical move here—in the course design I wanted to attend to their mental health by trying to strike a balance of lectures, readings, and assignments throughout the semester. Since many of our bigger assignments are due in the second half of the semester, I wanted to front load the lectures and readings in the beginning of the semester. I then told my students that when they are teachers, they should also consider things like this for their own students because teachers need to think about what is going on in students' lives *outside* of class and be responsive to that *inside* the classroom. (Weekly Reflective Notes, 10/20/2020)

In addition to incorporating digital media in the required readings, I also made sure to balance the due dates of major assignments throughout the semester; each student received extensive formative feedback before submitting work to be graded. I drew on my prior experience as a teacher educator to develop these considerations for course design. And, I found that being explicit with students about how my personal practical knowledge informed a balanced course design proved to be particularly useful in a remote class for modeling teacher thinking and responsiveness to students' lives outside of the classroom.

9.3.2 Improving One's Practice in Teacher Education

Teaching remotely reminded me of the need to center and prioritize systematic self-reflection and professional learning as a means to improving my practice in teacher education. After the immediate pivot to online coursework in the spring 2020 semester, I knew I needed to improve my skill set for online teaching. I, therefore, enrolled in a series of professional development workshops at my institution focused on improving remote pedagogical practices. In the workshops I learned how to utilize the chat feature in Zoom as means to solicit more participation and student engagement.

As a result, I leveraged the capabilities of the online platform to improve my practice and be more responsive to students in a remote setting. Specifically, I did not require students to keep their cameras on, although our institution urged us to, or to verbally participate; instead, I gave students options to use the chat feature—either to me privately or to the whole class—in addition to direct verbal participation through Zoom. For example, the lesson plan for week eight states that students will complete the Community Building activity in class.

> Share your 'wins' this week—what happened that gave you hope, brought you joy, or moved your work forward? Students should respond to the community building questions verbally to whole group, in the whole class chat, or in a private chat to me. (Lesson Plan, 10/20/20)

These choices reflect my identity as a relational teacher educator who does not value control, but rather honors the humanity of my students and their experiences.

These choices are also particular to the remote setting of my course, and as I reflect on my practice, I realize that I had never given students options for participation in traditional face-to-face settings because I never had the occasion to reimagine how such participation might look. My own identity as a relational teacher educator engaging in self-study encouraged me to see and appreciate these pedagogical changes.

9.3.3 Understanding the Landscape of Teacher Education

My knowledge of teacher education influenced how I revised and modeled classroom activities for students in an online environment. As a beginning teacher, I remember wishing that I had had more practical knowledge of teaching than the theoretical knowledge I gained in my teacher education program. In my current work with in-service teachers, they critique the emphasis of theory over practice in university settings. One of my pedagogical approaches, therefore, is to show prospective teachers how the content we discuss translates into *actual* classroom practice by modeling mini-lessons. On September 11th, for example, I wanted to model a virtual read-aloud of a 2002 children's book called *Fireboat* by Maira Kalman. This book provides a way for teachers or parents to engage children in conversations about tragic events, particularly those of September 11th, 2001. Each fall semester I model this mini-lesson but in a face-to-face environment.

Modeling this mini-lesson online required me to ensure the students could see the images and text in the book in much the same way they would have been able to in a traditional classroom; so I needed to first scan each individual page of the book and insert each scanned page as a slide on a PowerPoint presentation. I screenshared these with my students during our online class meeting. Before I read the book, I shared a Google document with students where they could post anonymous thoughts and questions before, during, and after our reading. After reading the book I made sure to address all of the anonymous questions from students. In this way, the prospective teachers now had a model for engaging in a virtual read-aloud and facilitating conversations about difficult topics.

Modeling classroom read-alouds of children's books is something I have always done, however, doing so in a remote environment gave me the opportunity to model a shared reading of a critical text using online tools. In this way, relational teacher education and my knowledge of the critiques we face as teacher educators influenced how meticulous and careful I was with modeling this activity; I wanted prospective teachers to remember this activity in the chance that they find themselves teaching young children online. As we all continue to embrace the new landscape of education at this moment, it is important for teacher educators to be responsive to the virtual elements of modeling how concepts translate into actual classroom practice.

9.3.4 Feeling and Conveying Respect and Empathy for Preservice Teachers

Teaching remotely altered *how* I conveyed respect and empathy for my preservice teachers by offering greater flexibility to them and explicitly focusing on their mental health and wellness; it also increased the degree of respect and empathy I felt for them because of the uncertainty of our times. Today's preservice teachers are not only experiencing radical shifts in the educational world, but they are learning to become educators with the knowledge that they themselves might be tasked with online or hybrid teaching in P-12 schools.

I respect and empathize with their situations and the challenges these radical shifts present. I convey respect and empathy with preservice teachers over time through my planning, feedback to them, and responsiveness to their needs. I devote attention to the organization of my course, the materials I select, the expectations I share with students, and the rituals I generate with them. I also demonstrate care in personal communication and correspondence with students and make myself accessible to them, inside and outside of class time. Taken together, this approach signals to students that I care about their growth and development.

To further convey my feelings to students, I implemented flexible due dates for assignments, which was admittedly outside of my comfort zone as a teacher educator. Any assignment for our course was due on Friday, but I would accept assignments as late as Monday without the need for students to request an extension. I told students this was intentional planning on my part to show that I wanted to "respect [their] weekend time but also allow [students] to use the weekends to work if [they] needed to" (Class Meeting Transcript, 9/8/2020). I also told students that if they needed time for any assignment beyond Monday, that they should email me, text me, or call me to request an extension. To this end, I had several opportunities to make good on my promise of flexibility. Below is an email which demonstrates how I used the flexible due dates and extensions to convey respect and empathy for students.

> Dear [Student],
> I completely understand the difficulties associated with this semester, the time overall right now, and the challenges with getting formal accommodations. You can absolutely have an extension. In addition to the extension, please let me know how else I can support your learning this semester. In my perspective as a former classroom teacher, each and every student has unique needs that may or may not be formally documented—I make accommodations either way. (Personal Communication, 10/31/2020)

This approach demonstrates the respect I have for my students as prospective teachers and the empathy I have for their new online learning environment. When teaching face-to-face, it never occurred to me to offer this degree of flexibility; teaching remotely provided the occasion for me to reconsider the degree of control I felt I needed and to reimagine the ways I convey respect and empathy for students.

Over time as I got to know more about my students and their needs, I realized that they needed a dedicated time and space for processing their experiences as remote learners. Around week five I began to open class with mental health/wellness check-ins. I would ask students to think about something that happened recently that moved their work forward, that brought them joy, or that gave them hope. In other instances, I asked students to think about how they processed their feelings, or how they were managing their time during this remote semester. In response to this pedagogical move that centers respect and empathy, one student wrote, "I love how Professor Morettini started every class with a 'mental health check in' to see how we were doing, or to share anything going on in our lives. It made me feel valued as a student" (Student Evaluation, 1/4/2021). In this way, I centered students' mental health and wellness as a way to convey respect and empathy for them as human beings.

Through a focus on the *particular* of this experience, I became more intentionally responsive by centering students' wellness and mental health; I ritualized this practice in my teaching and offered a way to model building meaningful relationships with students in a remote environment by creating a space for their mental health and wellness and then being responsive to students' needs. The analysis revealed that teaching remotely influenced my relational practices in that it deepened my efforts toward conveying respect and empathy.

9.3.5 Helping Preservice Teachers Face Problems

Helping preservice teachers face problems and reconcile the barriers to the teaching profession in the U.S. with their ambitions was unique in a remote environment because it required me to spend more structured, out-of-class time with them compared to when I share a physical classroom with them. In my years as a teacher educator working in a traditional face-to-face classroom, I would often address prospective teachers' problems while I set up for the day, often with their help, as they arrived for class. Since remote teaching lacked that informal space of togetherness, helping prospective teachers face problems emerged as a distinct need. During one of our remote class meetings, for example, I joined students in a Zoom breakout room and quickly noticed that they were not discussing the prompts I had assigned, but instead were engaging in a frenzied discussion about how to prepare for the upcoming Praxis exams.[2] Since the exams are high-stakes, they remain a significant source of stress and anxiety for the prospective teachers at my institution.

What is more, the Praxis Lab—the physical space at our institution that houses study guides and tutors—was closed because of COVID-19 restrictions. Rather than redirect students and try to assert control over their breakout room discussion, I showed them some online resources our university had and empathized that this was indeed a high-stakes and high-stress assessment. Then, after class, I wrote a message to all my students with Praxis study guides attached to the message. I realized, however, that a simple email was not enough and that I needed to redouble my supportive efforts.

I began to log onto Zoom for class 15 minutes early and told students we could use this time to chat informally and talk through issues; it was not required. Additionally, since students did not have easy access to their advisors on campus, I began setting up proxy advising sessions online with students, fielding questions about how to prepare for the Praxis exams and which courses students should take next semester to stay on track in their course sequence. Below is an excerpt from my reflective notes.

> Last week a student asked if she could call me to talk through some options for her schedule of classes next semester, since she did not pass the benchmark Praxis exams required to register for the next courses…she ended the conversation with a lot of gratitude. She said, "I talk to everyone in our cohort and we all feel the same way that you are so in touch with what we're going through this semester." (Weekly Reflective Notes, 11/5/2020)

Through this experience, I realized I needed to be more intentional about how I supported students in dealing with their problems. Being a relational teacher educator in a remote environment, then, required me to broaden the scope of support services I offered preservice teachers because other support services and resources were not readily accessible or available to them.

---

[2] The Praxis exams are a series of standardized tests of content knowledge and pedagogy for prospective teachers, and they are required for teacher certification in the state where this self-study was conducted.

9.3.6 Receptivity to Growing in Relationship

Freire (1998) reminds us that there is no teaching without learning, and so I opened myself up to learning and growing more comfortable with remote education in new ways by allowing students to co-construct assignments with me; thus, I situated preservice teachers as the experts rather than myself (Kitchen, 2005b). I am a product of face-to-face classrooms, and my socialization into the role of teacher educator occurred in the context of face-to-face classrooms. As I look back on previous semesters, I realize that I often told students about my willingness to learn from them without tapping into my students' skills and knowledge because I was cushioned by the familiarity of my classroom technologies.

To harness the potential of the online class environment, I leveraged preservice teachers' knowledge and skills to support my growth. My students are, admittedly, much more adept with technology than I am, and I was transparent with students from the first class about my own anxieties related to teaching remotely. I told students that I was "going to be learning alongside [them]" in the remote environment (Class Meeting Transcript, 9/1/2020). Thus, I laid bare my own vulnerabilities with students and invited students to draw on their burgeoning knowledge of teaching and technology to co-construct final assignment formats. The students surpassed my expectations; I received close-captioned videos, Jamboards, Padlets, and Google sites. And, the preservice teachers seemed genuinely excited to harness their technological skills in a professional way.

9.4 Reimagining My Self as a Relational Teacher Educator

Through intimate scholarship and personal history self-study, I gained new understandings of my self-in-practice (Fletcher, 2020) by revisiting and reimagining my previously-held manifestations of relational teacher education. From this study, I was reminded of the need to center and prioritize systemic self-reflection and professional learning as a means to engage in criticality of my teaching practice. I revised and modeled classroom activities for a remote environment and learned how remote teaching deepens my feelings of respect and empathy for preservice teachers. And, through this inquiry I realized that helping preservice teachers face problems in a remote environment required me to spend additional time with them to account for the loss of informal interactions before and after in-person classes.

By drawing on intimate scholarship and personal history methods, I see how teaching remotely actually broadened the scope of my role and enhanced the intentionality of my efforts to relate to students. In particular, there were instances when I took on the role of caregiver for students, transcending the role of teacher educator and providing support for preservice teachers even beyond the purview of our course. Further, I centered students' emotional well-being and mental health in a way I have never done in traditional in-person classes, which I am unsure I would have done if we had been together physically in a classroom. This study, therefore, prompted me to reimagine my relational self-in-practice in order to meet the demands of remote teaching. As a result, I will be more intentional and imaginative in my relational practices in both remote and face-to-face settings in the future.

For teacher educators, this study reminds us of our need to be responsive to the changing pedagogical *and emotional* needs of prospective teachers living and working in radical times. In framing my practices within the dimensions of relational teacher education, I learned that a remote setting does not erode my identity as a relational teacher educator if I reimagine how I manifest my relational practices. This study, therefore, provides a framework for other social-justice oriented teacher educators to reimagine their relational practices and their self-in-practice in remote settings. Future studies could revisit the construct of relational teacher education to extend and nuance what we know about its specific dimensions as remote teaching and learning become more commonplace.

9.5 Conclusion

At its core, this research demonstrates a commitment to improving my practice through self-study (Hamilton & Pinnegar, 1998; Loughran et al., 2004). In the self-study community, we acknowledge the self is always in the process of becoming, based on perspectives (Hamilton & Pinnegar, 2015), personal histories (Samaras et al., 2004), relationships (Beijaard et al., 2004), and contexts where self is formed (Biddle, 1979; Hordvik et al., 2021). This study contributes to conversations on ways we can use self-study methodology to learn about and enhance professional practice; the study also extends the self-study literature by providing an understanding of relational teacher education in radical times.

I am reminded that teachers are unfinished beings (Freire, 1998) and that self-study methodologies can provide valuable insights about areas in need of growth and renewal in my ongoing efforts toward social justice. Teaching in a new, remote context sparked my curiosities about how to maintain and reimagine my identity as a relational teacher educator. And, as a relational teacher educator with a commitment to social justice, the study prompted me to revisit criticality of my own practice as I entered into an epistemological space in which I was open to learning about and from *self* in new ways.

References

Barnes, D. (1998). Looking forward: The concluding remarks at the Castle Conference. In M. L. Hamilton (Ed.), *Reconceptualizing teaching practice: Self-study in teacher education* (pp. 9–14). Falmer Press.

Beijaard, D., Meijer, P. C., & Verloop, N. (2004). Reconsidering research on teachers' professional identity. *Teaching and Teacher Education, 20*, 107–128. https://doi.org/10.1016/j.tate.2003.07.001

Berry, A. (2008). *Tensions in teaching about teaching: Understanding practice as a teacher educator*. Springer Publishing.

Berry, A., & Kitchen, J. (2020). Self-study in times of radical change. *Studying Teacher Education, 16*(2), 123–126. https://doi.org/10.1080/17425964.2020.1777763

Biddle, B. (1979). *Role theory: Expectations, identities, and behaviors*. Academic.

Bowen, G. A. (2009). Document analysis as a qualitative research method. *Qualitative Research Journal, 9*(2), 27–40. https://doi.org/10.3316/QRJ0902027

Clandinin, D. J., & Connelly, F. M. (1999). *Shaping a professional identity: Stories of educational practice*. Teachers College Press.

Crenshaw, K., Gotando, N., Peller, G., & Thomas, K. (1995). *Critical race theory: The key writings that formed the movement*. The New Press.

Feldman, A. (2003). Validity and quality in self-study. *Educational Researcher, 32*(3), 26–28. https://doi.org/10.3102/0013189X032003026

Fletcher, T. (2020). Self-study as hybrid methodology. In J. Kitchen, A. Berry, S. M. Bullock, A. Crowe, M. Taylor, H. Guðjónsdóttir, & L. Thomas (Eds.), *International handbook of self-study of teaching and teacher education practices* (2nd ed., pp. 269–297). Springer. https://doi.org/10.1007/978-981-13-6880-6_10

Forgasz, R., & Clemens, A. (2014). Feeling feminist? A self-study of emotion as a feminist epistemology in education practice. In M. Taylor & L. Coia (Eds.), *Gender, feminism, and queer theory in the self-study of teacher education practices* (pp. 61–75). Sense Publishers.

Freire, P. (1998). *Pedagogy of freedom: Ethics, democracy, and civic courage*. Rowman & Littlefield.

Gonzalez, N., Moll, L. C., & Amanti, C. (2005). Funds of knowledge: Theorizing practices in households and classrooms. .

Greene, M. (1978). *Landscapes of learning*. Teachers College Press.

Greene, M. (1995). *Releasing the imagination: Essays on education, the arts, and social change*. Jossey-Bass.

Hamilton, M. L., & Pinnegar, S. (1998). The value and promise of self-study. In M. L. Hamilton (Ed.), *Reconceptualizing teaching practice: Self-study in teacher education* (pp. 235–246). Falmer.

Hamilton, M. L., & Pinnegar, S. (2015). Knowing, becoming, doing as teacher educators: Identity, intimate scholarship, inquiry. *Emerald*. https://doi.org/10.1108/S1479-368720140000026035

Hamilton, M. L., Pinnegar, S., & Davey, R. (2016). Intimate scholarship: An examination of identity and inquiry in the work of teacher educators. In J. Loughran & M. L. Hamilton (Eds.), *International handbook of teacher education* (Vol. 2, pp. 181–237). Springer.

Hordvik, M., Fletcher, T., Haugen, A. L., Moller, L., & Engebretsen, B. (2021). Using collaborative self-study and rhizomatics to explore the ongoing nature of becoming teacher educators. *Teaching and Teacher Education, 101*, 1–11. https://doi.org/10.1016/j.tate.2021.103318

Kitchen, J. (2002). Becoming a relational teacher educator: A narrative inquirer's self-study. In C. Kosnik, A. Freese, & A. Samaras (Eds.), Making a difference in teacher education through self-study. *Proceedings of the Fourth International Conference on Self-Study of Teacher Education Practices,* Herstmonceux Castle, East Sussex, UK, Vol. 2 (pp. 36–40). OISE University of Toronto.

Kitchen, J. (2005a). Looking backward, moving forward: Understanding my narrative as a teacher educator. *Studying Teacher Education, 1*(1), 17–30. https://doi.org/10.1080/17425960500039835

Kitchen, J. (2005b). Conveying respect and empathy: Becoming a relational teacher educator. *Studying Teacher Education, 1*(2), 197–207. https://doi.org/10.1080/1742596050028837

Loughran, J., Hamilton, M. L., LaBoskey, V. K., & Russell, T. (Eds.). (2004). *International handbook of teaching and teacher education practices*. Kluwer.

Martin, A. D. (2018a). Affective reverberations: The methodological excesses of a research assemblage. In K. Strom, T. Mills, & A. Ovens (Eds.), *Decentering the researcher in intimate scholarship: Critical posthuman methodological perspectives in education* (pp. 9–234). Emerald Publishing. https://doi.org/10.1108/S1479-368720180000031003

Martin, A. D. (2018b). Professional identities and pedagogical practices: A self-study on the "becomings" of a teacher educator and teachers. In A. Ovens & D. Garbett (Eds.), *Pushing boundaries and crossing borders: Self-study as a means for knowing pedagogy* (pp. 263–269). S-STEP.

Mayer, D., Mitchell, J., Santoro, N., & White, S. (2011). Teacher educators and 'accidental' careers in academe: An Australian perspective. *Journal of Education for Teaching, 37*(3), 247–260. https://doi.org/10.1080/02607476.2011.588011

Milner, R. (2012). But what is urban education? *Urban Education, 47*(3), 556–561. https://doi.org/10.1177/0042085912447516

Moll, L. C., Amanti, C., Neff, D., & Gonzalez, N. (1992). Funds of knowledge for teaching: Using a qualitative approach to connect homes and classrooms. *Theory Into Practice, 31*(2), 132–141. https://doi.org/10.1080/00405849209543534

Ravitch, S. M., & Carl, N. M. (2016). *Qualitative research: Bridging the conceptual, theoretical, and methodological.* Sage.

Samaras, A. P., Hicks, M. A., & Garvey Bergey, J. (2004). Self-study through personal history. In J. J. Loughran (Ed.), *International handbook of self-study of teaching and teacher education practices* (pp. 905–942). Springer.

Srivastava, P., & Hopwood, N. (2009). A practical iterative framework for qualitative data analysis. *International Journal of Qualitative Methods, 8*(1), 76–84. https://doi.org/10.1177/160940690900800107

Trout, M. (2018). Embodying care: Igniting a critical turn in a teacher educator's relational practice. *Studying Teacher Education, 14*(1), 39–55. https://doi.org/10.1080/17425964.2017.1404976

U.S. Department of Education. (2020). *Schools and staffing survey (SASS).* National Center for Education Statistics. https://nces.ed.gov/programs/coe/indicator_clr.asp

Yosso, T. (2005). Whose culture has capital? A critical race theory discussion of community cultural wealth. *Race Ethnicity and Education, 8*(1), 69–91. https://doi.org/10.1080/1361332052000341006

Brianne (Brie) Morettini, Ph.D., is an Associate Professor in the Department of Interdisciplinary and Inclusive Education in the College of Education at Rowan University. She teaches doctoral courses on research literature and analysis, and undergraduate courses on working with families and communities, inclusive education, and elementary education. She draws on a sociocultural theoretical framework to research beginning teacher identity development, beginning teachers' perspectives on teaching, and the use of self-study methodologies to uncover and acknowledge epistemological frames. She considers the intersections of theory and practice in her teaching and research. She has published her work in book chapters and peer-reviewed journals. She also presents her work at national and international research conferences.

Chapter 10
Not to Simply Intervene, but to Enact the Between: Urban Teacher Education as an Intra-Active Process

Mary F. Rice and Mariana Castañon

Abstract Urban teachers experience national pressure regarding their ability to serve diverse learners and enact socially just practices. Many also face criticism when they place criticality at the forefront of their practice because of racism and misunderstandings about how literacy develops. There are also assumptions about technological availability in urban areas versus rural ones, where urban teachers are assumed to have access to the resources they need for digital learning. As a collaboration between a teacher educator and an instructional coach, we use this chapter to unpack learning about supporting teachers across settings. Using Karen Barad's notions of intra-activity and diffraction as guiding concepts, we share an emerging praxis where instead of intervening with the teachers, we recognize ourselves as part of their worlds and help teachers understand that they produce and are produced by their contexts as well. Instead of moving between a rural teacher education practice and an urban teacher practice, we enact a practice based on ethics. Instead of reflecting challenges back to teachers, we invite them to see where the diffractions appear—as those are the most promising spaces for connectivity and agency.

Keywords Critical literacies · Diffraction in teacher education · Digital pedagogies in teacher education · Intra-active agencies in teacher education · Teacher educator identities · Urban teacher education

Success in teaching children in the so-called *urban educational setting* requires strong relational commitments and a social justice orientation (Brown, 2004; Kwok, 2019; Martin, 2020; Skerrett & Williamson, 2015). Urban teachers in the United States face criticism regarding presumptively neutral student achievement markers and they are disregarded when they draw attention to injustice in their schools due to racism and public disinterest in making school relevant to all students (Kohli,

M. F. Rice (✉) · M. Castañon
University of New Mexico, Albuquerque, NM, USA
e-mail: maryrice@unm.edu

2018; Skerrett et al., 2018; Zoch, 2015). Under such conditions, high attrition rates are unsurprising (Dunn & Downey, 2018; Hammonds, 2017; Kelchtermans, 2017).

The last 10 years has also seen an increase in digital learning, bringing new debates about technology's role in addressing inequity and highlighting technological availability in urban versus rural areas (McCloud et al., 2016). While rural teachers are often pitied for their lack of internet connectivity, urban teachers are presumed to have access to the technological resources and infrastructure they need for digital learning (Fernandez et al., 2019; Vega et al., 2020). In fact, many instances of comparisons between rural and urban education as a binary abound in the public discourse in the United States as well as other countries (Bernard, 2019 [Europe]; Chakrabarti & Mehta, 2019; [India]; Jun & Chudan, 2017 [China]; Looker & Bollman, 2020 [Canada]; Tieken, 2017 [U.S.]).

One of our goals for this chapter is to join others in challenging the utility of the binary between rural education versus urban education (Cloke & Johnston, 2005; McGlynn, 2018). Such a challenge is particularly important for a high poverty, under-resourced state like ours in the Southwestern U.S. where most challenges are shared across communities of various sizes. In this inquiry, our theoretical framework is based on the work of Barad (2007) and others (Deleuze, 2004, Forgasz & McDonough, 2017; Strom & Martin, 2017), which highlights intra-activity as an alternative means of thinking about rural and urban as separate spaces. Intra-activity refers to the fact that humans are never autonomous, but always operating in connection. Moreover, the stuff of our worlds, including technological stuff, also intra-acts with us: our devices use us as much as we use them (Rice, 2019). Such thinking trades questions about where the boundaries are on challenges on *urban* versus *rural* ones, and instead asks how tensions emerge and overlap in the lives of the people who learn and work in these contexts (Clandinin et al., 2009a, b; Murphy et al., 2020). Importantly, an intra-active approach can show how the challenges of teaching in what has been termed an urban area do not stem merely from being in a place with a large population or being in a place where that population is racially, linguistically, or culturally diverse. The challenges arise as an entanglement of goals, identities, understandings, and interpretations that exert force upon one another.

In this chapter, we define entanglement and share information about our context. Next, we offer traditional research perspectives on the perceived challenges of so-called urban teaching to show that what has been cloistered as *urban* is not as tidy as public discourse purports it to be. After that, we share our methods for learning about how we support the teachers in our context and provide the outcomes of our inquiry. Finally, we offer a discussion about how we and others in what have been termed *urban* areas might do to support teachers and teaching. Using Barad's (2007) new materialist notions of intra-activity and diffraction as guiding concepts, we share an emerging praxis for supporting teachers in understanding their contexts and ourselves in those contexts as well.

10.1 Entangled Contexts and Positions

We work in a state which consistently ranks low on standardized student assessment scores (Barnum, 2019). We, along with public schools and other teacher preparation entities in our state, bear criticism for this. In fact, there has been a recent legal case where the state department of education was found to provide insufficient access to appropriate educational supports for multiple student populations including English language learners (ELLs), students with disabilities, and indigenous students in rural and urban settings (Perea, 2018). Teaching and learning in our state have been further complicated during the COVID-19 pandemic, a time when our local schools used fully online learning from March 2020 until April 2021.

We are both long-term professionals in the field of education. Mary is in her fifth year as a faculty member at her university. She teaches courses at both the graduate and undergraduate levels. Her research and teaching focus on online learning and digital literacies. Many of her students are or will be teachers in K-12 schools. Her institution has a primary research mission. Even so, her college of education has a strong interest in providing effective teaching as part of teacher education. Mary grew up in Oregon, a relatively low population state in the Pacific Northwest of the U.S. She also taught from 2003 to 2013 in a town of 20,000 people at a junior high school with around 1500 students. Her dissertation was an exploration of rural English language arts teachers' curriculum-making with different types of technological devices (Rice, 2016). In that dissertation, she found that community pressure to use or not use technology was a more pressing challenge to teachers than the typically regarded issue of internet connectivity. Currently, Mary has a daughter who is a student at a local public school and a partner who is a public-school teacher in that same district.

Mariana organizes professional learning and is an instructional coach. She is originally from Eastern Europe. In her educator roles, she strives to empathize and work with the school's administration, staff, and community. Research shows, and Mariana's experience reflects, that instructional coaches are often assigned additional duties to support educators who struggle with learning how to teach in urban schools (Ramkellawan & Bell, 2017). The school Mariana works at is considered a highly diverse, urban school. At this school, 37% of the students have been classified as English learners and 33% of the student population has been classified into special education either because of a disability or because of giftedness. Almost every school in our state, including those in the urban area where Mariana works, has been designated as a Title 1 school, meaning that the schools qualify for federal funding to serve the high proportion of economically challenged residents.

In Mariana's school, 100% of the students qualify for free and reduced lunch, a proxy for socio-economic status at or below the poverty level. Most of the students are multilingual, coming from households that mainly speak Spanish as the primary language. However, there are many different language groups represented in the district. Mariana's professional responsibilities to plan learning opportunities for teachers, writing curriculum according to the needs of the school, and meeting with all teachers twice a week for 1 h during times when teachers are otherwise free of instructional duties. Prior to coming to her instructional coach role, Mariana taught in the district for a few years. However, most of Mariana's prior teaching experience was in the state of Minnesota, where she taught elementary and middle school-age students, in both rural and urban settings, for 16 years. She has two children attending the local public schools.

10.2 Perspectives on Urban Teaching

Terms like *urban school* and *urban teacher* draw on a complex set of historical understandings and notions (Ahram et al., 2011). In this section, we share more about the intra-active elements that produce urban school communities and urban teachers within these communities.

10.2.1 Intra-Active Elements in Urban School Communities

Many urban school communities share the characteristics of being dilapidated, serving students from diverse backgrounds who do not achieve high standardized test scores, and the community is regarded to be highly transient, unable, or unwilling to participate in school decision-making (Welsh & Swain, 2020). Many studies have taken the perspective that there are challenges with both the structure and the culture of urban schools (Ahram et al., 2011; Bower, 2000; Gehrke, 2005; Kraft et al., 2012; Olmedo, 1997; Sieben & Johnson, 2018). In an urban school community, teachers, students, and families are blamed for lower academic achievement and social problems (Amatea et al., 2012).

10.2.2 Intra-Active Elements that Produce Urban Teachers

As is the case with the whole of the urban school community, urban teachers are defined by what they are perceived to lack. Urban teachers are believed to enter their teacher preparation programs with limited understanding and perspectives about teaching students from disadvantaged circumstances (King & Swartz, 2018). Along with a perceived lack of understanding, teachers are also regarded to bring stereotypes related to the capabilities of diverse students and their families (Baldwin et al., 2007).

Urban teachers are blamed for educational outcomes due to their lack of instructional consistency, inexperience, poorly managed leadership, and low expectations for students in their classrooms (Ahram et al., 2011; Anyon, 2011). Under such circumstances, teachers are unable to draw on social and emotional resources and strategies, which means it is also difficult for them to support their students (Brackett & Cipriano, 2020). The touted solution to urban teachers' deficits is professional learning experiences (Morgan, 2017; Sieben & Johnson, 2018). These learning experiences are usually focused on raising standardized test scores and managing students, rather than helping teachers grow in their abilities to understand the needs of their students (Glass et al., 2018; Rice, 2021).

Finally, urban teachers are defined by the rate at which they leave the profession (Bower, 2000; Hammonds, 2017). Many teachers leave schools with students from poverty circumstances and seek to move to those with wealthier White populations that have higher achieving students (Kraft et al., 2012). Urban schools are then tasked with attracting and retaining effective and committed teachers (Kraft et al., 2012).

10.2.3 Entangled Understandings of Rural and Urban

In accordance with understandings about intra-activity and entanglement, rural schools share numerous challenges with urban ones. In research, they are also viewed as under-resourced, plagued by inadequate curriculum, and bereft of qualified staff (Logan & Burdick-Will, 2017). Struggles with relationship building are also documented (Corbett, 2016; Murphy et al., 2020). Ultimately, the tension between urban and rural school communities fails to serve children and families in either of those spaces.

At the heart of many critiques of urban school communities is an implicit notion that the quest to support cultural and linguistic diversity is too difficult or unnecessary because the curriculum should be neutral (Stoll, 2019). The perspective that the curriculum is not neutral, but biased, is regarded as radical in some communities (Gillies, 2021; Sabzalian et al., 2021). In communities of all sizes, small numbers of highly active individuals have been able to disrupt attempts to critique curriculum and acknowledge historical and contemporary biases (e.g., Colarossi, 2021). In such settings, students representing feared diversities (e.g., color, dis/ability, gender, language, religion,) are less safe in schools and their teachers may be in danger of punishment for meeting their needs. Under such circumstances, teachers are not positioned to determine which criticisms they should use to identity spaces for improvement and which they should classify as fearmongering and advocate against (Rice & Deschaine, 2021).

As both teachers in rural and urban spaces will be subject to public buffetings, the present task is to understand how overlapping agencies and contextual circumstances provide spaces for teacher support (Herman et al., 2020). In our study, we wondered how we, as a teacher educator and an instructional coach fit into these spaces. In what ways did our roles require multiple, overlapping commitments? What supports were we providing to teachers for urban contexts and how were we providing them?

10.3   Methods for Learning Intra-Actively

Much of what we as teacher educators know about teaching teachers is embedded in the curriculum we enact (Schwab, 1982). Further, curriculum emerges through the activities that we design and implement in our classroom contexts. It is also present in the interactions we have with our students before, during, and after teaching (Hamilton & Pinnegar, 2015). As we plan and as we act, much of what we do is tacit (Polanyi, 1967), embodied (Merleau-Ponty, 2013) and emerges moment to moment as we come into consciousness while teaching (Stern, 2004). In addition, teacher educators act on personal practical knowledge, where knowledge that was personal becomes practices (Clandinin et al., 2009a, b). The enactment of personal practical knowledge and tacit knowing, since they are non-consciously embodied in the practices of teacher educators, often does not emerge in research conversations on teaching or teacher education. Therefore, these ways of knowing and understanding only are visible in the actions of teacher educators as they teach, the documents they produce to direct their work, and publications by those who engage with self-study methodology.

If the teacher education field is to understand the insider knowledge in the work of preparing teachers and formalize it into an empirical discourse, there must be studies that uncover what teacher educators know about teaching teachers (Clandinin et al., 2009a, b; Hamilton & Pinnegar, 2015). Self-studies of teacher education practice can focus on improvement of practice as well as knowing embedded in practice (LaBoskey, 2004). For this project, we looked at accounts of our practice and our thinking about it in the urban context and determined to focus on understanding the knowing behind it. Understanding who we are, who we teach, why we teach our students, and how we are going to teach them are key elements of the knowing behind the practices for our urban educational settings.

Our study emerged from our interest in understanding the support we offer to teachers in our respective teacher education roles and contexts. Methodologically, we drew from Pinnegar and Hamilton (2009), who proposed self-study for learning about teacher education as a turn to the self. Within the frame of self-study research, Pinnegar and Hamilton (2009) suggested that teachers learn from their practices as they unpack their tacit knowledge. They defined tacit knowledge as "the kinds of things revealed not so much in our ability to articulate them as in the action or actions we take" (p. 17). Tacit knowledge is uncovered as teacher educators systematically examine the tensions that they encounter in learning to teach teachers (Berry, 2007; Polyani, 1967).

10.3.1   Data Collection

We collected data from each other in the form of discussion and stories for this work. Data analysis procedures relied heavily on a three-part dialogue between us, as well as Barad (2007) through her writings (Thomas, 2018). In collecting data, we focused on three elements: (1) evidence of collaborative, critical spaces, (2) documentation of practice for analysis, and (3) evidence of improvement to share with others.

10.3.1.1 Evidence of Collaborative, Critical Spaces for Learning

We were both approaching critical questions of practice from different perspectives (Loughran & Northfield, 2003; Pinnegar & Hamilton, 2009). While Mary was preparing prospective teachers and supporting practicing teachers in master's level courses, Mariana was working as an instructional coach and a professional learning resource in a local school district. Mary was able to understand more about the challenges teachers were facing as well as the challenges Mariana was working through and vice-versa. This collaboration provided opportunities for us to challenge one another. For example, we both thought that high quality professional learning experiences were important for teachers, but our various positions allowed us different perspectives on why that was difficult for prospective teachers and practicing educators in the district.

10.3.1.2 Documentation of Practice for Analysis

To learn from this study, we drew on multiple documents of practice (Berry & Loughran, 2002; LaBoskey, 2004). Our specific data sources included notes from our consultations and email correspondence between us. We also met together every other week during the spring 2021 semester to hold informal conversations. During these meetings, we told stories, asked each other questions, and tried to dig under the experiences we were having and the things we saw. For example, we discussed the high teacher attrition rate and the many classrooms in the district with no certified teacher in them and tried to think of all the forces acting in that context to contribute to that situation.

10.3.1.3 Verification of Improvement

We realized that we both are likely to continue to work in our present positions for some time. However, we also desired to share our learning and subject it to further critique from the field (Bannan-Ritland, 2003; Lunenberg & Samaras, 2011). For example, we used our collective learning to guide Mary as she planned summer course offerings and curriculum for summer and the fall semesters as well as consider what Mariana's research in schools might look like (Berry & Loughran, 2002; Pinnegar & Hamilton, 2009).

10.3.2 Data Analysis

We performed our analysis by seeking out diffractive learnings from the data we had gathered. To learn from data, we had to wrestle with Barad's (2007) definition of diffraction as an alternative to reflection. For Barad (2007), who was building on Haraway (1988), the goal of a reflective stance is to reproduce the original materiality at a distance and offer some assessment of it. Reflective stances require substantial control using language that articulates a value sameness or standardization. When evaluating educational circumstances from the discursive position of distance, performative orientations might seem optimal because they allow for reproduction of what can be seen. By contrast, diffraction is not concerned with reproduction. In diffraction, the focus is on differences that have specific effects. They must be differences that make a difference. To illustrate, over time, a wave of water colliding with a rock will eventually change both in drastic ways. This is what Barad (2007) referred to as *on-going becomings*. We viewed our data as the outcome of on-going becomings and then tried to go backward and trace their histories. Moreover, these were not histories that were clear, linear pathways, but instead were a very non-chronological, messy set of related thoughts about what contributed to understandings about the complexities of the present moment. For Mary, that meant thinking about her own upbringing, her teaching, and her dissertation research so-called rural communities, alongside her other experiences researching in what others (scholars and non-scholars) might think of as the urban setting.

During data analysis, it was also critical to return to the outward as a strategy to understand what was happening to the teachers we were working with and to understand ourselves as supporters of them. Limitless, layered contextual elements in educational systems operated simultaneously to produce intra-activity with effects that can be seen as diffractions (Barad, 2007; Haraway, 1988). In dyad, we discussed what the notes revealed about our critical understandings that were contextually embedded in the data. When we reached our conclusions, we revisited the data in relation to the themes and the evidence identified in our conversations. Building on the analytic documents produced, we created a document articulating our understandings about what we felt we were doing to support teachers and what understandings we had reached about the complexities of the contexts we were in. Together, we negotiated the description of and evidence for these findings. Finally, we developed a summary document with statements of knowing supported by evidence from the data. The summary of findings was reviewed with other teacher educators and then developed into a formal report.

10.4 Findings

The purpose of this self-study of teacher education practices (S-STEP) work was to document our attempts to support teachers. For both of us, that meant supporting teachers in the knowing behind their practices that would allow them to remain both solid and change as challenges emerge. By viewing our data through a lens of entangled intra-activity, we found that our support of teachers was more than a tidy list of lessons and professional learning workshops designed to "fix them". Instead of intervening with the teachers to change them into who we thought they should be, our data analysis revealed that we created roles centered on helping them understand that they produce and are produced by their contexts. Also, instead of moving between a rural teacher education practice and an urban teacher practice, we enacted a practice based on ethics where multiple aspects of the context at hand were considered. Finally, instead of reflecting challenges back to teachers, we invited teachers to see where the diffractions appear—because we felt that those spaces were the most promising for understanding connectivity and agency.

10.4.1 Recognizing Ourselves as Part of Their Worlds

Although Mary was not in the midst of teaching children, Mariana was simultaneously teaching children and supporting teachers, due to the teacher shortage during the pandemic year. That experience provided Mariana with the unique perspective and ability to not only see teachers struggle, but to live vicariously through them, allowing her the space to identify logical ways of helping teachers with their challenges. We are not only a teacher educator and an instructional coach—we are also mothers with children who are in the schools. In this way, we are part of the context as those who serve teachers, but we are also like the parents in those research studies who are positioned from a deficit perspective instead of a strength-based orientation. We explicitly shared our experiences with our own children with each other when we conducted this study. We also implicitly drew from those spaces as mothers and teachers as we worked to design strong learning experiences for teachers.

In one instance, Mary shared an experience she had as a mother monitoring remote teaching for her daughter. In the assignment, her daughter was supposed to conduct internet research to learn about a scientist and fill out a worksheet with questions. Her daughter saw only men's names on the worksheet and asked to learn about a woman scientist. She was then assigned Jane Gooddall. On the worksheet, all the questions used *he* stem (e.g., Where was *he* born?) and then many questions portended to family life (e.g., Whom did *he* marry? How many children did *he* have?). Jane Goodall had several important relationships with men that she never married, and her family life did not fit neatly on a single line or question in the worksheet.

These questions, about men, women, or non-binary people failed to portend to their scientific contributions. Not that family lives are unimportant, but the question set proposed such a narrow view of family configurations. We spent time thinking about this issue. On the one hand, we felt this curriculum was potentially damaging co-lateral learning about who should be a scientist and what scientists should be known for (Dewey, 1938). It was also a distressing use of a digitized traditional assignment, rather than a digital activity that made good use of the fact that the children were learning online.

On the other hand, Mary wanted to support teachers—the one her daughter had and then ones she was working with. Mariana also added that at her school, many of the classes did not have regular teachers and were occupied by substitutes who had been pressed into service from district positions or had teachers who were worn down and frazzled. Mary was not directly in that school, but she remembered her dissertation work in a rural district and how those teachers had found themselves teaching multiple subjects and combined classes for various periods of time without notice (as happens too often in urban contexts). Also, every teacher in her dissertation study had revealed that they were planning to leave the rural teaching setting and several left as the study neared completion. Keeping teachers teaching is vital, yet, when and how should teachers be prepared for critiques from administrators, their communities, and even society as a whole?

To understand how to support teachers and what it means in such a moment required us to consider all that matters merging simultaneously. For Mary, she helped her daughter fill out the worksheet as it was the best they could. Her daughter added -s to *he* on all the lines. Then, they also located images of Jane Goodall at different points in her life and in a variety of settings. When Mary's daughter presented her work, she shared a slide show focused on Jane's scholarship. Her classmates asked good questions and her teacher was appreciative. Mary's response marked a level-best attempt to act as a mother, a teacher, a teacher educator, a scholar, and community member. Just like Mary, many current educators and future teachers entering urban schools must juggle multiple identities. By being able to understand multiple simultaneous commitments, urban educators can carry those experiences into the classrooms where they can create safe spaces for students to not only learn content and grapple with their multiple overlapping identities.

10.4.2   Enacting a Practice Based on Principles and Values

We learned that it is one thing to have principles and values, but another to understand how those compete and conflict in our context. From the example above with Mary, there was an entanglement of commitments to various individuals and understandings about the challenging circumstances that teachers found themselves in because of the pandemic as well as the challenges they had always faced. Mary had a sense of herself as a friend of teaching and teachers and as a teacher educator and researcher with high expectations for teachers who come to her classes as students. Mariana also had similar understandings with teachers who were her friends, and she identified with them strongly. Even so, it was her job to help them learn to teach students.

Throughout data analysis, we sought out spaces of intra-activity where our principles and values came into tension. One place for Mariana was in the retention of teachers. Her school had more than a 30% turnover during the 2020–2021 school year. She found herself sacrificing time with her family and time she intended to devote to her doctoral studies because she was writing lesson plans and teaching combined classes. As a relational teacher (Kitchen, 2009), she felt stretched between her responsibilities to support the teachers, both those who were part of the school faculty and those who were serving in a substitute capacity. She often wrestled with feelings of frustration with the students, which is reflected in literature about urban students, and an understanding that many may have not been taught by teachers with credentials, but with a substitute teacher assigned to them for most of the year. In such circumstances, digital learning was considered a luxury that could not be provided.

Mary experienced another entanglement as she worked to support teachers in her online course about reading and writing digital texts. These practicing teachers had to return to in-person schooling with little notice on April 5, 2020. For the mothers who were teachers, that meant a scramble to find childcare when they had been teaching remotely with their young children in their home. For other teachers, it meant redesigning instruction for children physically present in the classroom and simultaneously for those who continued online learning. These disruptions were true for both the urban teachers and the teachers who taught further south in the rural school districts. In this context, what of Mary's class? Could teachers really be expected to keep going on with the class as if they had not been thrown into upheaval by the pandemic? Mary started each class by asking teachers how they were (even before the pandemic) as an indication of her relational commitment. But now, teachers were really taking that time to share their grief. One week, this sharing portion took up most of the class session, and Mary made no attempt to stop them. Of course, that meant shifting and canceling some of the work. Acknowledging the pain of teachers and recognizing the emotional toll these teachers were experiencing was a critical element of support. For these urban teachers, the best thing Mary could do for them was let them see that they cared about each other's struggles, and Mary cared, too.

Mary also had graduate students who were distressed at the criticism they were receiving for trying to make spaces in their curriculum to honor students of color. They felt that some parents and even some colleagues were over-reacting to their attempts to acknowledge multiple perspectives that included perspectives of people of color, including local indigenous groups. The graduate students asked Mary if they could make some digital materials to share when they were questioned. Even though making time to support the graduate students in their self-initiated task took time away from revising formal academic papers assigned to students by the department, Mary reworked the schedule to accommodate the teachers' immediate practical interest. Some of their papers did not turn out as strong in revision, but the teachers had generated shared materials to make a consistent, informed response to criticism they felt came from fear and misunderstanding. To Mary, the sacrifice of the polished paper revision resonated more strongly within the ethic of supporting teachers in being advocates for children and families. Others might disagree—and instead believe that learning to write about social justice within the academy will position the teachers better for long-term effects. Again, there is no perfect response—there are only opportunities to build ethical structures based on understandings from diffracted knowing.

10.4.3   Invite Teachers to See where the Diffractions Appear

Before the pandemic, teachers we worked with were being directed to incorporate more technology use in their classrooms. This was true for all teachers in the district, regardless of whether there was good internet connectivity in the schools, whether students had digital devices or not, and whether teachers were being offered support beyond "use this nifty tool" tweets or short talks by the district technology specialists. Rather than joining the chorus of people telling the teachers they must use the technologies, we both found ourselves working to help teachers understand their situation and determine where they could find space to act within the multiple overlapping agencies in their contexts. For example, many teachers admitted they lacked understanding about to locate and evaluate digital instructional materials, but instead of reflectively blaming themselves, they diffractively considered the lack of technological devices at their schools, the lack of professional learning experiences, the lack of time they were given to think and plan together, and the lack of understanding about what schools in their neighborhoods needed to successfully support digital learning.

Amid these understandings, the COVID-19 pandemic necessitated the sudden and immediate infusion of devices and programs into their contexts, but still, these were without adequate planning, sufficient time, and support. For example, the district purchased more digital devices than charging cords and not all students received a device they could re-charge once the battery was exhausted. Helping teachers understand the diffracted forces around them opened spaces for us to move them from self-blaming questions of "How do I not know this?" to "Let's help each other do this!"

After the teachers had considered their relationships to the technological resources that they had access to, they were prepared to imagine possibilities for delivering instruction that was supportive of students. Teachers who worked with Mariana began to ask deeper questions related to understanding students' cultural, social, and linguistic needs (Hollie, 2017) and built relationships with students both in person and in settings where classes were taught online out of necessity. Moreover, the teachers were also able to talk with Mariana about challenges connected to negative school culture, their own, their children's and their parents' understandings of achievement, and teachers' needs to recruit social and emotional support.

Mary experienced this need for social and emotional support when a teacher who was teaching online reported yelling at the children constantly. The teacher did not like herself when she yelled into her screen. The teacher also admitted she achieved little, but she was unable to stop herself on many occasions. Mary asked the teacher what message yelling sent about who she was as a teacher to the children, and their families who might be listening to the online instruction. The teacher shared that she wanted to convey her frustration so her students would complete their assignments. However, what she was potentially communicating was that her experience as a teacher was more important than their experiences as learners. Mary suggested that the teacher consider others in her professional or personal network who would be willing to listen to her frustrations on a regular basis or as needed, so her agency in the classroom could re-center on the actual learning goals for students. While not a flawless solution, (What if this teacher does not have a strong network of support from which to draw?) Mary's suggestion foregrounds an ethic where student and teacher experiences both matter but where students should not have to bear the weight of teachers' frustrations with the teaching context.

For Mariana, there was an intense urgency to support teachers emotionally to help them not only survive but thrive in their teaching during the pandemic and beyond. In her regular meetings with teachers, she asked them to consider what sustained them as educators. They reported their positive experiences with various agents such as students, parents, and even their technologies in terms of the devices the district provided and the applications to which they had access. Yet, they also commented that they were sustained in their desire to help individual students. Paramount to their happiness was a sense of working with administrators, rather than for them, to solve problems and address dilemmas related to teaching and learning. Mariana hoped that her diffractively-oriented purpose setting could become part of what teachers found gratifying about their work.

10.5   Discussion

Recognizing entanglement, using that entanglement to understand our values, and then inviting others see diffraction alongside us, helped us support teachers during this self-study work. Acknowledging entanglements release teachers from being in a persistent state of resistance or anxiety and puts them in a process of on-going becoming (Barad, 2007; Martin, 2020; Murphy et al. 2020; Strom & Martin, 2017). In short, intra-activity entangles contexts, identities, histories, and agencies while allowing knowledge to be fluid, evolving, and embodied (Clandinin et al., 2009a, b; Forgasz & McDonough, 2017).

Urban schools are often constructed within the discourse of failure (Ahram, et al., 2011; Welsh & Swain, 2020). Moreover, teaching is often blamed for children's apparent lack of academic success (Bower, 2000; Gehrke, 2005; Kraft et al., 2012; Olmedo, 1997; Sieben & Johnson, 2018). The pandemic has increased the intensity of these criticisms (Rice & Deschaine, 2021). What this self-study of teacher education practices revealed was that teachers may not have to remain subject to these discourses; moreover, when teacher educators help teachers to take a diffractive approach, teachers are better positioned to enact practices that have the potential for undoing inequities. Teachers are also diverted from a path where they might be tempted to shift blame onto children and their families. For us, managing these multiple simultaneous commitments in roles that include teacher, teacher educator, mother, and more is less draining when taking a diffractive perspective. It is less draining because there are more possibilities for action. We are also affirmed as we come to realize that we are not charged with solving problems. Instead, we support each other in managing dilemmas in ways that resonate with our social justice ethics and aims.

10.5.1   Implications for Teacher Education Practice

The findings from this self-study highlight the need for teacher preparation and teacher learning to incorporate understandings about entanglement and diffractive practices to help teachers understand their roles and their work. Understanding these nexuses is critical to instilling a sense of the relational in the work of teachers and in helping them realize that while they cannot undo injustice quickly in their contexts, they can make important contributions to others' (and their own) resilience. Indeed, the negative discourses often associated with urban schools and urban settings are challenged as teachers recognize the entangled assemblages that produce urban contexts and themselves as educators within these. The same would also seem to be true in rural schools that are defined by what they lack.

We have wondered how to make our entanglement more explicit with teachers in ways that would be useful to them. However, as part of the intra-activity and the understandings of overlap, connectivity, and the spaces between, we also understand that as a teacher educator and professional learning resource/instructional coach, we may more often be viewed as being apart from teachers' most immediate professional settings than being part of these contexts. This is especially important when navigating multiple commitments. Even so, we like the idea of being as explicit as we can about what matters to us and what matters to the contexts that we are in.

10.5.2   Implications for Researching Teacher Education

More self-studies are needed that illustrate the affirming outcomes that can emerge in urban schools when teacher educators work with practicing educators to explore issues in which they are mutually entangled. Indeed, teacher education research should take a stronger turn toward intra-active, entangled ways of knowing about teaching and learning in various school contexts. These self-studies should be undertaken by educators with diverse roles and provide detailed analyses of teaching and learning alongside the educational discourses that shape them.

Diffracted modes of research are important in examining issues such as: How can parents, teacher educators and others appropriately and productively participate in the co-construction of instructional materials and curriculum? How can we hold teachers to high standards of teaching *and* explicitly acknowledge and affirm our support of their teaching? How can teacher educators and teacher education programs respond when there is an abrupt, major overhaul for practicing teachers and preservice teachers (such as the shift to the online instructional modality)? Who is responsible (or who should be) for teachers' social and emotional support? Finally, we should be asking when and whether conversations about rural and urban areas are useful under the present discourses where many families and teachers are devalued in all spaces. Such future self-studies would support the preparation of all teachers—urban teachers and others—to notice and renounce injustices while responding to the effects of injustice in their contexts.

10.6   Conclusion

The purpose of this self-study of teacher education practices was to learn how our work as a teacher educator and professional learning/instructional coach provided materially important opportunities to supporting teachers in a space constructed as urban. We found that intra-active ways of knowing supported our thinking about how to understand what teachers do and what we are doing to enable educational experiences in our contexts. The findings of this self-study have implications for understanding how teacher educators and others who work in education can enact practices where they work to understand what is happening to teachers while also helping them find validation in what might be very troubling or challenging environments. Teachers and teacher educators need to adopt practices and engage in advocacy to disrupt inequities. As teachers and teacher educators understand how their identities and pedagogical practices are produced in the struggle to disrupt injustice, they can engage more purposefully in actions that address equity and social justice in classrooms and schools.

References

Ahram, R., Stembridge, A., Fergus, E., & Noguera, P. (2011). Framing urban school challenges: The problems to examine when implementing response to intervention. *RTI Action Network.* http://rtinetwork.org/component/content/article/12/465-framing-urban-school

Amatea, E. S., Cholewa, B., & Mixon, K. A. (2012). Influencing preservice teachers' attitudes about working with low-income and/or ethnic minority families. *Urban Education, 47*(4), 801–834. https://doi.org/10.1177/2F0042085912436846

Anyon, J. (2011). *Marx and education.* Routledge.

Baldwin, S. C., Buchanan, A. M., & Rudisill, M. E. (2007). What teacher candidates learned about diversity, social justice, and themselves from service-learning experiences. *Journal of Teacher Education, 58*(4), 315–327.

Bannan-Ritland, B. (2003). The role of design in research: The integrative learning designframework. *Educational Researcher, 32*(1), 21–24. https://doi.org/10.3102/2F0013189X032001021

Barad, K. (2007). *Meeting the universe halfway: Quantum physics and the entanglement of matter and meaning.* Duke University Press.

Barnum, M. (2019, January 28). Across U.S., graduation rates are rising with little connection to test scores. *Chalkbeat.* https://chalkbeat.org/posts/us/2019/01/28/graduation-rates-test-score-disconnect/

Bernard, J. (2019). Where have all the rural poor gone? Explaining the rural–urban poverty gap in European countries. *Sociologia Ruralis, 59*(3), 369–392. https://doi.org/10.1111/soru.12235

Berry, A. (2007). *Tensions in teaching about teaching: Developing practice as a teacher educator.* Springer.

Berry, A., & Loughran, J. (2002). Developing an understanding of learning to teach in teacher education. In J. Loughran & T. Russell (Eds.), *Exploring myths and legends of teacher education*. Proceedings of the 3rd international conference on self-study of teacher education practices (pp. 13–29). Queen's University.

Bower, R. S. (2000). A pedagogy of success: Meeting the challenges of urban middle schools. *The Clearing House, 73*(4), 235–238. https://www.jstor.org/stable/30189554

Brackett, M., & Cipriano, C. (2020, June 15). *Teachers are anxious and overwhelmed. They need SEL now more than ever*. EdSurge. https://www.edsurge.com/news/2020-04-07-teachers-are-anxious-and-overwhelmed-they-need-sel-now-more-than-ever

Brown, D. F. (2004). Urban teachers' professed classroom management strategies: Reflections of culturally responsive teaching. *Urban Education, 39*(3), 266–289. https://doi.org/10.1177/2F0042085904263258

Chakrabarti, S., & Mehta, S. (2019). Urban rural disparity in education in India. *International Journal of Research in Social Sciences, 9*(6), 639–650.

Clandinin, D. J., Downey, C. A., & Huber, J. (2009a). Attending to changing landscapes: Shaping the interwoven identities of teachers and teacher educators. *Asia-Pacific Journal of Teacher Education, 37*(2), 141–154. https://doi.org/10.1080/13598660902806316

Clandinin, D. J., Murphy, M. S., Huber, J., & Orr, A. M. (2009b). Negotiating narrative inquiries: Living in a tension-filled midst. *The Journal of Educational Research, 103*(2), 81–90. https://doi.org/10.1080/00220670903323404

Cloke, P., & Johnston, R. (Eds.). (2005). *Spaces of geographical thought: Deconstructing human geography's binaries*. Sage.

Colarossi, N., (2021, October 2). School board passes code to punish teachers over Critical Race Theory after funding threat. *Newsweek*. https://www.newsweek.com/school-board-passes-code-punish-teachers-over-critical-race-theory-after-funding-threat-1635021

Corbett, M. (2016). Rural futures: Development, aspirations, mobilities, place, and education. *Peabody Journal of Education, 91*(2), 270–282. https://doi.org/10.1080/0161956X.2016.1151750

Deleuze, G. (2004). *Desert islands and other texts, 1953–1974*. MIT Press.

Dewey, J. (1938). *Experience and education*. Kappa Delta Pi.

Dunn, A. H., & Downey, C. A. (2018). Betting the house: Teacher investment, identity, and attrition in urban schools. *Education and Urban Society, 50*(3), 207–229. https://doi.org/10.1177/2F0013124517693283

Fernandez, L., Reisdorf, B. C., & Dutton, W. H. (2019). Urban internet myths and realities: A Detroit case study. *Information, Communication & Society, 23*(13), 1925–1946. https://doi.org/10.1080/1369118X.2019.1622764

Forgasz, R., & McDonough, S. (2017). "Struck by the way our bodies conveyed so much:" A collaborative self-study of our developing understanding of embodied pedagogies. *Studying Teacher Education, 13*(1), 52–67. https://doi.org/10.1080/17425964.2017.1286576

Gehrke, R. S. (2005). Poor schools, poor students, successful teachers. *Kappa Delta Pi Record, 42*(1), 14–17. https://doi.org/10.1080/00228958.2005.10532079

Gillies, C. L. (2021). Seeing whiteness as property through Métis teachers' K-12 stories of racism. *Whiteness and Education*, 1–17.

Glass, R. D., Morton, J. M., King, J. E., Krueger-Henney, P., Moses, M. S., Sabati, S., & Richardson, T. (2018). The ethical stakes of collaborative community-based social science research. *Urban Education, 53*(4), 503–531. https://doi.org/10.1177/2F0042085918762522

Hamilton, M. L., & Pinnegar, S. (2015). *Knowing, becoming, doing as teacher educators: Identity, intimate scholarship, inquiry*. Emerald Publishing.

Hammonds, T. (2017). High teacher turnover: Strategies school leaders implement to retain teachers in urban elementary schools. *National Teacher Education Journal, 10*(2), 63–72.

Haraway, D. (1988). Situated knowledges: The science question in feminism and the privilege of partial perspective. *Feminist Studies, 14*(3), 575–599. https://doi.org/10.2307/3178066

Herman, K. C., Prewett, S. L., Eddy, C. L., Savala, A., & Reinke, W. M. (2020). Profiles of middle school teacher stress and coping: Concurrent and prospective correlates. *Journal of School Psychology, 78*, 54–68. https://doi.org/10.1016/j.jsp.2019.11.003

Hollie, S. (2017). *Culturally and linguistically responsive teaching and learning* (2nd ed.). Shell Educational Publishing.

Jun, W., & Chudan, G. U. (2017). The rural-urban differences in resources allocation of basic education and its social consequence. *Journal of East China Normal University (Educational Sciences), 35*(2), 33–42.

Kelchtermans, G. (2017). 'Should I stay or should I go?': Unpacking teacher attrition/retention as an educational issue. *Teachers and Teaching, 23*(8), 961–977. https://doi.org/10.1080/1354060 2.2017.1379793

King, J. E., & Swartz, E. E. (2018). *Heritage knowledge in the curriculum: Retrieving an African episteme.* Routledge.

Kitchen, J. (2009). Relational teacher development: Growing collaboratively in a hoping relationship. *Teacher Education Quarterly, 36*(2), 45–62. https://www.jstor.org/stable/23479251

Kohli, R. (2018). Behind school doors: The impact of hostile racial climates on urban teachers of color. *Urban Education, 53*(3), 307–333. https://doi.org/10.1177/2F0042085916636653

Kraft, M. A., Papay, J. P., Charner-Laird, M., Johnson, S. M., Ng, M., & Reinhorn, S. K. (2012). *Committed to their students but in need of support: How school context influences teacher turnover in high-poverty.* Harvard Graduate School of Education. https://citeseerx.ist.psu.edu/viewdoc/download?doi=10.1.1.501.7847&rep=rep1&type=pdf

Kwok, A. (2019). Classroom management actions of beginning urban teachers. *Urban Education, 54*(3), 339–367. https://doi.org/10.1177/2F0042085918795017

LaBoskey, V. K. (2004). The methodology of self-study and its theoretical underpinnings. In *International handbook of self-study of teaching and teacher education practices* (pp. 817–869). Springer.

Logan, J. R., & Burdick-Will, J. (2017). School segregation and disparities in urban, suburban, and rural areas. *The Annals of the American Academy of Political and Social Science, 674*(1), 199–216. https://doi.org/10.1177/2F0002716217733936

Looker, E. D., & Bollman, R. D. (2020). Setting the stage: Overview of data on teachers and students in rural and urban Canada. In M. Corbett & D. Gereluk (Eds.), *Rural teacher education* (pp. 21–73). Springer.

Loughran, J., & Northfield, J. (2003). *Opening the classroom door: Teacher, researcher, learner.* Routledge.

Lunenberg, M., & Samaras, A. P. (2011). Developing a pedagogy for teaching self-study research: Lessons learned across the Atlantic. *Teaching and Teacher Education, 27*(5), 841–850. https://doi.org/10.1016/j.tate.2011.01.008

Martin, A. D. (2020). Tensions and caring in teacher education: A self-study on teaching in difficult moments. *Studying Teacher Education, 16*(3), 306–323. https://doi.org/10.1080/1742596 4.2020.1783527

McCloud, R. F., Okechukwu, C. A., Sorensen, G., & Viswanath, K. (2016). Beyond access: Barriers to internet health information seeking among the urban poor. *Journal of the American Medical Informatics Association, 23*(6), 1053–1059. https://doi.org/10.1093/jamia/ocv204

McGlynn, N. (2018). Slippery geographies of the urban and the rural: Public sector LGBT equalities work in the shadow of the 'gay Capital'. *Journal of Rural Studies, 57*, 65–77. https://doi.org/10.1016/j.jrurstud.2017.10.008

Merleau-Ponty, M. (2013). *The phenomenology of perception.* (D. Landes, Trans.). Routledge.

Morgan, J. (2017). Too much professional development? Let's do something different. *Government Technology: Center for Digital Education.* https://www.govtech.com/education/too-much-professional-development-lets-do-something-different.html

Murphy, M. S., Driedger-Enns, L., & Huber, J. (2020). Rural schools as sites for ongoing teacher education: Co-making relational inquiry spaces between a principal and a beginning teacher. In M. Corbett & D. Gereluk (Eds.), *Rural teacher education* (pp. 171–181). Springer.

Olmedo, I. M. (1997). Challenging old assumptions: Preparing teachers for inner city schools. *Teaching and Teacher Education, 13*(3), 245–258. https://doi.org/10.1016/S0742-051X(96)00019-4

Perea. S. (2018, June 21). PED to grade state's teacher prep programs. *Albuquerque Journal.* https://www.abqjournal.com/1186603/ped-releases-report-card-grades-on-states-teacher-prep-programs.html

Pinnegar, S., & Hamilton, M. L. (2009). *Self-study of practice as a genre of qualitative research: Theory, methodology, and practice.* Springer.

Polanyi, M. (1967). *The tacit dimension.* University of Chicago Press.

Polyani, M. (1967). *The tacit dimension.* Doubleday.

Ramkellawan, R., & Bell, J. (2017). Raising the bar: Using coaching conversations to address issues of low expectations for students in urban settings. *The Educational Forum, 81*(4), 377–390. https://doi.org/10.1080/00131725.2017.1350238

Rice, M. (2019). Projections of identity: How technological devices become us and why it matters in ELA teacher education. *Ubiquity, 6*(1), 22–40. http://ed-ubiquity.gsu.edu/wordpress/wp-content/uploads/2019/12/Rice-6-1-Final.pdf

Rice, M. (2021). Reconceptualizing teacher professional learning about technology integration as intra-active entanglements. *Professional Development in Education, 47*(3), 524–537. https://doi.org/10.1080/19415257.2021.1891953

Rice, M. (2016). *A phenomenological inquiry into the technological curriculum making of secondary English Language Arts teachers in rural settings* (Doctoral dissertation). University of Kansas. https://kuscholarworks.ku.edu/bitstream/handle/1808/22029/Rice_ku_0099D_14861_DATA_1.pdf?sequence=1&isAllowed=y

Rice, M., & Deschaine, M. (2021). We need to help teachers withstand public criticism as they learn to teach online. In R. E. Ferdig & K. Pytash (Eds.), *What teacher educators should have learned from 2020* (pp. 101–110). Association for the Advancement of Computing in Education (AACE). https://www.learntechlib.org/p/219088/

Sabzalian, L., Shear, S. B., & Snyder, J. (2021). Standardizing indigenous erasure: A TribalCrit and QuantCrit analysis of K–12 US civics and government standards. *Theory & Research in Social Education,* 1–39.

Schwab, J. J. (1982). *Science, curriculum, and liberal education: Selected essays.* University of Chicago Press.

Sieben, N., & Johnson, L. L. (2018). Professional development pathways through social justice frameworks. *English Education, 50*(2), 108–115.

Skerrett, A., & Williamson, T. (2015). Reconceptualizing professional communities for urban pre-service teachers. *The Urban Review, 47*(4), 579–600. https://doi.org/10.1007/2Fs11256-015-0325-x

Skerrett, A., Warrington, A., & Williamson, T. (2018). Generative principles for professional learning for equity-oriented urban English teachers. *English Education, 50*(2), 116–146.

Stern, D. (2004). *The present moment in psychotherapy and everyday life.* W. W. Norton & Company.

Stoll, L. C. (2019). *Should schools be colorblind?* Wiley.

Strom, K. J., & Martin, A. D. (2017). *Becoming-teacher: A rhizomatic look at first-year teaching.* Brill/Sense.

Thomas, M. (2018). "The girl who lived": Exploring the liminal spaces of self-study research with textual critical partners. In D. Garbett & A. Ovens (Eds.), *Pushing boundaries and crossing borders* (pp. 327–333). Self-study of Teacher Education Practices.

Tieken, M. C. (2017). The spatialization of racial inequity and educational opportunity: Rethinking the rural/urban divide. *Peabody Journal of Education, 92*(3), 385–404. https://doi.org/10.1080/0161956X.2017.1324662

Vega, N., Stanfield, J., & Mitra, S. (2020). Investigating the impact of Computer Supported Collaborative Learning (CSCL) to help improve reading comprehension in low performing urban elementary schools. *Education and Information Technologies, 25*(3), 1571–1584. https://doi.org/10.1007/s10639-019-10023-3

Welsh, R. O., & Swain, W. A. (2020). (re)defining urban education: A conceptual review and empirical exploration of the definition of urban education. *Educational Researcher, 49*(2), 90–100. https://doi.org/10.3102/2F0013189X20902822

Zoch, M. (2015). "It's important for them to know who they are": Teachers' efforts to sustain students' cultural competence in an age of high-stakes testing. *Urban Education, 52*(5), 610–636. https://doi.org/10.1177/2F0042085915618716

Mary F. Rice, Ph.D., is an Assistant Professor of Literacy at the University of New Mexico. She earned her PhD in Curriculum and Teaching from the University of Kansas. At KU, Mary was a graduate research assistant at the Center on Online Learning and Students with Disabilities. In 2018, Mary was named an Emerging Scholar by the Online Learning Consortium. Prior to earning her doctorate, Mary taught general education English language arts, English as a Second language, and reading support in public schools. Her research and teaching focus on digital access and curriculum accessibility in educational settings. Mary has been working to draw on New Materialist frameworks alongside theories of literacies and identities. She has published over 100 items of scholarship on these issues.

Mariana Castañon, a Ph.D. student, currently resides in New Mexico as an Instructional Coach. She was born in Bulgaria, Eastern Europe, and immigrated to the USA with her family as a teenager. Her research interests include culturally responsive teaching, urban education, social-emotional learning (SEL) inclusive of all learners, and effective Middle School Advisory programs. This research was inspired by the needs of the teachers Mariana works with and her experience teaching in urban and suburban settings for the last 17 years. Mariana taught as an Elementary and Middle School ELA teacher for 14 years both in Minnesota and New Mexico, before starting her current Instructional Coach position and her Ph.D. work at the University of New Mexico. Mariana holds a Bachelor of Science degree from St. Cloud State University and a Master of Education from Hamline University in Minnesota. Mariana believes education is the key to humanity's existence.

Chapter 11
Materiality, Affect, and Diverse Educational Settings: A Collaborative Inquiry Between Urban and Rural Teacher Educators

Adrian D. Martin and Tammy Mills

Abstract Dominant conceptualizations of urban and rural education settings position these as distinct, with each presenting contrasting opportunities and challenges in the work of teachers. Consequently, it is unsurprising that teacher education research, focused on one of these settings, by and large fails to consider the commonalities that both of these contexts may in fact possess. In this chapter, the authors (an urban teacher educator and a rural teacher educator) report on a collaborative self-study they conducted that was focused on their teacher education practices in their respective settings. The purpose was to identify how an inquiry that attends to the materiality of these diverse educative and professional contexts could inform the preparation of future teachers and contribute to emergent perspectives on urban and rural teacher education. The inquiry is conceptually grounded in new materialism. As such, the authors not only investigated their teaching practices, but also how materiality and affect functioned to shape engagement with students, the institutional setting, and each other. Findings suggest that urban and rural teacher education possess shared commonalities, that the material structures in each setting serve to shape beliefs about teaching and learning, and that affect functions as an agentic force in the enactment of pedagogical practices. The chapter provides implications for teacher education and future research.

Keywords New materialism · Self-study · Urban education · Rural education · Materiality · Affect

A. D. Martin (✉)
New Jersey City University, Jersey City, NJ, USA
e-mail: amartin6@njcu.edu

T. Mills
University of Maine, Orono, ME, USA

© The Author(s), under exclusive license to Springer Nature Singapore Pte
Ltd. 2022
A. D. Martin (ed.), *Self-Studies in Urban Teacher Education*, Self-Study of
Teaching and Teacher Education Practices 25,
https://doi.org/10.1007/978-981-19-5430-6_11

The field of teacher education encompasses a wide spectrum of responsibilities in the preparation and development of educators. Among these are the requirements to satisfy licensure or certification demands, the promotion of pedagogies that advance equitable learning experiences for P-12 students, and supporting course-work and field experiences that integrate the content knowledge teachers and future teachers must possess to teach ethically and effectively (Cochran-Smith et al., 2013; Noddings, 2005; Oakes et al., 2013; Solbrekke & Sugrue, 2014). The scope and relevance of these endeavors has served to not only elevate the study and practice of teacher education from the margins towards the center of the scholarly community (Darling-Hammond, 2016; Kincheloe, 2011), but also forefronts the imperative to disrupt patterns on inequity in schooling (Martin, 2018b; Strom & Martin, 2017). To be sure, teacher education is vital to the advancement of systems of schooling that can respond to the needs, demands, and challenges of the twenty-first century.

Yet, despite the empirical and theoretical foundations that support the need for robust teacher education programs attentive to the challenges confronted by today's educators, much remains to be understood, particularly in relation to the role of materiality and affect. By and large, the insights gained through teacher education research attend to the role of the human (e.g., teacher and students), the actions undertaken (e.g., teaching practices), and the meaning-making of these in relation to the knowledge, skills, and dispositions educators should possess. Less is known about the role of the non-human (e.g., the physical classroom setting, teaching materials) and the more-than-human (e.g., computers, digital technologies) and their capacities to affect the work of teacher educators as well as the influence these bear upon the enactment of teacher education itself. Given the complexity inherent in teacher preparation, attention to materiality can provide greater texture and depth not only to teacher education scholarship, but also to teacher education practices themselves.

A growing number of teacher educator scholars (many of whom are part of the self-study of teacher education practices special interest group [S-STEP SIG]) are directly taking up these concerns (e.g., Martin, 2019a; Mills, 2017; Ovens, 2017; Strom & Martin, 2017; Rice, 2021). Acknowledging the confluence of activity that envelops the practices of teacher education both within and beyond the walls of the classroom, this emergent knowledge base adopts an onto-epistemological shift that allows for a complex, situated, and affirmative orientation beyond linear conceptions of teaching and learning. Much of this work is aligned with a new materialism paradigm, a conceptual lens that breaks from humanism's assumptions that humanity is the sole shaping element in social relations and discourses, and in the partition of the natural world from human activity (Fox & Alldred, 2014; Taylor & Ivinson, 2013). A new materialist perspective situates teacher education and the practices that teacher educators enact as enmeshed and affected not only by researchers and education stakeholders, but by the substance (i.e., the materiality) of the world itself (Martin, 2019b; Snaza et al., 2016).

Grounding ourselves in this conceptual orientation, we conducted a self-study to learn more about teacher education within our own and each other's respective settings. As an early career urban teacher educator (Adrian) and an early career rural teacher educator (Tammy), we are aware of how our contexts shape and inform the work of the teacher candidates and in-service educators that we teach. As former P-12 educators ourselves, we are familiar with teachers' daily practices and circumstances in our geographic settings. For Adrian, this meant classrooms with culturally and linguistically diverse students and learning environments that were not always adequately funded. For Tammy, this also meant contexts that may have lacked sufficient funding, but largely consisted of White students with minimal exposure to diverse cultures and languages. Recognizing that research about teaching and learning between urban and rural teacher educators is an area in need of scholarly attention (Knight & Oesterreich, 2011) and the lack of inquiries on materiality and affect in teacher education, we wondered what insights could be gained by collaboratively exploring our teacher education contexts with each other, and how this might inform our future pedagogies and understanding of selves as teacher educators. With the aim of putting philosophy to work (Martin & Strom, 2015, 2019; Strom & Martin, 2013), we explored our professional settings, practices, and identities with new materialism. Our research question was: How does the materiality of urban and rural teacher education affect our work and understanding about teacher education?

We begin by describing new materialism as the conceptual framework. We highlight new materialist concepts as guiding analytics in our inquiry. We then report on our methodological approach, grounded in the tenets of self-study and intimate scholarship. We provide our findings, and offer what we learned individually and collaboratively. We follow with implications for teacher education practice and self-study research.

11.1 Theoretical Framework

New materialism was the conceptual frame that informed our inquiry. This lens attends to matter in its myriad permutations and how it functions to produce phenomena (Coole & Frost, 2010; Fox & Alldred, 2017). It shifts attention away from human-centered actions and discourses towards matter, and how matter exerts agency in the doing of "something." New materialism positions matter as lively, active, and as having a shaping effect upon other forms of matter. As such, a new materialist framework calls for the researcher to attend to the scope of material resources in a given context and how these mingle with particular ecologies of action or thought (Taguchi, 2014). Such a lens allows for "models of causation and explanation that can account for the complex interactions through which the social, the biological, and the physical emerge, persist, and transform" (Frost, 2014, p. 69).

Given this focus on matter as active, lively, and vibrant, new materialism posits a monistic ontology, one that problematizes humanistic conceptions of a discrete self in favor of a self that is "an impure human-nonhuman assemblage" (Bennett, 2010, p. xvii). Instead, the self encompasses "...a turbulent field in which various variables and materialities collide, congeal, morph, evolve, and disintegrate" (Seres,

2001, as cited in Bennett, 2010, pp. xi). As such, explorations of the self expand to include flows of activity between and amongst matter in its different forms. The self is examined neither in isolation nor devoid of context; the self is a composite of a multitude of material elements whose ontological status emerges through the interplay of said elements.

This interplay surfaces through affect. Affect refers to the Spinozist notion in which an entity has a capacity for activity or responsiveness (Braidotti, 2013; Massumi, 1987; Martin, 2018a). This should not be conflated with human intention. Affect is matter's "...efficacy...[to] do things...to make a difference, produce effects, alter the course of effects" (Bennett, 2010, p. viii). Affect extends beyond the realm of the rational or logical. It is trans-sensory and unencumbered by discourse (Coleman, 2012). Many scholars have taken up investigations of affect in relation to matter (e.g., Bennett, 2010; Helmsing, 2016; Martin, 2019a). These investigations have highlighted the role of matter beyond the human in the working of something (e.g., classroom practices, energy distribution, food production). Adopting affect supported us in centering our own sensory experiences and how multiple forms of matter shaped these experiences. In this self-study, we began to recognize the affects produced by matter, and how these not only informed our teaching practices in our respective settings, but also the ways that these shaping elements contributed to our understanding of self as teacher educators.

Bennet's concept of "thing-power" is a productive analytic that captures matter's affective capacities in the non-human and more than human (e.g., digital tools' affordances and limitations in the classroom). Thing-power centers "...how things do in fact affect other bodies, enhancing or weakening their power" (Bennett, 2010, p. 3). Thus, deploying new materialism and attending to matter's affects via thing-power necessitated a conscious and deliberate magnification of the world. This empirical investigation explored matter in our urban and rural settings, and allowed us to compare and contrast how these contribute to urban and rural teacher education.

To support this aim, we adopted Bennett's (2010) new materialist principles for systematic inquiry. We viewed the events and circumstances in our inquiry as encounters between and among materiality in multiple forms. Thus, we ourselves were affecting and affected by matter. Additionally, attentiveness was given to the non and more-than human. While we considered our intentions, desires, hopes and perspectives, we focused on forms of matter and the thing-power exerted by these to shape our teaching practices and teacher educator selves. Further, we veered away from the notion of providing concrete, stable, and coherent findings in favor of articulations that incorporate the non and more-than human as affective and integral to our work. Thus, this work extends beyond the scope of much teacher education research as it attends to more than discourse and human-centered activity. This expanded lens can serve as a conceptual template for other education researchers seeking to engage in such work.

11.2 Methodology

Our inquiry drew from the tradition of intimate scholarship (Pinnegar & Hamilton, 2015; Strom et al., 2018a, b) and employed self-study methodology (Kitchen et al., 2020; Kosnik et al., 2006; Tidwell et al., 2009), framed through LaBoskey's (2004) criteria for investigating teacher education practices with S-STEP methods. First, our study was self-initiated and focused; we ourselves were the researchers and the research focus. This veers away from positivist conceptions of research, disrupts notions of authentic objectivity (Martin & Kamberelis, 2013), and takes seriously the generation of teacher educator knowledge and practice produced through processes of inquiry, reflection and collaboration with a critical other (Kastberg & Grant, 2020; Mills et al., 2020). We initiated this inquiry, and set out to capture our understandings and meaning-making as valuable resources in the development of our practice and in the framing of our professional selves. After numerous initial conversations, we narrowed our focus and decided to collaboratively explore ourselves and our pedagogies as part of urban and rural teacher education.

Second, the inquiry was improvement aimed. Our utilization of self-study served to simultaneously promote understanding of the educational contexts we were situated in and to create change for the better, both within our immediate capacities as teacher educators, but also in relation to the larger teacher education scholarly community with whom this inquiry is shared. New materialism propelled us to extend towards these broader environments and explore the ways our contexts are positioned via policies, discourses, events, and practices. By engaging with the materiality of rural and urban environments, we sought to elucidate the ways interactions with matter (and with each other) could produce teacher education differently.

Third, we engaged with multiple qualitative research methods. Conducting this work over the course of a semester, we drew from narrative research approaches (Clandinin & Connelly, 2000; Reissman, 2008) and maintained individual journals via Google Drive. Through these journals, we documented our teaching experiences, our embodied experiences, and reflections on new materialist literature that we collaboratively read (e.g. Bennett, 2010; Snaza et al., 2016). We also responded to each other's journal entries in the form of comments. These comments often proceeded as separate, ongoing conversations that expanded our data pool. Additionally, we discussed these data sources during our monthly Zoom meetings, which were transcribed.

While productive, these data sources centered on the discursive, and given our attention to matter and affect, we turned to walking-methodologies (Springgay & Truman, 2019). Walking methodologies (i.e., systemic inquiries where the embodied experience of navigating through a particular context is critically analyzed) provided an opportunity to attune to the environment and our sensory encounters. We engaged in numerous "affect walks" in our settings. We walked about our respective settings and consciously attuned ourselves to the myriad forms of matter around us. To move away from the discursive and "capture" the material, we took photographs and recorded videos using our smartphones. We explored these contexts and pondered the affects that were produced. We wondered, "How does this material matter? What is this affect? How does this interact with my teacher education practice? How does this affect effect urban/rural teacher education?"

During our walks, we made individual choices as to what we recorded as representative of the material affects surrounding us. We then added our photos and videos to our Google drive and wrote reflective narratives about our walks. Having collected our artifacts and shared our narratives, we then discussed each other's data sources to help us challenge our assumptions and biases about our contexts, reveal inconsistencies, and expand our perspectives (Mena & Russell, 2017). We systematically reviewed each other's artifacts, viewed and listened to the recordings, and wrote additional reflections about what we noticed in relation to our own and each other's settings.

Fourth, we employed a set of interactive structures and activities throughout our data collection process. We interacted with each other, with our individual data sources, and with each other's data sources. We interacted with materiality in our affect walks. The turn to the sensory and to our embodied experiences necessitated an engagement and interaction between our senses and settings. In this way, while this work is self-study, it is not a self-contained or isolated investigation. This self-study is connected to and interactive with the amalgam of where we were and what was a part of/with the material substance of our surroundings.

Our analytic process was interactive as well. We conducted multiple rounds of reading, rereading and discussing the individual data sources. We proceeded to "walk" with these (Eakle, 2007), as a means of highlighting the affective and the sensory. We consciously applied the notion of affect to consider how our contexts were informing our sense of self and our pedagogy, and thing-power to deliberately highlight the agency of matter and how matter was exerting its influence. In this way, we began to discern salient features of the urban and rural teacher education setting and how these worked to produce our professional practices and identities. Thus, we shifted away from codifying (i.e, a reduction of the complexity of where we were) towards conceptualizing a complex model of multiple affective movements and flows we identified as being caught up in.

Fifth, we established trustworthiness through engagement with each other as critical friends and through the narratives of our analytic process as exemplar-based validation (LaBoskey, 2004). Our stories, accounts, reflections, and embodied knowing functioned as artifacts of experience. We set out to document "normal practice" (Kuhn, 1970), the typical materiality of our respective environments, the ordinary, taken-for-granted, and often not considered. To be sure, the account of our methods provides transparency to the reader, who can determine the value of this chapter for their own research and pedagogical practice.

11.3 Findings

Our emergent themes cast light on materiality's shaping effect/affect on ourselves and our practices in urban and rural teacher education. This inquiry suggests that despite their differences, urban and rural teacher education are material permutations rather than mutually exclusive fields of practice and study. Our emergent themes are: (1) material issues and phenomena transverse the "borders" of urban and rural teacher education; (2) materiality's affects informed our embodied experiences as teacher educators; and (3) materiality affected discursive constructions of our teacher education practice and scholarship. We discuss these in the following sections.

11.3.1 The Borders of Urban and Rural Teacher Education

Our self-study led us to realize that the borders (both physical and conceptual) that are set up to distinguish between urban and rural education (and teacher education) are porous and, in some respects, illusory. The materiality of each context affects the other, suggesting a need to rethink how we prepare future educators. Borders are meant to divide, parse, and separate. Urban teacher education is conceived as training for teaching in diverse, densely populated areas. Rural teacher education is concerned with preparing future teachers for culturally homogenous, sparsely populated settings.

Throughout the self-study process, we pondered these conceptions and how they informed our understanding of the purposes for teacher education. We were both concerned with issues of equity and social justice for students and teachers who (especially in the United States) are all too often denigrated and maligned as quasi-professionals responsible for the nation's economic challenges. For us, taking up equity issues in our pedagogy included supporting critical consciousness among our education students, and supporting an understanding of the connections between race, class, gender, sexual orientation, and dis/ability in relation to teaching and schools as institutions of the state. These were salient themes in how we each approached curriculum development and classroom instruction.

Yet the turn to the material highlighted that it is not only these aims or purposes that we shared and that carried across urban and rural borders, but also the effects/affects of the natural world. The affect walks provided a non-discursive window into our own and each other's context. Tammy's video and photos showcased buildings in expansive fields, an abundance of trees, and a body of water. The rustle of leaves and the sweep of the wind were audible in the video, and it was clear that the human-made elements (e.g., buildings, benches, lamp posts) were positioned and constructed without diminishing the sublime in the natural landscape.

Adrian's video and photos also highlighted trees, plants, and shrubbery. However, unlike in Tammy's setting, the human-made (i.e., buildings, cars, paved walkways) dominated the setting, while the natural elements were purposefully and intentionally curated. The water fountain, bushes, and a canopy of trees brought the natural world to the academic setting. Yet these were secondary elements in the composition of the urban environment. A sweeping expanse "bordered" Tammy's rural setting, while Adrian's urban setting was "bordered" by gates and fences, surrounded by avenues with heavy traffic. Facets from one type of setting could be found in the other, not just physically present, but actually doing *something*. Tammy's comments from our October 2020 Zoom session illustrate our observations:

> It is interesting to think as you were talking, I was writing. What does water quality do? What does air quality do, and when you are in an assemblage and air quality is part of that assemblage? What is air quality doing? Oh, I'm just really interested in those kinds of things, because I have to tell you…I live in a state where everybody romanticizes and idealizes what life is like here, and what it looks like here. What it feels like to live here. But, materially when you live here, you have to realize that there are these paper mills that just spew the most noxious smelling horrible pollutants into the air. Also, we are the recipients of all the pollutants that blow across the country from neighboring states, and nearby big cities. And you know, I love my lake and it's crystal clear, but I would never in a million years drink that water. Even though everybody goes "Awe your lake is so clean"…you know, this pollution will come up here. You can't come to me and think that this is a whole idea of borders…for me, you just go, you know, the borders are not real, and everybody knows that. But nobody really acknowledges that.

Detrimental environmental conditions in relation to schooling are often associated with the urban setting in the United States. As Tammy's comments highlight, the environmental conditions and concerns of the urban setting affect the rural. Concerns about air and water quality are routinely discussed in reference to urban schools. Yet water and air pollutants exert their own agency, their capacity to affect, and fail to respect the "borders" that are established by humans. Conceptualizations of teacher education for distinct settings must therefore expand; what affects and causes effects in one setting carries over into others. This example, focused on the natural world and the damages caused by human-activity, forefronts the need for all teacher educators to more carefully (and purposefully) consider the consequences of human activity not just locally, but how this activity extends into other settings. It is not just our values that surfaced as salient dispositions across geographic regions. The affect of matter did so as well. As teacher educators, this led us to more fully evaluate how we were positioning teacher preparation as embedded with material consequences that extend beyond physical and discursive borders.

11.3.2   Materiality's Affect/Effect in Our Embodied Experiences

Our self-study led us to recognize the affects of materiality on our embodied experiences as urban and rural teacher educators and how we understood ourselves in these roles. In alignment with Barad's edict that we are not "in the world, but of the world" (2012, p. 8), we recognized how we participated with other forms of materiality in the teacher education assemblage. Our actions, discourses, and engagement with the world around us contributed to the "doings" or "happenings" of teacher education as jointly produced. Our analysis, especially the experiential contemplations of our affect walks, helped us recognize how matter exerted an agentic force. For Adrian, this was emphasized through the confluence of listening to diverse languages, the sweep of the wind, and sirens. For Tammy, it was the rustling of the leaves, the sounds of a musician, and the sight an American elm tree. Turning away from a concentration on our actions, words, and dispositions (even momentarily) towards the vibrancy of these "things" helped us to attune to the multiplicity of material elements that shape who we are and what we do. Adrian's affect walk journal entry from Sept. 2020 illustrates this.

> Today, the campus was missing the usual overlap of voices and conversations from students, staff, and visitors because of the Covid pandemic. I found myself focused on the light bearing down upon the stone bricks that pave the walkways, the sound of the wind as I headed towards my office building, and the shadows cast by the trees. The leaves rustled, and I couldn't help but think the leaves are protesting the coming of the cold weather, their descent from the high branches overhead towards the pavement, where they will dry up and cover the surfaces that I and others walk on. I heard a few students speaking. The voices were not in English, and I do not know the language. As I walked, I did not think about this. But now, I cannot help but make note that linguistic diversity and hearing a plurality of languages is characteristic of my lived experience, here in the urban setting.
>
> I also heard sirens. I do not know if these were police sirens, an ambulance, or firefighters as I could not see the source of the sound…The photos and videos of the affect walk have elicited these as another feature of my urban setting, and I am starting to grapple with how these sounds enact their "thing-power" on my experience as an urban teacher educator. What does it mean when the sounds of alarms are routine, a fixture of background noise? It mingles with all else I see and hear and feel…I cannot help but feel that the trees and leaves, the shrubbery, the grass, the dirt and even the water (when there is water) in the fountain hearken and call out (just as the sirens are calling out). These material permutations are reminders of connections to the earth and to the world beyond my immediate scope. It calls me to think about how I and my students will not only engage in teaching practices in urban settings that will affect the urban context as normatively conceived, but also the world beyond. The demarcation of urban, suburban, and rural are social constructs…The trees and the buildings are permutations of the same "thing", although they might be doing different things. The sounds called out, be they sirens, or the wind, or the running water.
>
> I feel these affects, and am reminded of the settings my students will likely teach in. The size and shapes of the classrooms I use, the class size itself, the long hallways similar to those of P-12 school buildings are all there, reflected as I walk into the building, as I enter the classroom, as I hold a piece of chalk or wipe a marker board, as I start a lesson….these are all echoes of what I am aiming to prepare my students to do.
>
> And so, thinking about this, about words and sentences in languages I do not know and do not understand, about the chalk in my hand, about the sounds of my steps in the hallways and the air flowing through opens windows, these all filter to the back of my awareness, like the rustle of the leaves and the sirens of the vehicles speeding by. I am reminded of difference, of material differences, differences in matter, and the beauty of human diversity. The collectivity of difference in the urban setting is compelling, and causes me to consider difference as affirmative (to borrow from Braidotti) and vital to success.

11.3.3 The Inter/Intra-Play of Materiality and Discourse in Teacher Education

Our self-study led us to rethink the shaping effect of discourse upon materiality and materiality upon discourse in teacher education. Intra-play is a concept advanced by Barad (2012) that suggests discourse and materiality do not exist in isolation from one another or solely interact; rather, each surfaces through intra-play (i.e., the coming together of each in disparate ways) and through this an object, individual, or notion gains ontological status. The material and the discursive are mutually co-constructed and constituted in webs of affective mangles. How we talk about teacher education shapes the *thingness* of teacher education. How we do teacher education informs how we define it, and one cannot be separated from the other.

We recognized this inseparability through our discussions on the challenges of standardized and high-stakes testing. Teacher licensure programs in the United States require teacher candidates to pass a variety of standardized assessments. While these assessments vary from state to state, an underlying commonality is that in order to gain employment as an educator, candidates must successfully complete the assessments. Despite the differences in where we teach, both of us experienced common affective responses to the tensions and challenges in not only preparing our students to possess the knowledge, skills, and dispositions necessary for the teaching profession, but also in preparing them with the knowledge and skills needed to pass these tests. We struggle with this, as we each know that failing high-stakes tests could result in a teacher candidate being unable to obtain licensure. In addition, we know of the dangers in curriculum being narrowed to solely address what is being assessed, resulting in fewer learning opportunities and experiences for teacher candidates (Au, 2007). Yet, failure to address what is covered in these assessments will make entry into the teaching profession all the harder for our students.

Our self-study led us to identify how rubrics, checklists, inventories, assessments, and grades function as material resources that we employ and as apparatuses our students must master in order to advance academically and professionally with material consequence if they fail to do so. These instruments shape and affect what we do in our teacher education classrooms. We simultaneously work with them by providing scaffolded supports to our students in our coursework and assignments. The demands of these instruments complicate our ontological sense of self as teacher educators and compels our practices in directions that we may not have otherwise taken up. Grappling with these themes, in the December 2020 Zoom session, Tammy shared:

> Because we know, we understand, that learning isn't linear and it's not measurable, it is unpredictable. It's potentials and possibilities. It's about affect. So I'm thinking spatially in terms of our teacher education programs where if they don't get a certain grade, they can't continue in the program. If they get a low grade, it'll pull down their GPA and then they're not eligible to continue….And the sad thing is…the people who have to follow this the closest are usually the most marginalized populations…They need to know how to do so, how to perform on these measures, in order to gain access to power.

The excerpt highlights how the material implementation of high-stakes assessments shape the discourses that we employ and utilize to make meaning of our contexts. Our meaning-making emerged from our practices, our social-justice orientation and the environments we were in. We also recognized that, for our most underprivileged students, many of these tests serve as concrete measures that reflect what is needed in order to achieve success (e.g., doing well on a course or gaining entry into the teaching profession). While our practices and the use of these tools affected our teacher educator identities and propelled us to more fully consider actions and steps we could take to advance equitable schooling experiences for all students (both P-12 and teacher candidates), we also realized the material implications for our students should these measures be revoked. This consideration surfaced in the December 2020 Zoom session, where Adrian remarked:

> It's making me think, Tammy, about grading and the grades. How grading and grades can function as a means to include or exclude, and what this suggests for students from marginalized backgrounds or those who possess marginalized identities. For students of color or working class backgrounds or financially disadvantaged backgrounds, because they have to satisfy what's on these rubrics and on these standards or earn these grades in order to gain access to the profession, and for many and as you said, what if all that is removed, right? And none of that is there, then the question might become, for those communities, for those students, *What do I have to do right now that there's no grades or rubrics or exams for me to show what I know or can do? What do I have to show in order to move forward? What's the measure? How much?* It's like now, even though we know many assessments are culturally insensitive or biased, if assessments or such tools aren't used, then what is the measure for teacher candidates, urban or rural, to become teachers, to show what they know? Does it turn to cultural capital? Which, for many from marginalized backgrounds, they do not possess.

Exploring the issues of testing and measurements of learning in our practices shed light on the ways accountability and compliance initiatives function to contour the discourses we employed, and how these discursive constructions affected our practices and the material consequences for us and our students. We know that teachers and students in rural and urban contexts are affected differently by policies of accountability, compliance, and surveillance, often enacted within structures of evaluation and accreditation. For us, advancing equity and social justice in our teacher education classrooms means that we not only explore what we do, but also attend to the inter/intra-play between and among the constructs, materiality, and discourses of what we know.

11.4 Discussion

In our self-study of materiality and affect in urban and rural teacher education, we attempted "to linger in those moments during which they find themselves fascinated by objects, taking them as clues to the material vitality that they share with them" (Bennett, 2010, p. 17). Analysis of data collected from this lingering demonstrated that we can not take our students' perspectives (or our own) of urban and rural spaces for granted. We can not make assumptions about the contexts in which we teach or are going to teach, namely that they are singular and separate from others. There needs to be a critical, material analysis of the affects produced by the contexts of where we prepare teachers. We recognize that our own students will typically teach in settings similar to their teacher education contexts. Although discussed as "urban" and "rural" in policy and institutional discourses, pedagogical constructions, and informal conversations, our self-study sheds light on how contexts, normatively conceived as mutually exclusive, are entangled, leaking through porous boundaries into each other. Colonizing practices and discourses, industry, bodies of water, human bodies, and weather thread and co-mingle, often with disregard to the human-constructed notion of boundaries.

As Tammy walked through the leafy spaces of trees, grass, rocks, and dirt of the rural setting and Adrian walked in similar spaces of his urban setting, we noted the different feelings this produced, both in the "doing" and the "viewing" of each other's walking. Both settings offered what would be considered natural spaces that were assemblages of human, non-human, and discursive elements, but they produced different affects in us as teacher educators. The rural setting seemed to invite more possibilities for immersive human material interaction, while the urban setting seemed to offer a curated "view only" activity with less access, as the natural space was minimized by constructed boundaries (e.g., paved streets, highways, densely spaced housing). These differences may influence what affect is produced in rural and urban students and how they understand, feel, and interact with their campus spaces as preservice teachers. It may inform a view of these as bounded spaces. They may feel different embodied affects related to who is allowed access, who creates boundaries, who curates the contents, and the relationship between power and pedagogical practices. Thus, recent calls for the implementation of socio-emotional learning in schooling systems (e.g., Hansen, 2019) does not sufficiently highlight the scope of influences upon teaching and learning. To more fully gain insight of the processes of teaching and learning, teacher education must attend to the shaping affects of embodied knowledge in the learning of teacher candidates, and how material circumstances produce different kinds of teaching and learning experiences.

For example, Tammy's rural students may have a different relationship with the land surrounding their rural campus than Adrian's students. These relationships are complex and may be rife with systemic racism (Zamudio et al., 2010) that some may not realize without a critical analysis of the spaces they occupy. Such critical analysis would be productive when considering Tammy's rural context, which includes recently installed signs in some areas that are written in English and in the Native Wabnaki language as a way to let all people on campus know that the land they have access to is located on "Marsh Island in the homeland of the Penobscot Nation, where issues of water and territorial rights, and encroachment upon sacred sites, are ongoing." (Land Acknowledgement, University of Maine, 2018). Thus, the unfettered, unquestioned, unbounded access to "natural spaces" may serve to perpetuate colonial systems of White supremacy that historically have failed to acknowledge the rights and privileges of others. Considering that Tammy's students, the majority of whom are from dominant culture backgrounds, will more than likely teach in rural areas, among trees, bodies of water, a history of resource extraction, decreasing wages, and an aging demographic, this critical understanding of the relationship with the embodied experience in one's surroundings is an important step towards dismantling oppressive systems and structures. As teacher educators drawing on these perspectives, we are better able to prepare our students not only for their own respective contexts, but other settings as well, conscious of the value to consider how the doings of one setting relate to others, and the interconnectedness between/among forms of matter, both near and far.

We believe this kind of inquiry supports our work with pre-service teachers and the commitment to supporting affirmative views of P-12 students' backgrounds and experiences. As with P-12 teachers and their students, teacher educators need to adopt affirmative views about the backgrounds and experiences of their own teacher candidates (Sleeter & Carmona, 2017). Our self-study contributes to this perspective with the ethical imperative to consider how materiality, affects, and educational discourses exert agency and can be experienced differently by diverse bodies. The codification of educational practice through discourses that seek to regulate teacher and student autonomy and agency often address issues such as dress codes, discipline, evaluation, and standardized curricula (Giroux, 2011). In fact, recent American educational reforms to standardize schooling, when broadly implemented, disregard alternative ways of knowing and learning specific to rural life (Kassam et al., 2017) and those in urban settings as well (Ladson-Billings, 2014; Villegas & Lucas, 2002). Correspondingly, the design of many academic standards seek to ensure the curriculum's genericity and severance from the materiality of students' place based understandings (Kassam et al., 2017). Just as our own embodied and embedded experiences shaped our engagement with our settings and informed an understanding of what we do in our teacher education classrooms, the lived experiences and understandings of teacher candidates, beyond the normative discourses of schooling, also serve as a shaping affect.

Learning to unearth those affects and question the current status quo knowledge and practices of evaluation, assessment and curriculum implementation, and inquiring into what these do to the bodies of all learners in schools and communities is one essential practice to dismantle systems of oppression. For example, our insights of the affects of evaluation, assessment, and grading in rural and urban education contexts, shifted beyond identifying similarities and differences towards understanding how current evaluation systems are often divorced from the places in which teacher candidates learn, and instead are more often are linked up to larger systems of neoliberalism and marginalization (Strom & Martin, 2015). Working with self-study and new materialism demonstrated how standards, standardized curriculum, and evaluation systems are complex and entangled with markers of status quo school achievement with material-corporeal consequences.

As self-study researchers, we engage in scholarship of our teaching practices with the aim to improve future instruction. We believe that this research on teaching has implications for advancing equitable schooling experiences and teacher education programs/practices that can more readily provide nuanced and socially just learning opportunities to teacher candidates. The effects (and affects) of material circumstance have lived consequences. When preparing teacher candidates for diverse classrooms, it is vital to consider and attend to how materiality mitigates the learning experience. Self-study methodology is an appropriate and highly efficacious tool to promote this knowledge and the development of such practices. Future self-study researchers could conduct similar inquiries in their own settings to identify the role of materiality and affect and how embodiment is experienced through the intra-play of matter.

This self-study explored ourselves in relation to the material. While much self-study is grounded in assumptions of a "self" that the researcher can gain access to through reflection on data gathered about one's professional practices as a teacher educator, we viewed ourselves as part of a research assemblage, elements among elements in a constellation of the human, non-human, and discursive that came together to produce particular knowledges and practices (Martin, 2018a; Martin & Strom, 2017; Strom et al., 2018a, b). This self-study illustrates an approach to explore one's connectedness to objects, things, sensations, settings, and spatio-temporal relationships. Given the affordances to attending to emotions, past history, socio-cultural identities, and discourse, this work builds upon the body of self-study literature in exemplifying how matter matters. Thus, our collaborative approach to new materialist self-study allowed us to question foundational assumptions and binary discourses associated with teacher education in urban and rural contexts. Ultimately, self-study is a liberating methodology that enabled us to highlight the role of matter in teacher education. Future self-study research could expand upon this work and consider materiality, the pedagogical encounter, and affect.

11.5 Conclusion

This collaborative self-study provides insight of how materiality transverses the borders of urban and rural teacher education, how affects informed our embodied experiences as teacher educators, and the affects upon teacher education discourses. To be sure, this work represents a starting point for each of us. We learned about ourselves, we learned about each other, and we learned how things in the spaces we occupy can inform what we do and how we know. We proceed from this work with a greater appreciation for what our students understand, what they bring to our classrooms, and how we can provide meaningful learning opportunities for a more socially just, equitable, and sustainable future. As we contemplate the future (both in research and in our teaching practices) we acknowledge how this inquiry was bound to a single semester and took place during the Covid-19 pandemic. While not the focus of this work, such a context certainly informed some of the circumstances and events that we experienced. Future research can take up the material and affect in less unusual times. We invite other researchers to engage in self-study projects of their own, and employ or adapt what is described herein to meet their research and pedagogical needs. We hope others find this chapter of relevance and productive in the development of a pedagogical repertoire, and that the salience of matter and affect as agentic can aid in explorations of teaching and learning.

References

Au, W. (2007). High-stakes testing and curricular control: A qualitative metasynthesis. *Educational Researcher, 36*(5), 258–267. https://doi.org/10.3102/0013189x07306523

Barad, K. (2012). *What is the measure of nothingness? Infinity, virtuality, justice.* Hatje Cantz Verlag.

Bennett, J. (2010). *Vibrant matter.* Duke University Press.

Braidotti, R. (2013). *The posthuman.* Polity Press.

Clandinin, D. J., & Connelly, F. M. (2000). *Narrative inquiry: Experience and story in qualitative research.* Jossey-Bass Publishers.

Cochran-Smith, M., Piazza, P., & Power, C. (2013). The politics of accountability: Assessing teacher education in the United States. *The Educational Forum, 77*(1), 6–27. https://doi.org/1 0.1080/00131725.2013.739015

Coleman, C. (2012). Affect. In A. Parr (Ed.), *The Deleuze dictionary* (pp. 11–14). Edinburgh University Press.

Coole, D. H., & Frost, S. (Eds.). (2010). *New materialisms: Ontology, agency, and politics.* Duke University Press.

Darling-Hammond, L. (2016). Research on teaching and teacher education and its influences on policy and practice. *Educational Researcher, 45*(2), 83–91. https://doi.org/10.310 2/0013189X16639597

Eakle, A. J. (2007). Literacy spaces of a Christian faith-based school. *Reading Research Quarterly, 42*(4), 472–510. https://doi.org/10.1598/RRQ.42.4.3

Fox, N. J., & Alldred, P. (2014). New materialist social inquiry: Designs, methods and the research-assemblage. *International Journal of Social Research Methodology, 18*(4), 399–414. https://doi.org/10.1080/13645579.2014.921458

Fox, N. J., & Alldred, P. (2017). *Sociology and the new materialism: Theory, research, action.* SAGE.

Frost, S. (2014). The implications of the new materialisms for feminist epistemology. In H. E. Grasswick (Ed.), *Feminist epistemology and philosophy of science: Power in knowledge* (pp. 69–83). Springer.

Giroux, H. A. (2011). *On critical pedagogy.* Bloomsbury.

Hansen, C. B. (2019). *The heart and science of teaching: Transformative applications that integrate academic and social-emotional learning.* Teachers College Press.

Helmsing, M. (2016). Life at large: New materialisms for a (re)new(ing) curriculum of social studies education. In N. Snaza, D. Sonu, S. E. Truman, & Z. Zaliwska (Eds.), *Pedagogical matters: New materialisms and curriculum studies* (pp. 137–151). Peter Lang.

Kassam, K. S., Avery, L. M., & Ruelle, M. L. (2017). The cognitive relevance of indigenous and rural: Why is it critical to survival? *Cultural Studies of Science Education, 12*, 97–118. https://doi.org/10.1007/s11422-016-9745-5

Kastberg, S., & Grant, M. (2020). Characteristics of critical friendship that transform professional identity. In C. Edge, A. Cameron-Standerford, & B. Bergh (Eds.), *Textiles and tapestries: Self-study for envisioning new ways of knowing.* EdTech Books. Retrieved from https://edtech-books.org/castle_conference_2020/chapter_17

Kincheloe, J. (2011). The knowledges of teacher education: Developing a critical complex epistemology. In J. Kincheloe, K. Hayes, S. R. Steinberg, & K. Tobin (Eds.), *Key works in critical pedagogy* (pp. 227–243). Essay, Brill I Sense.

Kitchen, J., Berry, A., Bullock, S. M., Crowe, A. R., Guðjónsdóttir, H., & Thomas, L. (Eds.). (2020). *International handbook of self-study of teaching and teacher education practices* (2nd ed.). Springer.

Knight, M. G., & Oesterreich, H. A. (2011). Opening our eyes, changing our practices: Learning through the transnational lifeworlds of teachers. *Intercultural Education, 22*(3), 203–215.

Kosnik, C., Beck, C., Freese, A. R., & Samaras, A. P. (Eds.). (2006). *Making a difference in teacher education through self-study: Studies of personal, professional and program renewal.* Springer.

Kuhn, T. S. (1970). *The structure of scientific revolutions*. University of Chicago Press.

LaBoskey, V. K. (2004). The methodology of self-study and its theoretical underpinnings. In J. J. Loughran, M. L. Hamilton, V. LaBoskey, & T. Russell (Eds.), *International handbook of self-study of teaching and teacher education practices* (pp. 817–869). Springer Publishing.

Ladson-Billings, G. (2014). Culturally relevant pedagogy 2.0: A.k.a. the remix. *Harvard Educational Review, 84*(1), 74–84. https://doi.org/10.17763/haer.84.1.p2rj131485484751

Martin, A. D. (2018a). Affective reverberations: The methodological excesses of a research assemblage. In K. Strom, T. Mills, & A. Ovens (Eds.), *Decentering the researcher in intimate scholarship: Critical posthuman methodological perspectives in education* (pp. 9–23). Emerald.

Martin, A. D. (2018b). Professional identities and pedagogical practices: A self-study on the "becomings" of a teacher educator and teachers. In A. Ovens & D. Garbett (Eds.), *Pushing boundaries and crossing borders: Self-study as a means for knowing pedagogy* (pp. 263–269). S-STEP.

Martin, A. D. (2019a). The agentic capacities of mundane objects for educational equity: Narratives of material entanglements in a culturally diverse urban classroom. *Educational Research for Social Change, 8*(1), 86–100. https://doi.org/10.17159/2221-4070/2018/v8i1a6

Martin, A. D. (2019b). Teacher identity perspectives. In M. Peters (Ed.), *Encyclopedia of teacher education*. Springer.

Martin, A. D., & Kamberelis, G. (2013). Mapping not tracing: Qualitative educational research with political teeth. *International Journal of Qualitative Studies in Education, 26*(6), 668–679. https://doi.org/10.1080/09518398.2013.788756

Martin, A. D., & Strom, K. J. (2015). Neoliberalism and the teaching of English learners: Decentering the teacher and student subject. *The SoJo Journal: Educational Foundations and Social Justice Education, 1*(1), 23–44.

Martin, A. D., & Strom, K. J. (2017). Using multiple technologies to put rhizomatics to work in self-study. In A. Ovens & D. Garbett (Eds.), *Being self-study researchers in a digital world: Future oriented pedagogy and teaching in teacher education* (Self-study of Teaching and Teacher Education Practices) (Vol. 16, pp. 151–163). Springer.

Martin, A. D., & Strom, K. J. (Eds.). (2019). *Exploring gender and LGBTQ issues in K12 and teacher education: A rainbow assemblage*. Information Age Publishing.

Massumi, B. (1987). Translator's foreword and notes [foreword]. In G. Deleuze & F. Guattari (Eds.), *Thousand plateaus: Capitalism and schizophrenia* (pp. ix–xix). University of Minnesota Press.

Mena, J., & Russell, T. (2017). Collaboration, multiple methods, trustworthiness: Issues arising from the 2014 international conference on self-study of teacher education practices. *Studying Teacher Education: A Journal of Self-Study of Teacher Education Practices, 13*(1), 105–122. https://doi.org/10.1080/17425964.2017.1287694

Mills, T. (2017). Mangling expertise: Using post-coding analysis to complexify teacher learning. *Issues in Teacher Education, 26*(3), 128–144. https://www.itejournal.org/issues/fall-2017/12mills.pdf

Mills, T., Strom, K., & Abrams, L. (2020). More-than critical friendship: A posthuman analysis of subjectivity and practices in neoliberal work spaces. In C. Edge, A. Cameron-Standerford, & B. Bergh (Eds.), *Textiles and tapestries: Self-study for envisioning new ways of knowing*. EdTech Books. Retrieved from https://edtechbooks.org/castle_conference_2020/chapter_14

Noddings, N. (2005). *The challenge to care in schools: An alternative approach to education*. Teachers College Press.

Oakes, J., Lipton, M., Anderson, L., & Stillman, J. (2013). *Teaching to change the world* (4th ed.). McGraw-Hill College.

Ovens, A. (2017). Putting complexity to work to think differently about transformative pedagogies in teacher education. *Issues in Teacher Education, 26*(3), 38–51.

Pinnegar, S. E., & Hamilton, M. L. (2015). *Knowing, becoming, doing as teacher educators: Identity, intimate scholarship, inquiry*. Emerald Publishing.

Reissman, K. (2008). *Narrative methods for the human science*. Sage Publications.

Rice, M. F. (2021). Reconceptualizing teacher professional learning about technology integration as intra-active entanglements. *Professional Development in Education, 47*(2–3), 524–537. https://doi.org/10.1080/19415257.2021.1891953

Sleeter, C. E., & Carmona, J. F. (2017). *Un-standardizing curriculum: Multicultural teaching in the standards-based classroom*. Teachers College Press.

Snaza, N., Sonu, D., Truman, S. E., & Zaliwska, Z. (Eds.). (2016). *Pedagogical matters: New materialisms and curriculum studies*. Peter Lang.

Solbrekke, T. D., & Sugrue, C. (2014). Professional accreditation of initial teacher education programmes: Teacher educators' strategies—Between 'accountability' and 'professional responsibility'? *Teaching and Teacher Education, 37*, 11–20. https://doi.org/10.1016/j.tate.2013.07.015

Springgay, S., & Truman, S. E. (2019). *Walking methodologies in a more-than-human world: WalkingLab*. Routledge.

Strom, K. J., & Martin, A. D. (2013). Putting philosophy to work in the classroom: Using rhizomatics to deterritorialize neoliberal thought and practice. *Studying Teacher Education: A Journal of Self-study of Teacher Education Practices, 9*(3), 219–235. https://doi.org/10.1080/1742596 4.2013.830970

Strom, K. J., & Martin, A. D. (2015). Deterritorializing neoliberal thought and practice in the classroom. In M. Abendroth & B. Porfilio (Eds.), *Understanding neoliberal rule in higher education: Educational fronts for local and global justice* (Vol. 2, pp. 171–186). Information Age Publishing.

Strom, K. J., & Martin, A. D. (2017). *Becoming-teacher: A rhizomatic look at first- year teaching*. Brill/Sense Publishers.

Strom, K., Mills, T., Abrams, L., & Dacey, C. (2018a). Thinking with posthuman perspectives in self-study research. *Studying Teacher Education, 14*(2), 141–155. https://doi.org/10.108 0/17425964.2018.1462155

Strom, K. J., Mills, T., & Ovens, A. (Eds.). (2018b). *Decentering the researcher in intimate scholarship: Critical posthuman methodological perspectives in education*. Emerald Publishing.

Taguchi, H. L. (2014). New materialism and play. In L. Brooker, M. Blaise, & S. Edwards (Eds.), *The SAGE handbook of play and learning in early childhood* (pp. 79–90). Sage.

Taylor, C. A., & Ivinson, G. (Eds.). (2013). *Material feminisms: New directions for education*. Routledge.

Tidwell, D. L., Heston, M. L., & Fitzgerald, L. M. (Eds.). (2009). *Research methods for the self-study of practice*. Springer.

University of Maine. (2018, May 10). *Land grant acknowledgement*. https://library.umaine.edu/about/university-of-maine-land-acknowledgement/

Villegas, A. M., & Lucas, T. (2002). *Educating culturally responsive teachers: A coherent approach*. State University of New York Press.

Zamudio, M. M., Russell, C., Rios, F. A., & Bridgeman, J. L. (Eds.). (2010). *Critical race theory matters: Education and ideology*. Routledge.

Adrian D. Martin, Ph.D., is a faculty member in the College of Education at New Jersey City University. Dr. Martin's scholarly agenda attends to equity, social justice, inclusion in education and, more specifically, in teacher education. Grounding his research in diverse theoretical and conceptual frameworks, Dr. Martin engages with multiple methodologies to explore the work of teacher educators, critical pedagogies, and teacher preparation. An active member of the American Educational Research Association (AERA) Self-Study of Teacher Education Practices (S-STEP) special interest group, he served as the 2019–2021 program co-chair. Dr. Martin's research has been published in multiple peer-reviewed journals, including *Action in Teacher Education, Studying Teacher Education, Teachers College Record*, and *International Journal of Qualitative Studies in Education*.

Tammy Mills, Ph.D., is an Assistant Professor of Curriculum, Assessment, and Instruction at the University of Maine. Tammy is a teacher educator/researcher who puts complex, non-linear theories to work in the areas of teacher education, development, and leadership. Tammy's most recent work includes a chapter creating a framework of discomfort and vulnerability for those who do work perceived as risky in neoliberal institutions of higher education. She also co-authored a complex framework that examines the concept of and development of teacher leadership throughout a teacher's career. She co-created the Teacher Leadership Collaborative, a grant supported network of Maine teachers that supports each other in creating and carrying out various inquiry projects focused on more equitable and inclusive practice. Prior to moving into higher education, Tammy taught multiple grades, K-9, and held various leadership positions in schools around the United States.

CPSIA information can be obtained
at www.ICGtesting.com
Printed in the USA
LVHW080854200922
728816LV00003B/11